Visual Basic
Deployment Handbook

Rick Delorme
Fabio Claudio Ferracchiati
Kevin Hoffman
Billy Hollis
Nick Manning

® Wrox Press Ltd.

Visual Basic .NET Deployment Handbook

First published September 2002

Published by Wrox Press Ltd,
Arden House, 1102 Warwick Road, Acocks Green,
Birmingham, B27 6BH
United Kingdom
Printed in the United States
ISBN 1-86100-771-X

Trademark Acknowledgments

Credits

Authors
Rick Delorme
Fabio Claudio Ferracchiati
Kevin Hoffman
Billy Hollis
Nick Manning

Additional Material
Andrew Polshaw

Technical Reviewers
Damien Foggon
Mark Horner
Erick Sgarbi
Matt Snailham
David Whitney

Technical Editors
Nick Manning
Andrew Polshaw

Commissioning Editor
Nick Manning

Managing Editor
Jan Kolasinski

Project Manager
Beckie Stones

Production & Layout
Neil Lote

Index
Michael Brinkman

Proof Reader
Chris Smith

Cover
Natalie O'Donnell

About the Authors

Rick Delorme

Rick Delorme is currently a software developer in Ottawa, Ontario, Canada for prairieFyre Software Inc, a Microsoft Certified Solutions Provider. Almost all his development is done on Windows platforms leveraging Microsoft products. Rick is a Microsoft Certified Professional and has been working with Visual Studio .NET since Beta 1. When he's not working, he enjoys hitting the greens and fighting off those terrible bogeys.

> *Thanks to Wrox for the opportunity to work with them. I would like to thank my wife of less than 2 months for putting up with me while I work so much and for supporting me through all my professional endeavors.*

Fabio Claudio Ferracchiati

Fabio Claudio Ferracchiati is a software developer and technical writer. In the early years of his ten-year career he worked with classic languages and old Microsoft tools like Visual Basic and Visual C++. After five years he decided to dedicate his attention to the Internet and all the related technologies. In 1998 he started a parallel career writing technical articles for Italian and international magazines. He works in Rome for CPI Progetti Spa (http://www.cpiprogetti.it) where he develops Internet/Intranet solutions using Microsoft technologies. Fabio would like to thank Wrox for the chance to write this book.

> *Dedication to Danila: As in every book I write and (I hope) will write, a special thanks goes to my unique love. You can't imagine how important it is to have a woman like her near me in the happy and sad moments that life gives to us. I love you so much…*

Kevin Hoffman

Kevin Hoffman is a Software Engineer and Architect working with .NET and Web Services in Houston, Texas. He started programming when his grandfather gave him a Commodore VIC-20 that he'd managed to repair after his uncle found it in the trash. Since then, he's done everything from writing head-to-head DOS games for 2400-baud modems to building enterprise e-commerce web applications in ASP. Ever since he got his hands on the first beta of .NET he's been completely hooked on playing with his favorite new toy: C#.

Billy Hollis

Billy Hollis first learned BASIC over 25 years ago, and is co-author of the first book ever published on Visual Basic .NET, VB.NET Programming on the Public Beta, from Wrox Press, as well as several other .NET books. He is a frequent speaker at conferences, including Comdex, TechEd, Microsoft's Professional Developer Conference (PDC), and the Visual Basic Insiders Technical Summit (VBITS), often on the topics of software design and specification, object-based development in Visual Basic, and Microsoft .NET. He was chosen by Microsoft to train all 200 instructors for its 2001 .NET Developer Tour.

Billy is MSDN Regional Director of Developer Relations in Nashville, Tennessee for Microsoft, and was named Regional Director of the Year for 2001 by Microsoft. He has hosted Developer Days in Nashville for the last four years. He has his own consulting company in Nashville that focuses on training, consultation, and software development for the Microsoft .NET platform.

> *My family has been supportive as always as I've squeezed in the time to write for this book, often at their expense. Those of us in the software industry love this time of intense innovation, but I'm sure Cindy, Ansel, and Dyson will be happier when things get back to the normal pace of change.*

Nick Manning

Nick is a technical editor and author at Wrox Press in Birmingham, UK. After a successful career in accountancy, he moved to IT a few years ago and joined Wrox in April 2001. He is an FCCA, MCSD, MCDBA, and MCSE, and has been involved with .NET since the Beta 1 stage. When he's not working, Nick enjoys home improvements, watching old sci-fi programs, and supporting Aston Villa Football Club.

VB.NET

Deployment

Handbook

Table of
Contents

Table of Contents

VB.NET

Deployment

Handbook

Introduction

Introduction

No matter how great your design and build of a .NET application is, it won't be of any use until you deploy it to the users it is intended for (unless you plan to run everything from your own development machine). Deploying your .NET applications correctly is as important as developing them correctly, and .NET brings many advantages to the deployment phase of software development. However, we often need to do much more than XCOPY our files from development to production machines as this book will show. Deploying your applications efficiently will not only benefit your users, it will benefit you with fewer calls to your help desk.

Who is this Book For?

All books in the Visual Basic .NET Handbook series are aimed at practicing Visual Basic .NET developers who need to learn how to complete a specific task. This book is no different and will be the ideal companion to any developer who needs to deploy the application that they've spent much time and effort in developing. This means that the book is suitable to virtually all developers whether they are in-house Windows application developers, third-party component developers, independent consultants, or anyone needing to deploy a Visual Basic .NET application.

To gain the most from this book, you will need a copy of Visual Basic .NET Standard Edition, or better, or any copy of Visual Studio .NET.

What Does this Book Cover?

This book covers all the ground that a developer needs to know in order to deploy their applications. Below is an outline of what each chapter contains.

Chapter 1 – Deployment Strategies

In this chapter we will discuss the various classic deployment scenarios and introduce the advantages that .NET brings to the deployment arena. Anyone who has been developing Windows software over the past few years will be well aware of the term "DLL Hell", and this chapter will explain how .NET was designed to overcome this and other problems.

Chapter 2 – Deployment Options in .NET

This chapter details the various options available to the developer when they are deciding how to deploy their applications. We cover the minimum requirements for .NET applications to run on a client computer, and introduce Windows Installers and the other methods of deployment. We also take a look at third-party deployment products.

Chapter 3 – Windows Installer Features

Having introduced Windows Installers in the previous chapter, this chapter covers them in detail. We explain how the various editors available, such as the File System editor, can be used to customize your setup packages. The chapter concludes with a complex example that illustrates many of the features discussed in the chapter, including how to install a custom database along with your application.

Chapter 4 – Configuring and Securing Applications

This chapter discusses the important issues of configuring and securing your applications. We start by explaining the building blocks of all .NET applications, namely Assemblies. We show you how to build assemblies and how to view their contents once they are built. Then we move on to using configuration files effectively in your applications. The second half of the chapter is devoted to securing your application and covers areas like Code Access Security and the .NET Framework Configuration tool.

Chapter 5 – Maintaining and Updating Applications

Shared assemblies form an important part of many .NET applications. In this chapter, we see how to create shared assemblies, including how to create a strong name. We explore the Global Assembly Cache, the machine-wide repository for shared assemblies that exists on all computers that have the .NET Framework installed. We cover the vital topic of Versioning that allows us to have multiple versions of the same assembly installed on the same computer without all the problems associated with DLL Hell.

Chapter 6 – Licensing

Once you have developed your application, you need to license it to ensure that only valid users benefit from your hard work. We cover the various licensing options available and show when and how to use them. The second part of the chapter is devoted to the topic of developer-to-developer licensing where one developer creates a component that is licensed to a second to use in their applications.

Chapter 7 – Protecting Your Intellectual Property

In this chapter we cover how to protect your work. We define what intellectual property is and detail some of the methods that other people may use to benefit from it without your consent. We look at some of the common methods (legal and technical) used to foil the potential thief or hacker.

Appendix A – Using Active Directory to Deploy the .NET Framework

For any computer to run a .NET application, it must first have the .NET Framework installed. This appendix details how the Windows 2000 Active Directory can be used to deploy the .NET Framework to client computers within a domain.

Appendix B – Deploying the .NET Framework with an Application

You may need to provide the .NET Framework to your clients at the same time as your application's setup package. This appendix shows how the two can be combined into one package.

Appendix C – An AutoDeploy Component

This appendix has been taken from the Wrox Press book *Visual Basic .NET Solutions Toolkit* (ISBN: 1-86100-739-6) and was written by Rockford Lhotka. It shows how to load and execute code from both DLLs and EXEs on a client computer without the need to manually copy any files.

Appendix D – Support, Errata, and Code Download

This appendix tells you of the support available from Wrox for this book, how to view or submit any errata, and how to download the code available at the Wrox web site.

Nick Manning
Editor – VB.NET Handbook Series, Wrox Press

VB.NET

Deployment

Handbook

1

Deployment Strategies

Software comes into existence on a development machine. To be useful, however, software must reside on appropriate production machines, which may be anything from web servers to user workstations. The process of getting the software onto the systems where it's needed is what we call **deployment**.

The Impact of .NET on Deployment

.NET has many effects on how we create and use software. Its transparent support for Internet technologies allows new application architectures using Web Services. ASP.NET and Web Forms bring rapid application development to web sites. From multi-language integration to mobile device support to easier smart client development, there's no shortage of changes wrought by .NET.

Yet the changes .NET brings to deployment are as important as any of these. .NET offers a host of deployment options that were not available for COM-based software. These options completely change the economics of deployment. The changes are so important that they can even alter the preferred architecture for a system written in .NET.

To see why this is true, let's first look at typical deployment scenarios in pre-.NET Visual Basic systems, and discuss their strengths and weaknesses.

Classic Deployment Scenarios

Visual Basic has existed since 1991, and the architectures used for systems written in VB have evolved considerably during that period. The major architectural patterns used include:

❑ Standalone client

❑ Client-server

❑ N-tier

❑ N-tier with browser-based interface

It's an oversimplification to restrict discussion to this list, but it will suffice to discuss the typical deployment challenges faced by pre-.NET Visual Basic systems. All of these architectures are still in use today for different systems, and all will be appropriate for certain new systems written in .NET.

Prior to the NT architecture, the Windows environment ran on top of MS-DOS. The deployment model for pre-Windows 9x applications mirrored the ease of deployment allowed by DOS. To deploy an application, the minimum requirements were simply to create a directory and copy the application's files into it.

With the advent of 32-bit systems, things became much more complex. Microsoft introduced the Component Object Model (COM), which eventually became the basis for much of Microsoft's 32-bit computing infrastructure. COM had some advantages, but easy deployment was not among them.

General Deployment Problems Caused by COM

Microsoft's COM standard was developed for use on small systems with limited memory (compared to today) running Microsoft Windows. The design tradeoffs for COM were oriented around sharing memory, and quick performance on hardware we would now consider slow.

This meant that **Dynamic Link Libraries (DLLs)** in COM are shared between applications, and a binary interface standard is used to give good performance. To allow the system to quickly find the components needed to run an application, DLLs have to register their class IDs in the local Windows Registry.

This requirement means that even simple applications using COM needed a sophisticated installation program. Such a setup program has to recognize whether necessary DLLs are already present and registered, and perform the registration if they are not. If the DLLs are to be shared with other programs, the installation program must also locate the DLLs in an appropriate location, which is, by a commonly used convention, a subdirectory of the main Windows directory.

Besides the registration logistics needed to make DLLs work at all, COM components have another huge deployment problem. They can easily be rendered inoperable by versioning issues. The resulting morass of problems related to versioning is known colloquially as "DLL Hell".

The need to register components locally also results in other limitations. It is not possible for a COM application to be placed on a CD-ROM or a network drive, and then run from that location without an installation procedure. The necessary local registration of components makes the installation procedure mandatory.

The problems of COM deployment haunt systems even when an application is no longer needed. Uninstalling a COM-based system is a major challenge. It is necessary to remove all the relevant Registry entries, while being careful not to remove any still needed by other systems. Determining what applications use a shared component and when the component is no longer needed by any active application is so difficult that most systems over time build up a large number of "orphaned" COM components in their shared component directory.

The impact of COM's deployment problems is huge. For example, it has caused major problems for packaged software vendors, some of whom report that half or more of their technical support calls are related to DLL conflicts. As we shall see below, the high cost of COM deployment on client machines drove the adoption of browser-based interfaces, even when such interfaces were not optimal for users.

Because of the ubiquitous nature of COM, all of the major architectural patterns mentioned in the list above suffered deployment drawbacks. Let's look at each pattern, and discuss a bit about its deployment.

Standalone Client

The earliest VB applications were mostly self-contained local applications. Some recent applications still use this model, usually because the application requires a smart user interface and contains no data that needs to be shared online with other users. Prototypical examples of such applications include a drawing or charting program, a word processing program with document layout capabilities, or a game.

Such applications might use a database, but it is typically located on the same machine as the application. The Microsoft JET Engine, on which Access is based, has historically been the most common database technology used for this architecture, typically accessed with Data Access Objects (DAO) or ActiveX Data Objects (ADO).

Such applications may or may not be componentized. Early applications, written in VB3 or earlier were not necessarily, because Visual Basic could not be used to build components then. Non-componentized standalone applications, in which the user interface logic, the business logic, and the data access logic are indiscriminately mixed, are often called *fat clients*. In fat client applications, all the logic sits in one large EXE, or possibly a small number of such EXEs.

Even with only EXEs to install, fat client applications built with classic VB for 32-bit Windows pose deployment challenges. Even if the application is not made up of COM components, it still must use COM components for such operations as data access. The VB4-VB6 libraries themselves are COM-based. The application might also use other third-party DLLs such as ActiveX/OCX controls. Therefore such applications still require installation technology. However, the installation of a fat client is not as complex as with some of the later architectures. For in-house fat-client applications, the Visual Basic Package and Deployment Wizard is the most commonly used tool to create an installation program. If the application must be installed on a large number of client machines (for example, a commercial software program, or an application used throughout a large corporation), a more robust installation program built using third-party tools is preferred.

Maintenance of such applications requires replacing the entire EXE that is affected. Even minor bug fixes need a large module to be distributed to each client.

Client-Server

Fat client applications were sometimes extended to place the data on a shared server. The multi-user databases used for this have more capability than the Jet engine, offering functionality such as stored procedures.

As fat clients shifted some processing to the shared database server, they evolved into *client-server* applications. The deployment issues for client-server applications in classic Visual Basic resemble those for fat clients. It's still necessary to install a data access technology (typically ADO) to each client machine, and for further configuration to occur so that a connection to a remote database can be made. In some cases, deploying such applications involves additional work to deploy the database elements on the server (starting data, stored procedures, etc.).

Client-server applications introduced a new deployment issue. If business logic were in the client code rather than in a stored procedure (common for such applications) then the same business logic might be on hundreds of separate machines. Changes to the business logic thus required all of them to be maintained and updated, and it was often necessary to do this in a coordinated fashion so that all systems were running the same business rules.

Client-server applications can be componentized, but most early ones were not. This complicated the "duplicate-code" problem because business rule updates often meant updating the entire client application just to make sure that updates were company-wide. As these systems became more complex, and as component technologies became more available in newer versions of Visual Basic, components began to be used extensively in client-server applications.

N-Tier

As the trend towards componentization took hold, a new application design began to be used. It was initially called 3-tier, because it added an additional layer between the client and the server. This layer ran on a shared server and encapsulated business rules in components on that server, which was often called an "application server". Later, the middle tier began to be segmented into multiple layers, and the more generic "n-tier" description become common.

The n-tier architecture helped simplify the maintenance of business logic to an extent. Since business logic in an n-tier system is mostly in business objects on the server, it is easier to change that logic without affecting the client machines. However, moving the business logic to the server added a new deployment challenge. The middle tier layers usually consisted of complex sets of inter-related components. The problems inherent in COM made deploying and maintaining these sets of components quite difficult.

N-tier architecture with COM-based client code combines the worst of COM's deployment problems. The high number of client machines requires an expensive, large-scale deployment effort for installation and maintenance, and the complex tier of COM components on the application server exposes the worst of COM's versioning and compatibility problems.

Browser-Based Interfaces

Something had to give in this world of expensive n-tier deployment. In 1996-1997, an alternative presented itself. Internet technologies became widely available, offering a means to host a user interface in a web browser with essentially zero deployment costs on the client systems. Systems using a browser-based interface also had the advantage of wide availability even when users were geographically distributed.

The new application model used the same n-tier design as described above, with a thinner user interface layer running completely in a browser. Such systems essentially turned the client machines into visually pleasing versions of old-style IBM 3270 or Wyse terminals, because the processing capabilities of the client machines were very lightly used.

The deployment of browser-based applications was the same as the n-tier scenario above for the middle tier and data tier. The client tier was contained in elements running on a web server, and was commonly written with Active Server Pages (ASP). Therefore, the necessities of web servers drove the deployment of the client tier for browser-based systems, requiring, for example, the creation of virtual directories for the web application to use.

The server-based deployment of browser-based applications is not simple. The complexities of COM make the application servers difficult to install and maintain, and the tier of the application running on the web server often contains COM components with the same problems. Web sites often contain static content developed outside the software development team, and coordinating content changes with software changes is an additional complexity.

At least these deployment problems are restricted to the servers, however. Once a web application is up and running, the application has no responsibility for deploying anything to the client. Responsibility for installing the browser lies with the vendor creating it, not with the application.

There are two situations that require attention during client deployment of web applications. If the application uses such technologies as plug-ins, applets, or ActiveX controls, then client deployment of these technologies is involved. And if the web application is targeted at a particular browser or family of browsers, then it may be necessary to facilitate the installation of a compatible browser by pointing users to a source for installation.

Dealing with the complexities of deployment to a web server is often handled with a chain of locations that receive new or changed parts of an application. The most common setup looks like this:

Figure 1

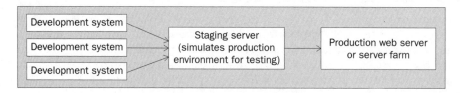

Client Deployment Mechanisms

As previously mentioned, browser-based systems can have complex deployment, but it is restricted to the servers. Applications containing a client-side tier of logic still face the difficulty of deploying to the client. The approach taken to solve that problem will vary with the number of clients and the complexity of the application.

In-house Corporate Deployments

Many COM-based systems produced for in-house corporate use are deployed to a fixed, relatively small number of users. It is not economic to invest huge amounts of money in deployment technology, so a simple installation program is used. It may not work for every user, but if it works for most of them the others can be tweaked manually to complete the installation.

VB Package and Deployment Wizard

The most common tool used for creating an installation program for a VB6 system that will be used by a relatively small number of client machines is the VB Package and Deployment Wizard (sometimes called the Setup Wizard). A VB6 project is used as the starting point, and the wizard also gathers a list of the components and other files included in the system, including the VB6 runtime files. Then the Package and Deployment Wizard creates an installation program that copies the necessary files, registers the components, and creates a menu of shortcuts. The starting point of the installation is a Setup.exe application. This is not a Visual Basic program, so it can run before the VB6 libraries are installed.

The VB Package and Deployment Wizard can easily encounter problems with DLL conflicts if used on a wide variety of clients with different versions of the operating system and various other products installed. However, the typical corporate scenario has only a few operating system versions and a small list of other products to worry about, so it's manageable to overcome the problems that arise as long as the number of client systems is not too large and they are not too geographically dispersed.

Off-the-Shelf Installation Technologies

For installing a VB6 application to a large number of clients, it is usually desirable to have better installation technology than the Package and Deployment Wizard can produce. There are vendors that offer products specifically for producing installation programs. The best known such products are InstallShield and Wise Installer.

These products offer the ability to write installation scripts, giving a lot more control over the installation process. They can detect the version of the operating system, for example, and alter their behavior depending on the OS being used. They also have mechanisms for detection and correction of errors encountered during installation, and for the rollback of the installation if it cannot be completed successfully. Finally, they automatically create technology to uninstall the application when necessary.

Later versions of these installation products interface to the Windows Installer technology introduced by Microsoft in 1999. Windows Installer works by packaging software into files with an extension of .msi. The Windows Installer technology is built into Windows 2000 and onwards, and it can be retrofitted to older 32-bit Windows operating systems.

Commercial packages almost always use these advanced installation products, and many use the Windows Installer technology. The wide variety of machines and environments into which packaged software will be installed dictates very smart installation technology. It is not unknown for commercial package vendors of COM-based software to spend up to thirty percent of their development expenses on installation and deployment technology.

A Continuum of COM-Based Applications

All of the architectural choices listed earlier are still used in various circumstances. To see why, we can consider applications as residing on a continuum. In the vertical dimension, applications at one end have simple user interfaces, and at the other applications require more sophisticated user interfaces. In the horizontal dimension, applications range from a small number of users to a large number. Here's a diagram of the continuum of COM-based applications:

Figure 2

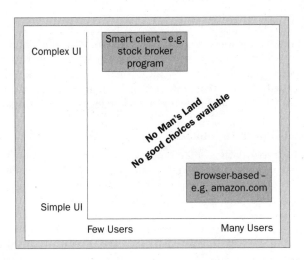

At two corners of this continuum, the preferred choice of architecture is clear. On the bottom right end, a browser-based interface is required to control deployment costs, and is entirely suitable because the UI is simple. On the top left, the application requires a smart client tier to gain the sophisticated user interfaces needed, but there are not too many users, so deployment costs are under control.

Other positions on the continuum must make tradeoffs. To get the low deployment costs, browser-based applications relinquish the ability to have a slick, responsive user interface. To get the intelligent user interface, smart client applications give up the wide availability and low deployment costs of browser-based applications.

In the middle of the continuum is a no-man's land, where neither choice is anywhere close to ideal. In today's COM-based world, the browser-based choice becomes the default for most applications in this no-man's land, because the low cost associated with browser-based deployment trumps the more intangible gains of a smart user interface.

This conundrum is solved to a great degree by .NET. As you'll see in the next section, .NET dramatically reduces deployment costs for many different kinds of architecture. We'll revisit this continuum of applications later in the chapter and discuss the implications .NET has for it.

Deployment Advantages of .NET

When Microsoft began to design .NET, it was aware of the deployment problems of COM. Because of these problems, .NET was designed to eliminate many of these. In particular, .NET does not require the components to be registered in the Windows Registry, and is capable of running an arbitrary number of DLLs with the same interface side by side.

It is hard for an experienced Windows component developer to see how anything can work without registration, GUIDs, and the like, but .NET does. Simple applications produced in .NET can be designed to install with a simple copy. Just copy the files onto the disk and run the application. Windows programmers haven't seen this since the days of DOS.

But there are many additional deployment improvements in .NET. Versioning is simpler and more flexible, and uninstalling .NET applications is dramatically easier. However, before we can discuss these deployment improvements, we need to discuss some basics of how .NET is structured.

The Major Elements of .NET

The word ".NET" has become attached to many things, but when we refer to .NET in this book, we mean the .NET Framework. This is the software that resides on a machine and provides a new platform for application development and execution.

There are two major parts of the .NET Framework: the **Common Language Runtime** (often abbreviated the CLR), and the **Framework Base Classes**, usually just called the base classes, or class library.

The CLR is an execution engine that loads, manages, and executes programs created by .NET compilers. The way the CLR operates has a huge impact on .NET's deployment features. We will look at it in detail shortly.

The Framework Base Classes comprise a large library of pre-written functionality. These classes provide .NET with capabilities such as:

❑ Data access

❑ Security checking

❑ Thread manipulation

❑ Math libraries

❑ Graphics operations to the screen

❑ Internet communication

❑ XML access and manipulation

❑ Encryption and decryption

This list just touches the surface of the Framework Base Classes. Using this library, applications don't need to contain as much code as on previous platforms. The Framework Base Classes take care of a great deal of lower level, "infrastructure" code, allowing .NET applications to concentrate on the necessary business rules and operations.

Many of the Framework Base Classes wrap functionality that was previously available through the Windows API and other low-level interfaces. Wrapping this functionality provides a more usable, consistent format to the programmer, and speeds application development. For example, to get the name of the current logged-in user, it isn't necessary to go through a Windows API call. A .NET Framework component can be easily instantiated that exposes the current user as a property.

The Framework Base Classes affect deployment because they allow even small programs in .NET to be quite powerful. Once the .NET Framework, with this vast library, is installed to a system, actual application systems can be modestly sized.

Since .NET applications are fairly compact, it is feasible to deploy them in new ways. They can be deployed on the fly over the Internet for example, as will be shown later in the chapter.

Some of the base classes are particularly important for deployment. Those that allow compiled modules in .NET to be examined internally and manipulated, for example, are used for various deployment-related purposes. These classes are in a namespace called Reflection – the full name of the namespace is System.Reflection.

Except for special classes in the Framework Base Classes that are used for deployment purposes, we won't need to discuss the Framework Base Classes in any more detail in this book. But we do need to look in some detail at the CLR.

The Common Language Runtime

The key to understanding deployment in .NET is to understand how .NET's execution engine, the Common Language Runtime, works. You can get details on that from many sources, but here's a quick overview.

Assemblies and Metadata

All code in .NET is compiled from the source language to a compact byte-code format called **Intermediate Language**, or IL for short. However, compilers in .NET are responsible for more than simply creating this byte code. Compilers in .NET must create an entire unit, called an assembly, which contains both compiled byte code and all the information needed to run the code. This information embedded in an assembly is called **metadata**.

Metadata includes information such as:

❑   The name and version of the assembly

❑   The other assemblies this assembly needs to run (its dependencies)

❑   The classes contained in the assembly and their interfaces

❑   Security permissions the assembly needs to run

❑   Copyright and trademark information

There is a great deal of additional information in the metadata, but this listing will be sufficient to explain .NET's deployment model. Assemblies and their structure are discussed in more detail in Chapter 4.

The concept of metadata is not new. COM components use a form of it called a type library, which contains metadata describing the classes exposed by the component, and is used to facilitate OLE Automation. Using the facilities of COM+ also requires supplying more metadata to specify, for example, whether a component supports transactions.

One of the drawbacks to metadata in COM and COM+ is that metadata is stored in different places, and outside the component. A component's type library may be stored in a separate file and the component's registration GUID (which would be considered metadata related to identification of the component) is stored in the Windows registry.

In contrast, the metadata in .NET is stored in one place – *inside* the component it describes. Metadata in .NET also contains more information about the component, and is better organized.

This metadata is key to the easy deployment in .NET. When a component is upgraded or moved, the necessary information about the component cannot be left behind. Metadata can never get out of sync with a .NET component because it is not in a separate file. Everything the CLR needs to run a component is supplied with the component.

Structure of the CLR

As the execution engine, all .NET code runs in the context of the CLR. It must be present on the system before any .NET code can run. If a .NET application is being deployed to a system, and there is no certainty that the .NET Framework is already present, then installation of the .NET Framework must occur first, if it is not already present. Installation of the .NET Framework places both the CLR and the Framework Base Classes on the target machine.

In the future, operating systems from Microsoft are expected to contain a version of the .NET Framework built-in and so it should be less of an issue when deploying .NET applications. However, in the near term, installation of the .NET Framework will be one of the responsibilities of a good deployment system.

The Execution Cycle

The way the CLR executes code is not obvious, because it works differently from most previous runtime architectures. In particular, the CLR does not interpret the IL byte code. Instead, there is a step performed automatically by the CLR to further compile the byte code to binary code for the current machine; the code goes through a just-in-time (**JIT**) compiler. The code that actually runs in .NET is thus fully compiled binary code, which results in good performance. However, the assemblies containing IL byte code are compact, and have a degree of portability to future .NET execution environments on other systems.

.NET compilers must be able to create assemblies containing IL code and metadata. These assemblies are then executed by the CLR. When an assembly is loaded, it first goes through the Just-In-Time (JIT) compiler. The assembly's byte code is compiled as necessary, on the fly, to machine-specific binary code. This binary representation is cached for the current execution of the application. However, it is lost and must be re-created the next time the application runs.

Provided in the .NET Framework SDK, is a utility to force the binary compilation of an assembly, and to store that compiled binary version indefinitely. The pre-compiled binary is then used instead of going through the JIT compiler at execution time. This results in faster loading of the assembly, and is a good way to increase performance for frequently used modules. This utility is called Ngen.exe, and it can be invoked from the command line. Install scripts can use Ngen.exe to pre-compile an entire application to binary to possibly improve the application's performance. Details on that are in Chapter 7. Please note that using Ngen.exe doesn't mean that a self-contained executable is created. The CLR is still necessary to execute it, but the code being executed doesn't have to be passed through the just-in-time compiler (JITed) before execution.

Fixing the Limitations of COM

Because of the way the CLR loads, manages, and executes code, .NET applications do not have most of the deployment drawbacks of COM applications. Here is an overview of how .NET handles the most serious deployment limitations of COM. More details on these subjects are included in later chapters.

Side-by-Side Installations

COM components are located only by using a GUID in the Registry. This points all applications on a single machine to the same version of a particular DLL. However, in .NET, DLLs can reside in the application directory, and they will be automatically loaded from there. Since there is no registration required for such DLLs, as many of them as necessary can exist in separate application directories, and each will be loaded for its corresponding application. Some of these DLLs may be the same, others may have differences, but they all load and execute side-by-side. The CLR manages which DLL is used by which application automatically.

.NET includes many capabilities to manage versioning and side-by-side execution of DLLs and Chapter 5 goes into detail on these capabilities.

End of DLL Hell

COM interfaces are binary, and even minor, seemingly insignificant changes can easily break the ability of an application to use a component. COM DLLs have a strict versioning scheme to keep things in order, but this introduces the problem of easily introducing an incompatible DLL, or several of them, when doing maintenance. This combination of problems yields a situation where it may be close to impossible to sort out the interfaces and their versions. This is DLL Hell.

.NET interfaces are type based, and have a resilient binding mechanism that doesn't allow insignificant binary differences to prevent compatibility. This relieves DLL Hell because it becomes much harder to break a tier of interrelated components with minor changes. When problems do occur, .NET's binding mechanisms more precisely pinpoint the source of the problem, making it easier to fix.

Application Directory vs. GAC

The **Global Application Cache** (usually called the GAC) is the .NET analog of the Windows Registry (as mentioned earlier), at least for purposes of locating centralized components. However, it only needs to be used for components shared among applications. Components intended for a single application (or even for two or three applications) can be placed in the application directory (as previously discussed), and do not need to be registered in the GAC. The GAC also has facilities for loading multiple versions of the same component as if an assembly's metadata points to an assembly in the GAC, then it will always include the version.

Chapter 5 deals in detail with the GAC and how to manage programs in it. That chapter also discusses versioning in more detail.

Easy Uninstall

For a simple .NET application, uninstalling just means deleting the application's directory. Because .NET does not place entries in the Registry, uninstalling a .NET program does not involve removal of these entries. Configuration information for .NET is not normally installed in the Registry either. It is placed in a configuration file residing in the application's directory, and is therefore deleted with the rest of the application.

It is also not considered good practice to place shared .NET DLLs in locations such as the Windows\System32 directory, so it's easier to avoid "orphaned" DLLs. Using Reflection, it is relatively easy to create utilities that can scan a disk and see what shared DLLs are not in use, making it easier to identify and delete these shared DLLs.

It may still be appropriate to create an uninstall program for a .NET application, but it is normally far simpler than an equivalent program for a COM application. This relative simplicity of removing a .NET application from a system is sometimes expressed by saying that a .NET application has a "no-impact install", or a "low-impact install".

New Deployment Options in .NET

Because .NET fixes many of the deployment limitations of COM, it offers a wider array of deployment options. It also offers some new options, such as Internet deployment, based on technologies specifically built into .NET for deployment.

Keep in mind that all of these deployment options assume that the client machines have the .NET Framework installed. Here are some of the new options:

- ❑ Install an application by copying its modules into a directory, and then immediately execute the application.

- ❑ Run an application directly from a shared drive on a network.

- ❑ Run an application directly from a CD-ROM or DVD with no installation procedure.

- ❑ Deploy a standalone application from a web server, but run it locally on the client machine. This is often referred to as Internet deployment.

Let's go into more detail on these new options.

Copying into a Directory

We have already discussed the option of copying files into a directory and immediately running the application by clicking on an EXE. The files usually originate from one of two alternatives – a CD-ROM or a shared location on a network. In many respects, this option resembles deployment under MS-DOS.

As you'll see later, if you move beyond simple applications, you may still need an installation program. But it is guaranteed to be far simpler than its pre-.NET equivalent.

Running from a Shared Drive

Many organizations have a network that makes resources such as printers and shared disks available to all client machines. While such a network could be used to make the installation of COM applications more convenient, it was still necessary to go through the usual registration process for each component. This made it necessary to have an installation program. If a DLL on the shared drive was changed, another registration process was necessary for client systems to use the new DLL.

.NET needs no registration of an application's components, so an application can run directly from a shared network location with no installation process (except any necessary configuration of the application to an individual user). Users can just point to the application on the network and execute it.

If a DLL is changed on the shared drive, that DLL is then used by all client systems the next time it is needed. Nothing special needs to happen on the client system to make the new DLL active. It will automatically be used the next time the application is begun.

There is one limitation to using deployment this way in .NET. The individual client systems must have their security policy configured to allow applications to run as expected from a non-local drive. By default, applications running from a non-local location are not fully trusted and the CLR restricts what the code can do. This is discussed in more detail in the section on security later in this chapter.

Running an Application from Removable Media

Suppose you have a CD-ROM or DVD that contains a large amount of archived data. You might want to place an application program on the media with the data that would allow the data to be searched or browsed. If you create such a program with COM-based tools, it must be installed from the media to the local machine before being used. Registration issues force this step.

However, as with applications on a shared drive, .NET doesn't need registration, so the program can be run off the CD-ROM or DVD (or floppy or other removable medium) with no installation process. Because these drives are considered part of the local file system, it is not even necessary to configure security permissions for this capability to work.

Internet Deployment

The options above are not as convenient for an application that must be installed on a set of client machines that are geographically dispersed. The obviously desirable mechanism to deploy such applications is the Internet.

Fortunately, .NET also includes the capability to deploy an application over the Internet. This capability is especially applicable to Windows forms applications because they carry their own user interface along with them.

How Internet Deployment Works

To use Internet deployment, the client machine must have the .NET Framework installed and an Internet connection. At the other end, the system used for deployment must be a web server with .NET and Internet Information Server (IIS) on it.

The application to be deployed is placed in a directory on the server that can be located with a URL. Then the application can then be launched in one of two ways:

❑   Click on a link in a web page that points to the application's startup EXE on the server.

❑   Use a small "launcher" application to point to the main application on the server. This launcher is essentially a local shortcut to the application. It must be located on the local file system, and it usually gets there by being copied via FTP or e-mailed as an attachment.

As you'll see, it is more common to use the second mechanism because it allows the security policy to be set more easily. However, both mechanisms work very much the same from the point at which the application is launched. In particular, both mechanisms cause the application to be downloaded from the Internet and executed locally.

Here is a diagram showing the steps in this process of deployment and execution. For this example, we will assume that:

❑   The application on the web server resides in two separate DLLs

❑   The application should start with a form named StartForm in AppDLL1.dll

❑   The application contains another DLL named AppDLL2.dll, and this DLL contains a form named OptionsForm

❑   We are using a launcher program that has already been copied to the local file system

Figure 3

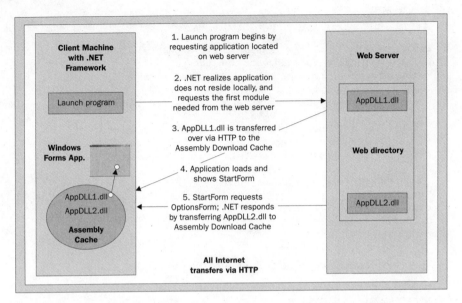

Since this chapter has not presented any real code so far, we'll take this opportunity to cover the process of Internet deployment in detail, including how to write the code in the launcher program to start the process.

Here are the steps needed to build a Windows forms application that will be deployed over the Internet with a launcher program:

1. Create the forms-based application in exactly the same way you normally would develop a Windows forms app.

2. When you have finished developing the application, change the compile option for all the Windows forms projects in the application to create a DLL. Windows forms applications normally compile as an EXE, but you can change the compilation model for a project in its Project Properties. Under the Common Properties | General tab, there is an option called Output type. You should set it to Class Library to create a DLL that contains the Windows forms application. We assume this was done for AppDLL1.dll in Figure 3.

3. Copy all the DLLs containing the application into a web folder. This includes the DLL containing the startup Windows form for the application, plus any DLLs that contain components or other forms needed in the application. DLLs that are part of the .NET Framework should not be included.

4. Create the launch program. Start a new Windows forms application, and place a button on the blank Form1. In the button's Click event handler, place the following code:

```
Try
    Dim sLocation As String
    sLocation = "http://MyWebServer/MyDeploymentDirectory/AppDLL1.dll"

    Dim objStartAssembly As [Assembly] = [Assembly].LoadFrom(sLocation)
    ' This line needs to change to include
    ' the namespace and name of your starting form.
    Dim FormType As Type = _
        objStartAssembly.GetType("MyProjectName.StartForm")

    ' Create an instance of the Form as a generic object
    Dim objStartForm As Object
    objStartForm = Activator.CreateInstance(FormType)

    Dim Form2 As Form = CType(objStartForm, Form)
    Form2.Show()
Catch ex As Exception
    MsgBox(ex.Message)
End Try
```

5. Place the following line at the top of the form code:

```
Imports System.Reflection
```

6. In the above code, change the URL for the DLL that contains the first form needed to the location on your web server. Also change the name of the form in the line that begins Dim FormType to your project name coupled with the name of your form.

7. Compile the launch program and transport it to the machine to which the application will be deployed (preferably a machine separate from your development machine). That machine must have the .NET Framework installed. Run the launch program, and press the button. The application will start, but you will need to change security settings to make it fully functional. Security will be discussed in more detail later.

What is Happening Behind the Scenes

When the launch program executes, it requests the loading of classes from assemblies that do not yet exist on the client. At that point, as we saw in the diagram earlier, the assembly is automatically fetched from the deployment web server and placed on the local client machine. It resides on the client machine in the application download cache.

Once the assembly has been placed in the application download cache on the client, classes from the assembly can be loaded and run. That includes any forms needed (since Windows forms are just classes in .NET), or any other objects that are part of the application. You can see the assemblies in the download cache by opening a command window from the Visual Studio .NET menu, and entering the command:

```
> gacutil /ldl
```

We can step through the code above to get a better idea of what is happening. At the top of the launch program code we placed the line:

```
Imports System.Reflection
```

As mentioned earlier, the `Reflection` namespace is used to work with assemblies, their interfaces, and their metadata. It contains a number of classes, including the `Assembly` class, which refers to a particular .NET assembly. This class is used in the code above to load an assembly from a web server.

Inside the `Try` block, the first two lines of code set the location of the web server that will be used for deployment. As previously mentioned, you'll need to change the URL to point to the DLL that contains the first form in your application.

Then an `Assembly` object is instantiated using the `LoadFrom()` method of the `Assembly` class. That method allows a reference to an assembly to be loaded from a URL or a file's pathname. The brackets around the word `Assembly` are there because the word `Assembly` is also a reserved word in VB.NET, so the brackets inform the compiler that you want the `Assembly` class (in the `System.Reflection` namespace) instead of the `Assembly` keyword.

If the assembly that is being referenced is not in the download cache, it is fetched from the web server and a copy is placed in the download cache. Then the assembly object is ready for use in the code.

The next line of code (which must be changed to show the correct namespace path) is:

```
Dim FormType As Type = _
    objStartAssembly.GetType("MyProjectName.StartForm")
```

This line uses the `Assembly` object to fetch a type from the assembly. In our case, the type is the `StartForm` type for the Windows form we want to load. The definition of this type is placed into a `System.Type` object.

The next two lines of code are:

```
Dim objStartForm As Object
objStartForm = Activator.CreateInstance(FormType)
```

This is one of the few cases in .NET where you use anything other than the New keyword to instantiate a class. This code instantiates a form object using the type of StartForm just fetched from the assembly. The instantiation is done with the System.Activator class, which contains methods to create types of objects, either locally or remotely. The CreateInstance() method of the Activator class is roughly analogous to the CreateObject() function in VB6 and VBScript.

The final two lines in the Try block are:

```
Dim Form2 As Form = CType(objStartForm, Form)
Form2.Show()
```

The first of these two lines is used to cast the generic object objStartForm to an object of the specific type System.Windows.Forms.Form. This will allow early binding of the object. The next line just shows the form and the application is started.

At this point the launch program is done. The application is under the control of the form that was loaded from the web server. It can carry out operations and load additional forms as necessary. If it loads additional forms from the same assembly, those forms are automatically loaded without any special logic. If it loads additional forms from other DLLs on the web server, then those DLLs are also automatically deployed as necessary. This allows the application to be deployed a piece at a time as individual assemblies are needed, as long as an Internet connection is available.

Versioning

When .NET checks the download cache for an assembly, if it finds the assembly, then it checks the assembly's version. It also checks the current version of the same assembly on the web server (assuming an Internet connection is available). If there is a new version of the assembly on the web server, that new version is transferred to the download cache and used instead of the earlier version. This enables a new version of an assembly to be deployed by just copying it to the deployment web server. The rest of the deployment sequence for the new version is automatic.

If an application happens to be in offline mode, it will skip the test for current version and just use whatever version it has in the download cache. This enables the application to continue working if an Internet link is unavailable.

How .NET Changes the Economics

These new options for deployment under .NET significantly reduce the deployment costs of an application. This is certainly helpful in the case of server-based applications, but in that case the relatively small number of machines limits the potential savings. Where .NET really changes the economics of deployment is applications that install to many client machines.

Let's revisit our continuum of applications, and see how things change under .NET.

Figure 4

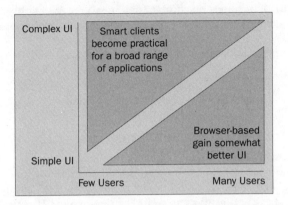

The lower right corner of this continuum gets some changes because ASP.NET allows browser-based interfaces to become more capable without an inordinate amount of work. However, the big changes are in the upper left corner The dramatically lower costs of deploying to a large number of clients makes it practical to use smart client interfaces for a far broader range of applications.

The Resurgence of the Smart Client

We didn't stop making smart client, forms-based interfaces because users didn't like them. We stopped making them because they were just too expensive to deploy compared to the browser-based alternative. With those economics now changed, smart client applications are poised to retake much of the ground lost to browser-based applications in the last five years.

Users can certainly benefit from smart client interfaces that are fast and responsive. Smart client interfaces can far more effectively use the intelligence of the client machines. Security is better on smart clients. The user interface can be controlled down to a keystroke-by-keystroke level to make it optimum for the user.

Distributed Smart Client Architecture

It's important to recognize that "Internet enabled" does not equal "browser-based". Internet enabled simply means that applications communicate over the Internet. It is quite feasible for smart client applications to get their data over the Internet using mechanisms such as Web Services.

The new combination of Internet deployment, smart client interfaces, and web services for data is a powerful one. It combines the best of many technologies. Many .NET applications, especially those that are both geographically distributed and require excellent interfaces, will use this new model.

Distributed smart client architectures are a prime example of a case where deployment under .NET affects the choice of application architecture. In COM, it was usually not practicable because of the high deployment cost, but with that cost dramatically reduced under .NET, it becomes practicable for a broad range of applications. It should be evaluated as an alternative to a browser-based architecture for many scenarios, including:

❑　Geographically distributed corporate applications

❑　Extranet applications

❑　Internet applications involving complex media

Implications for Packaged Software

If you are in the world of commercial software, you know that COM has not been kind to packages. Vendors of commercial software spend an immense amount of time and money on COM-related installation and deployment issues. .NET promises to change the economics for these applications as well. The deployment changes alone make .NET a much better platform for commercial software than COM.

Classic Architectures Revisited

Each of the classic architectures for VB programs changes its deployment under .NET. Let's summarize the changes:

Standalone Client

The standalone client application can use the deployment options mentioned above. Its deployment characteristics are similar to the smart-client case.

If the smart client is a stable application with many modules, it probably makes sense to use one option to create an application directory and copy in the files, with other minor installation chores if needed. There are no compelling reasons to use Internet deployment in this case, and the Internet deployment does exact a small performance penalty when the application starts up.

Client-Server

The deployment options above are all possibilities for client-server applications. Since many client-server apps are inside organizations and run on the organization's network, the shared network drive is one of the better options. If network traffic is a major consideration (because the application is used by a very large number of users, for example), it may be more practical to install the application to each client via one of the other mechanisms discussed earlier. If each client has a local installation into an application directory, an automated process to check for updates may be desirable.

N-Tier

The n-tier deployment changes are a superset of those for client-server. The smart-client tier is installed as previously discussed. The middle tiers are usually installed with more manual methods, using .NET's capability to run DLLs straight out of application directories, and to replace them on the fly.

If the n-tier application needs to scale to enterprise levels or support distributed transactions, then the middle tier components many need to be deployed to use COM+ Services. The `System.EnterpriseServices` namespace in .NET provides classes that allow .NET to work with COM+ Services. *Professional VB.NET Transactions* from Wrox Press (ISBN 1-86100-595-4) has more information on using COM+ Services from VB.NET.

Browser-Based Interfaces

N-tier applications with browser-based interfaces get the same middle-tier deployment advantages discussed above. For the client-tier, .NET's ability to change DLLs on the fly has big implications. It means a new DLL on the web server can be copied over the old one without stopping the web server. Older page instances will continue to use the old DLL classes, and new ones will begin using the new DLL automatically.

However, the big change for browser-based interfaces is that they are not needed as much. In many cases, they can be replaced by a distributed smart client application to give the user a better, more productive interface. The deployment costs of such smart clients are not quite as low as a browser-based client, but they are far lower than with COM and are economical for many more applications.

Limitations Imposed by Security Requirements

As applications become more distributed over the Internet, security assumes more and more importance. Recognizing this, .NET has a very sophisticated security infrastructure. The objective of .NET security is to distinguish legitimate code from potential malicious code, and to possibly impose limitations on even legitimate code so that it can only perform appropriate operations. Legitimate code can be recognized via a variety of characteristics, including its location, origin, publisher, and hashed key value. The publisher of a module can be identified with a public encryption key.

The information that allows .NET to recognize trusted applications and to configure their permissions is called its **security policy**. Chapter 4 goes into considerable detail on security in .NET. However, it's helpful to have a brief overview at this point to understand the general limitations security poses on deployment.

By default, .NET applications running from the local file system are completely trusted. Once code is copied form any source to the local file system, the default security policies of .NET will allow it to access any resources on the local system, within the security restrictions imposed by the operating system. This default policy can be changed for a client system to impose any security constraints.

.NET applications that are running from a shared network drive, or that are deployed using Internet deployment, have completely different default behavior. The original released version of the .NET Framework gives this code a minimal set of privileges, including only the ability to execute and display windows. In Service Pack 1 of the .NET Framework, the default security settings completely disable this code until permission to run it has been specified in the local machine's security policy. Intranet and Internet applications are two different kinds of application that can be given separate security settings, but are set the same by default when the .NET Framework is installed.

For code deployed via these mechanisms, it is mandatory to alter the security policy for each client machine. This is not as bad as it sounds. It is possible to allow a client machine to run all applications from a given shared drive or web site in one operation, for example, by giving such applications an appropriate level of trust. But this step must be considered when planning deployment using these mechanisms.

Configuration Issues

We previously mentioned that configuration information for .NET applications normally does not go in the Windows Registry. .NET has its own configuration files in an XML format.

In many respects, these .NET configuration files can be considered analogous to old-style INI files. However, the hierarchical capability of XML makes these new configuration files much more flexible.

Using .NET Configuration Files

Let's look at the format Microsoft uses in its XML-based configuration files for .NET. In this format, the root element is named Configuration and the first-level elements correspond to the sections in an INI file. Each section can then have attributes, which correspond to the key-value pairs in an INI file. There is a section called configSections that names the other sections that will be used in the configuration file. There is also a section called appSettings that is the most commonly used location for application parameters, and it has shortcut means of access (shown in the following example code).

Here is an example configuration file using this format:

```
<configuration>
  <configSections>
    <section name="MySection"
             type="System.Configuration.SingleTagSectionHandler" />
    <section name="AppSettings"
             type="System.Configuration.SingleTagSectionHandler" />
  </configSections>

  <MySection MyFirstEntry="Value for First Entry"
             MyLastEntry="Value for last entry" />

  <appSettings>
    <add key="AppSettingsEntry1" value="First App Settings Value" />
  </appSettings>

</configuration>
```

More complex configuration files are possible. It is possible to do hierarchical storage of configuration information, for example. However, the simple form above will be sufficient for our discussion and examples.

Such a configuration file is named with the name of the application's EXE file plus the suffix `.config`. The file is located in the directory as the application's EXE file. For example, if the application is named `MyApp.exe`, the configuration file should be `MyApp.exe.config`, and it should be in the same directory in which `MyApp.exe` is located. The `ConfigurationSettings` class, as seen in the example in the next section, loads configuration information from a file, which has the appropriate name and location. `ConfigurationSettings` does not have a method to load from any other source.

In the sections below, we will just look at the basics of reading and storing key-value pairs in attributes as shown above.

.NET Framework Classes for Configuration

If you just want to read the information in these configuration files from Visual Basic .NET, there is a set of classes in the .NET Framework to do that. However, those classes don't let you set up your own sections in the configuration file and write to them – you have to do that manually. The classes are in the `System.Configuration` namespace.

Here is a simple example using these classes to read key-value pairs for an application section. This is the code needed to read the application configuration file shown above, and to display the value in the `MyFirstEntry` attribute of the `MySection` element:

```
Imports System.Configuration
Imports System.Collections
  . . .
    ' This code goes further down in the module, e.g. behind a button
    Dim MyTable As IDictionary
    Dim sValue As String
    Dim value2 As String
    Dim value3 As String

    MyTable = CType(ConfigurationSettings.GetConfig("MySection"), _
       IDictionary)
    sValue = CType(MyTable("MyFirstEntry"), String)
    MsgBox(sValue)

    Dim MyAppSettings As _
       System.Collections.Specialized.NameValueCollection
    MyAppSettings = ConfigurationSettings.AppSettings
    sValue = CType(MyAppSettings("AppSettingsEntry1"), String)
    MsgBox(sValue)
```

This code uses the `ConfigurationSettings` class and retrieves a collection of key-value pairs in `MySection`, storing them in `MyTable`. Then the item in `MyTable` for `MyFirstEntry` is fetched and placed in a message box.

The code also loads the settings from the `appSettings` section and displays the value for the one named `AppSettingsEntry1`. If you have trouble running this code, make sure you have correct capitalization in the `appSettings` section of the XML configuration file. "appSettings" should have a lower case "A", and neither "key" nor "value" should be capitalized.

Adding or changing configuration values in the .NET configuration files can be done manually, or in code with standard XML operations (using the capabilities in the `System.XML` namespace). Examples are beyond the scope of this book. Installation programs in .NET must often fix configuration settings for an application to customize it to the user.

Why You Still Need Installation Programs

.NET dramatically reduces amount spent on installation technology, but does not eliminate the need. Here are a few of the actions an installation program may need to take to install a .NET application:

❑ Setting up database connections or other configuration information

❑ Placing icons in appropriate places

❑   Installing shared assemblies to the Global Assembly Cache (GAC)

❑   Registering legacy COM components (including ActiveX controls)

❑   Installing the .NET Framework itself

This book assumes that in most cases, you will need to write an install program. Depending on complexity, it may be done using the built-in installation capabilities in Visual Basic .NET, or it may require more powerful third-party installation technology. Both options are covered in this book.

Why You Still Need to Worry about COM

.NET offers easy access to legacy COM components. It is very easy to refer to a COM component from a .NET application. .NET creates a wrapper assembly, called a Runtime-Callable Wrapper, which exposes the COM component as if it were a .NET component. This capability is usually referred to as COM Interop.

You may still need to be concerned about COM deployment if your system uses COM Interop to access any COM components. Some of the reasons you might require COM Interop include:

❑   **You are using ActiveX controls** – Your project may require ActiveX controls that do not have .NET equivalents. For example, System.Windows.Forms does not contain a web browser control or the Microsoft Media Player control. Some third-party ActiveX controls also do not have .NET equivalents.

❑   **You are using third-party COM components** – ActiveX controls are not the only form of pre-packaged functionality that can be purchased from third-party vendors. COM-based components, often running on application servers, are also integrated into many applications. Such components must still be used until they have .NET equivalents. Some may never get them.

❑   **You have legacy COM components needed by your new .NET application** – If you have upgraded your system from VB6, in some cases it makes sense leave certain components in VB6. These components may still be needed for other systems that have not been migrated, for example. Or it may be impossible to migrate the components because the source code has been lost.

If your system contains any COM or ActiveX components, all of them must still be installed according to the rules of COM. The .NET wrapper assemblies that interface .NET to these COM components require no special treatment – they are normal .NET assemblies.

We won't be covering COM deployment in this book. If you already have such components, you should already be familiar with the deployment issues you face. For more information on COM Interop, see the Wrox Press book *Professional Visual Basic Interoperability*, ISBN 1-86100-565-2.

Summary

One of the most important effects of .NET is to reduce deployment costs and to multiply deployment options. .NET thus changes the economics of deployment for a wide variety of applications.

These changes are so significant that they even change the preferred architecture for some systems. In the world of COM, browser-based systems, in particular, are often chosen because of their low client deployment costs. In .NET, many of these systems could logically be replaced by smart client alternatives.

Understanding these new deployment options is important. You need to be aware of all the available options and their relative costs so that you can choose the right application architecture and the right deployment model for a given scenario.

You must also understand the relationship between deployment and security to be effective. Different deployment models have different security implications, and while .NET's security model offers a wide range of functionality, it comes with considerable complexity.

Now you are ready to dive into the details, starting with a simple deployment scenario, and then going on to more complex options. Later chapters will deal with configuration, security, versioning, licensing, and protecting your intellectual property.

VB.NET

Deployment

Handbook

2

Deployment Options in .NET

Some of the first questions that developers ask themselves are:

❑ What do I have to do in order to install this application on other computers, now that I have created it?

❑ Which operating systems are supported?

❑ If my application uses database access, do I need to install a specific database package?

At the end of this chapter you will be able to satisfactorily answer these questions. Moreover, you will be aware of the new tools provided by Visual Studio .NET in order to assist in the preparation of a Windows Installer package (MSI file), as well as of some third-party products.

This chapter is an introduction to the various deployment options open to you. If you have never deployed an application using the various tools provided by .NET, then this chapter will prove very useful. If you have, then read on as there will likely be some areas that you haven't seen before. By the end of this chapter, you will have been given an overview of the full scope of deployment tools available to you, the developer, and will be able to put the more detailed topics covered in the next chapters into context.

Below is a summary of what is covered in this chapter:

❑ **What you need to install .NET applications**: typical installation requirements, as well as software and server application requirements.

❑ **Windows Installer**: implementing Visual Studio .NET tools to create a simple application with a setup project.

- ❏ **Other deployment projects**: a brief introduction on other deployment projects, such as Web Setup, CAB file, and so on.

- ❏ **XCopy**: for easy web projects you will see how simple it is to deploy applications using the straightforward method of copying the files and the directory structure they're contained within.

- ❏ **Third-party deployment solutions**: a brief introduction to the "Wise for Visual Studio .NET" tool.

Let's start with installation requirements.

Installation Requirements

The Microsoft .NET Framework 1.0 is the core of all .NET applications and must be present on any target computer where you want to install your application. The Framework contains the Common Language Runtime engine (CLR) and class library, necessary to consume the intermediate language (MSIL) contained in the assemblies and executables created with the compilers.

So the first step needed in installation is to check that the .NET Framework 1.0 is present on the target computer and, if necessary, install the .NET Framework. At the Microsoft site (http://msdn.microsoft.com/downloads/default.asp?URL=/downloads/sample.asp ?url=/msdn-files/027/001/829/msdncompositedoc.xml) you can find the .NET Framework Redistributable package that contains all the necessary files to execute any .NET code. You can find the same file on the Windows Component Update CD within the Visual Studio .NET package, on the .NET Framework SDK CD, and within Windows update online with Windows XP.

> The `dotnetfx.exe` file contains the .NET Framework redistributable files, but from the Microsoft site you will receive the `dotnetredist.exe` file. Decompress it in a temporary folder and use the resulting `dotnetfx.exe` file in your installation packages.

To install the .NET Framework on the target computer, just execute the `dotnetfx.exe` file and follow the instructions. There are some software installation requirements that you must comply with. These are: the version of Windows must be one of Microsoft Windows 98 or NT 4 (Service Pack 6) or higher, and you need Internet Explorer 5.01 or greater.

Depending on your application requirements you might also need to install the following:

❑ **Microsoft Data Access Components 2.7** (**MDAC**). If your application uses database access with managed providers, you will have to install MDAC components. You can find the last version of the MDAC components at the http://www.microsoft.com/data/download_270RTM.htm site. You can also download the localized version of the MDAC component from this location.

❑ **Internet Information Server 5**, or later. If you have created an ASP.NET application you have to be sure that this is present in the target platform. If not, you have to install it before launching the .NET Framework installation.

Microsoft has already released the second service pack for the .NET Framework, so you should include it in your installation package regardless of whether you used it to create your application.

Recommended Software and Hardware

Other than the typical installation requirements listed in the previous section, you will have to consider installing some other components. In fact, if you are planning to install your .NET application on Windows 98 or Windows NT 4, you may need to install the Windows Management Instrumentation (**WMI**) CORE 1.5 library (Windows Me, Windows 2000, and Windows XP have it already installed). Microsoft released WMI in order to implement Web-Based Enterprise Management (**WBEM**) – an industry initiative to develop a standard technology for accessing management information in an enterprise environment. You can find the WMI components redistributable file at: http://msdn.microsoft.com/downloads/?url=/downloads/sample.asp?url=/msdn-files/027/001/576/msdncompositedoc.xml&frame=true.

Finally, you will have to consider hardware requirements in order to ensure that your application works as expected. The following table lists minimal hardware requirements, running on a low-end operating system, such as Windows 98 for the client, and Windows NT 4 or 2000 for the server.

Scenario	CPU	RAM
Client or desktop application	Pentium 90 MHz or faster	96 MB or better
Server application	Pentium 233 MHz or faster	256 MB or better

---

**The .NET Framework redistributable installer will stop the
installation when minimal requirements are not encountered.**

Using the .NET Framework Redistributable

The .NET Framework redistributable is a single-file Windows Installer package that
launches an internal `Install.exe` program when you execute it. The installer checks
for Windows Installer version 2.0 on the target machine, installing it when not present.
Then, the Windows Installer will launch the internal MSI file, which starts a wizard.

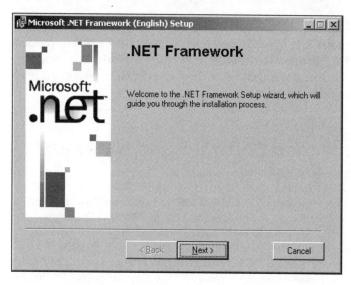

You can also use a command-line version of the redistributable, specifying options that
customize installer behavior. Let's see the syntax:

```
> dotnetfx [/q:a] [/c:"Install [/l][/q]"]
```

You specify `Install` with the various switches after the `/c:` parameter. In the
following table you can see these command-line options' meaning:

Option	Description
/l	Using this option causes all the installer's operation and installation errors to be logged in the `netfx.log` file contained in the `%temp%` directory.
/q	This option specifies quiet installation mode. This will launch the Install program within the package without displaying messages and dialog boxes. You have to specify the `/q:a` option in order to avoid the .NET Framework redistributable showing its own messages and dialog boxes.

In the following example a quiet installation has been executed:

```
> dotnetfx /q:a /c:"install /q"
```

Localized Versions of the Redistributable

When your target operating system is not an English version, you might wish to install the localized version of the .NET Framework redistributable file. Here follows a list of the available non-English versions:

- ❑ Chinese (Simplified)
- ❑ Chinese (Traditional)
- ❑ French
- ❑ German
- ❑ Italian
- ❑ Japanese
- ❑ Korean
- ❑ Spanish

If the target operating system is Windows 98, then you must install the localized version of the .NET Framework. For all the other operating systems you only need the English version.

In order to test your installation package, when created, you have to reserve a hard disk partition, or another computer, for a new installation of your target operating system (you should consider trying the installation on all operating systems that your application may be deployed to). Consider the possibility of using the VMware tool, which creates one or many virtual machines in which you can install further operating systems, such as Windows 98, Me, NT, and so on. You can test your installation package in the virtual machine without creating new partitions or using other computers. You can find more information and obtain a trial version of this program at http://www.vmware.com.

Windows Installer

Microsoft's Windows Installer is an installation and configuration service included in recent Microsoft operating systems. Microsoft Windows 2000, Millennium, and XP provide this service natively, whereas 9x and NT 4 require a service pack.

The Windows Installer uses an **installation package** to install, uninstall, and repair applications on target computers. The installation package is contained within an `.msi` file, which consists of an installation database that contains tables with file paths, dependencies, and data streams. Moreover, an installation package can contain internal and external files, such as script files – useful to check for the presence of a particular application, or to create and populate a database.

The installation of an MSI package can be subdivided into three phases:

1. **Acquisition**: When the user launches the setup program, the Windows Installer queries the installation database in order to retrieve specific information and generates a script with every step to follow in deployment.

2. **Execution**: During this phase the information retrieved is passed to a high priority thread that starts the installation.

3. **Rollback**: If something goes wrong, or if the user breaks the installation, then the Windows Installer restores the original state of the computer. This is possible because the Windows Installer creates a rollback script during the acquisition phase, backing up every file that it deletes or modifies during the installation. This script allows installations to be handled in a transacted manner; they either complete in their entirety, or they completely fail. There is no middle ground, or partial installation. When an error occurs, the system is rolled back to its pre-installation state.

If Windows Installer detects that a system reboot is needed, a message box will appear with the relevant restart message as installation completes. A reboot is usually needed when an upgraded file is in use and the installer can't replace it. Also, if a file is moved or deleted by the user, Windows Installer will attempt to reinstall this file next time the application is launched. When uninstalling, the database is queried to ensure that no other installed application is using any of the files that may be removed.

Because of these features, developers can create their own installation packages with the following advantages:

❑ **Resilience**: The installer can detect and reinstall damaged components without reinstalling the entire application. It queries an application file list from the installation database, restoring the original structure from the backed up files.

❑ **Install on demand**: Your application can use modules that are only installed the first time that they are required by the user – we'll see an example of this in Chapter 6.

❑ **Advertisement**: The Windows Installer can advise users about new applications that will be installed only when they launch them. Imagine your application has alternative skins; you can show shortcuts to these skins without having installed them on the computer, yet. When the user selects that shortcut an install on demand installation starts setting up all the necessary skins.

40

❏ **Customization**: You can produce a unique installation package that has different installation behavior depending on different users and groups. For example, you can decide to provide application functionalities to only the finance group, while hiding them to the rest of your company.

❏ **Patching and upgrading**: You can easily distribute an updated version of your application using the installation package.

Creating a Windows Installer Package

As previously mentioned, the Windows Installer is a service contained in the operating system and it can be used through its own library. In order to install your application you have to plan where to deploy your files, where to create directories, whether to create registry keys, and so on.

We could do this manually by inserting all this information into a blank installation database using the correct tables to store directories information, files information, and so on (you can find a copy inside the Platform SDK that you can download at: http://www.microsoft.com/msdownload/platformsdk/sdkupdate). However, this procedure is difficult to perfect and out of scope for this book.

In this section, we will see how simple it is to create a Windows Installer package using the Visual Studio .NET setup tool. In the next chapter, we will look in detail at every tool provided by Visual Studio .NET. This section serves as introduction to show you how Visual Studio .NET makes the creation of an installer simple.

A Simple Windows Application

Once you have launched Visual Studio .NET you can select a new project from either the start page or from the File | New Project... menu. The following dialog box will be shown allowing you to select the Windows Application project template.

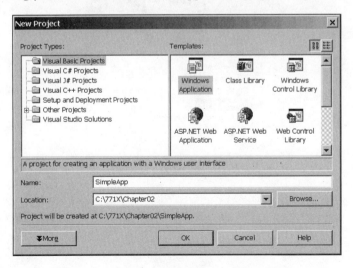

Once you have chosen the application location and the application name (we'll use
SimpleApp), and pressed the OK button, Visual Studio .NET will generate a new form
called Form1 and an AssemblyInfo.vb file used to specify information on the
application, such as version, author, and so on (covered in detail in Chapter 5). In this
first simple demonstration there is no need to add any functionality to our application,
so you can add the Setup Project template by selecting Add Project | New Project.... The
following dialog will be displayed:

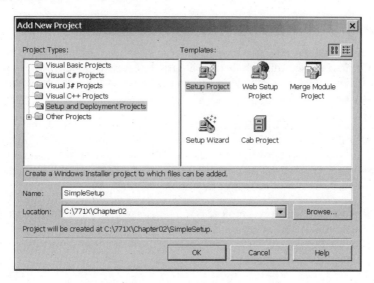

Once you have chosen the name and location for your setup project and pressed the
OK button, a new project will be added to the solution and displayed in the Solution
Explorer window:

Selecting the project in the Solution Explorer, the Properties window will be populated
with all the properties and values that characterize the application. For example, in
order to change the title of the installer you can change the Title property (by default
it takes the project's name). We'll be examining this in Chapter 3.

In the main window, Visual Studio .NET should now be showing the File System window that allows the developer to add files, directories, shortcuts, and more to the setup application (we will examine the editor in more detail in Chapter 3).

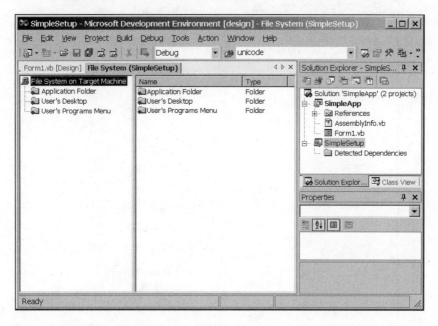

Since users may have installed their operating system in a non-default location, the File System dialog shows three folders that represent general system folders. It will be the Windows Installer's responsibility to retrieve the system folder paths so you do not need to be concerned with the retrieval of such information. The meaning of each tree node is described below:

❑ **Application folder**: This represents the folder chosen by the user in which to install the application.

❑ **User's Desktop**: This represents the desktop folder of the target computer.

❑ **User's Programs Menu**: This represents the Programs menu of the target computer (the one accessible from the Windows's Start menu).

You can add other system folders right-clicking on the File System on Target Machine tree root, and selecting the Add Special Folder menu (see Chapter 3 for more details).

As you'll want to deploy your simple application to the application folder, you need to add a shortcut to the desktop of the target computer, and then a menu as a child of the Programs menu. Let's start adding the project output to the application folder.

Right-click on the Application Folder node, and select the Add | Project Output... menu:

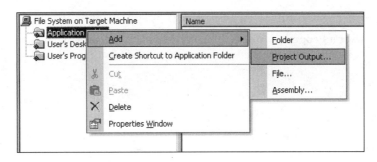

Project Output... specifies the current project output you want to deploy in the application folder. You can choose your Windows Application, called `SimpleApp`, from the Add Project Output Group dialog box:

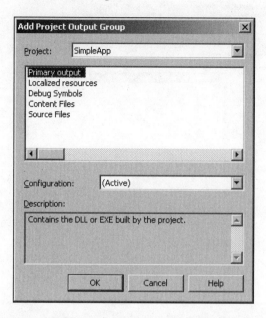

Using the Add Project Output Group dialog, you can select one or more groups of possible resources to deploy to the target computer; these are shown below:

❑ **Primary Output**: by selecting this group you will deploy the final executable or DLL built by the selected project.

❑ **Localized Resources**: if your application uses satellite assemblies that contain localized resources, such as different output languages, you can select this group to include them in your installation package.

❑ **Debug Symbols**: by selecting this group you can deploy files necessary to debug your application.

❑ **Content Files**: by selecting this group you can deploy all your content files, such as report, images, and so on.

❑ **Source Files**: by selecting this group you can distribute your source files, which might do for educational or open source projects.

This simple application doesn't use external resources or content files so just add a primary output group:

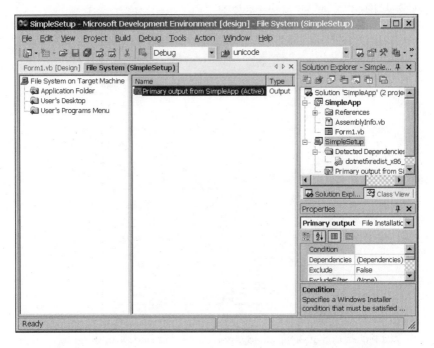

Now you can add a shortcut to the User's Desktop tree node to configure the MSI package to tell the Windows Installer to create a shortcut pointing to the application located on the user's desktop. When you select the User's Desktop node in the Tree View, the Name section at the right of the TreeView is still empty. Therefore, right-click it and select Create New Shortcut from the context menu.

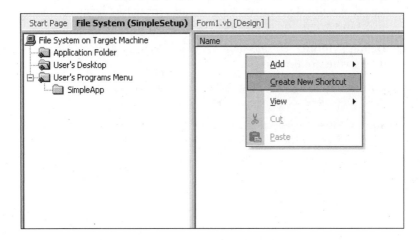

The Select Item In Project dialog box will appear. By using it, you can select the output pointed to by the new shortcut.

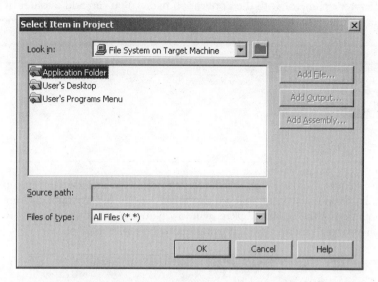

Since the application executable will be deployed to the application folder, you have to select Application Folder in the Look in: combobox (you can double-click on the folder as well).

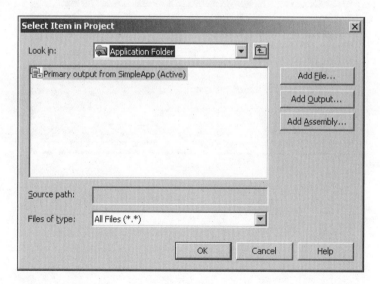

Once the primary output has been selected, you have to rename the shortcut. In fact, the installer will create a shortcut with a specified name (Shortcut to Primary output from SimpleApp (Active) is the default one).

You can now repeat this operation to create another shortcut to be placed in the Start | Programs menu. An installer will usually create a new folder named either with the manufacturer's name or with the application name. You can add a folder by simply right-clicking on the User's Programs Menu tree node selecting the Add | Folder menu.

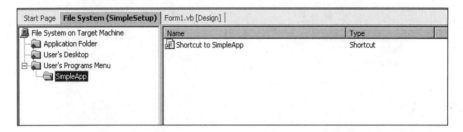

The last step required to create an installation package is to include the Setup project in the configuration manager so that we can build the MSI file. By right-clicking on the Solution root node in the Solution Explorer window, you can select the Configuration Manager... menu. The following dialog box will be displayed:

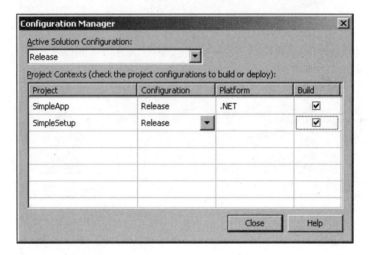

You have to check the Build checkbox corresponding to the Project that you want included in the building process. Now select Build | Build Solution (or press *Ctrl+Shift+B*) and both the application and installation package will be created. Inside the folder containing the built solution, you will find the following files:

❑   InstMsiA.exe: The ANSI version of the Windows Installer executable running on older operating systems, such as Windows 98.

❑   InstMsiW.exe: The Unicode version of the Windows Installer executable for more recent operating systems, such as Windows 2000.

❑   Setup.exe: The installation launcher. It checks for the operating system version and runs the ANSI or the Unicode version of the Windows Installer, passing the installation package contained in the Setup.ini file.

❑   Setup.ini: It is the configuration file for the setup program.

❑   SimpleSetup.msi: The installation package that contains our application.

The Windows Installer queries the installation database within the MSI file and starts the deployment. There are no substantial differences between ANSI and Unicode versions (other than the code page of any text); setup checks for Unicode support in the target operating system and if it is not supported, then it executes the ANSI installer version.

Running a Windows Installer Package

Launching the setup.exe file you will start the installation. A welcome screen should appear:

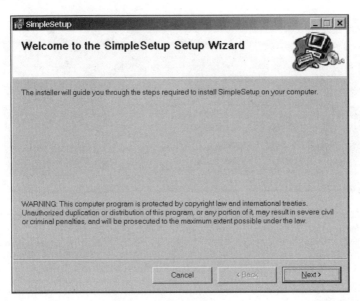

As you can see, the setup project title has been inserted in the welcome message. All the messages and icons can be modified using the various editors in Visual Studio .NET, detailed in Chapter 3. By pressing the Next button you go through the next step:

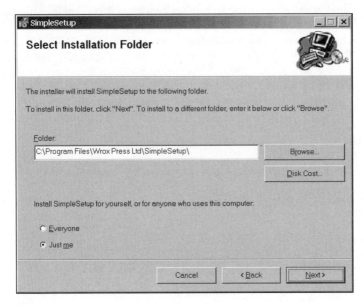

In this step the user will choose the application folder in which to install the application. The user can decide to install the application for everyone using the computer, if so desired. The user must have administrative rights to be able to write to the All Users folder. By pressing the Disk Cost... button, the user can see how many bytes are required from the application, choosing an alternative path destination if the drive does not have sufficient space.

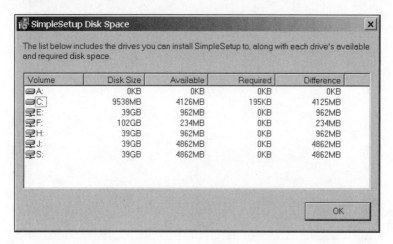

After pressing the Next button, a confirmation message will be displayed to give the user a final chance to go back and change some installation parameters.

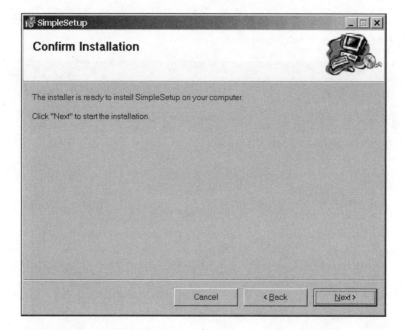

After this, a progress dialog box is displayed showing the installation progress and any relevant information, before the Installation Complete dialog box is shown.

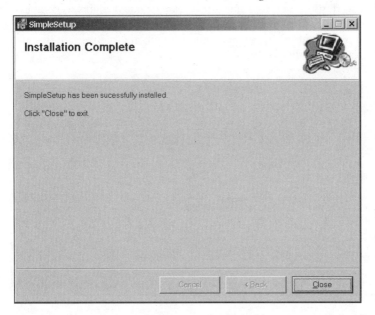

As you can see from the following screenshot, a shortcut has been added to the user's desktop with the name specified in the project. By selecting the Start | Programs menu, you can see that a new SimpleApp folder has been created, and a shortcut to the application has been added (obviously running the application will not be that interesting as all you will get is an empty form).

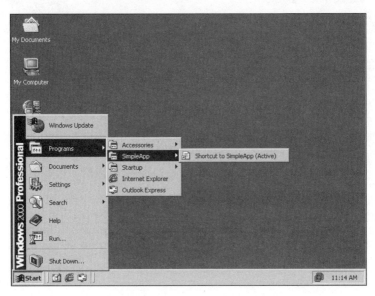

Uninstalling Applications

You can uninstall the `SimpleApp` application by using the Add/Remove Programs option in Control Panel:

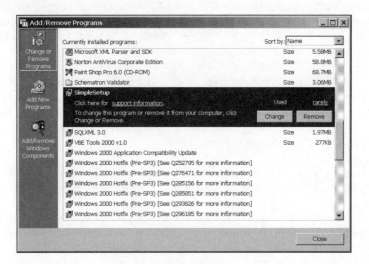

If you click on the support information link you are presented with the following dialog that provides some information, such as the publisher and version, and the ability to repair the application if it is not working correctly:

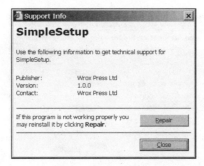

Other Types of Installation

You have seen one of the most used installation type, the Windows application setup, but Visual Studio .NET offers other templates to build different installations, such as web installation and merge modules creation. In this section you will see an example for each installation template, concluding with XCopy, which can be very useful for fast and easy deployment.

Web Setup Project

Visual Studio .NET introduces a great innovation to the development scene – the Web Setup project template. Developers of ASP will be familiar with the difficulties in deploying their applications. ASP developers will have to copy all the ASP pages to a brand new web site or virtual directory, copy and register any external component (DLLs), create a database, if used, with tables, views, and stored procedures, manage Internet Information Services settings, and so on.

Using a Web Setup Project, you can create an installation package that handles registration and configuration issues automatically. Then you can either distribute the MSI file using traditional media, or deploy it using a web server. In the last case you just have to copy the installation package into a web server directory and optionally create an HTML page with a link to it.

In order to deploy a simple web application, you must first add a Web Setup Project to the Web Application project. This can be found under the Add Project dialog.

Once you have chosen the name and location for the project, a new setup project will be added to the solution. Web Setup projects are very similar to Windows setup projects; you can use editors to add files, register components, and so on (see Chapter 3 for more details). Of course, in a Web Setup project you can choose a virtual directory to deploy the application to, and the initial page to show. These properties and much more can be defined in the Properties window after having selected the project in the Solution Explorer:

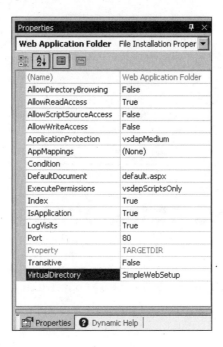

Apart from choosing the virtual directory and the default document, you can set Internet Information Services settings, such as to allow directory browsing, read and write access, and to choose the execute permissions level.

After having added the project output to the setup and added the project to the build process you can build the solution by selecting the Build | Build Solution menu (or by pressing the *Shift+Ctrl+B* key combination); you will obtain the same set of files as produced by a Windows setup application. You can deploy the setup files using traditional media, such as compact discs. In addition, you can copy the MSI file to a web server and create an HTML page with a link to it. In this latter case you would assume that the target computer already has the necessary files to launch a Windows Installer package. If not, you can specify an alternative directory where you have already copied the `InstMsiA.exe` and `InstMsiW.exe` setup launchers

If you select the Properties menu from the context menu that appears when you right-click on the Web Setup Project name within the Solution Explorer, the following window will appear:

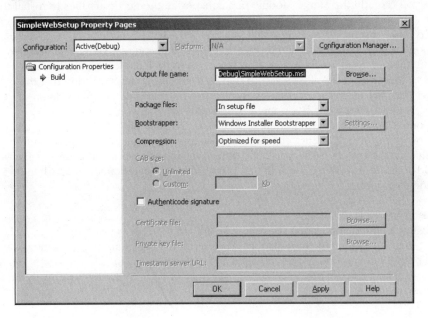

By selecting Web Bootstrapper from the Bootstrapper: combobox, you can specify URLs for the setup.exe and InstMsiX.exe files (you can find more details for this window in Chapter 3). The following dialog box allows you to specify these URLs:

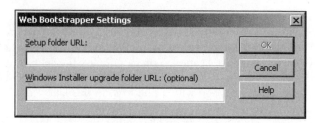

Merge Modules Setup Project

Merge Modules are reusable installation components. A merge module contains all the necessary resources to install a single component (for example, if your application uses GDI+ you can add the Merge Module that contains all the necessary files to install the GDI+ component on the target machine). Merge Modules store the files, dependencies, registry keys, resources, and more that guarantee the correct installation of a single component. The Merge Module has the .msm file extension and cannot be installed directly in your target operating system, but it has to be included in other setup projects. Merge Modules allows you to deploy your component ensuring that the correct versions are installed. That's why you should distribute another version of your Merge Module when your component is updated. Imagine you create a shared component that is used by different applications. Because of the "side-by-side" .NET Framework feature, different versions of the same component can be successfully installed on the system. So, if you build a new version of your shared component, you should create a new Merge Module that installs the new component (read Chapter 5 on updating/versioning for more details).

Microsoft has created a library of Merge Modules that can be included in setup projects. For example, if the application uses the ATL library, then the setup project can include the VC_atl70.msm merge module that contains all the necessary files to deploy the ATL library. You can find merge modules in the Program Files\Common Files\Merge Modules directory of your computer, or directly on the Microsoft web site.

Let's start examining what we have to do in order to create our merge module. Create a new Merge Module project, from the New Project... dialog:

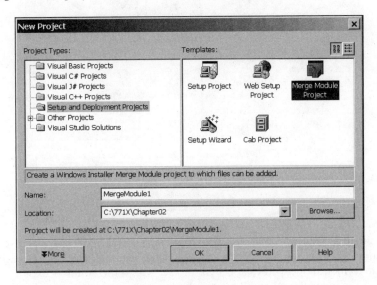

Once the name and location textboxes are filled in, the Visual Studio .NET main window will be filled with the File System editor, which shows just two folders:

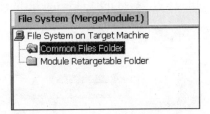

If you add your component to the Common Files Folder, it will be deployed to the Common Files system folder. If you add your component to the Module Retargetable Folder, you will give the opportunity to select the directory in which deploy your component by the setup installer. From the application setup you have to select the Merge Module Project in the Solution Explorer. In the Properties window the KeyOutput parameter allows you to select the destination folder from the list of available folders in the File System editor.

CAB Setup Project

CAB files are a useful way to deploy components from a web server to the web browser because they contain compressed files for easier distribution. Creating a Cab Project in Visual Studio .NET you can easily build a CAB file you can copy to your web server so it can be deployed as required. In the New Project... dialog you can create a new Cab Project:

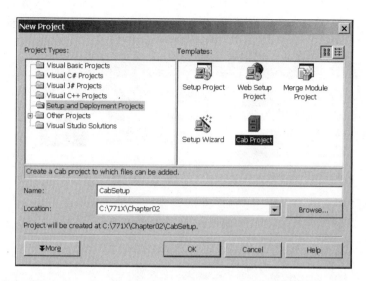

The first thing that you will notice upon creation is that no editors are available in the Visual Studio .NET IDE. From Project | Add, you can select the Project Output and File menus. The former allows you to specify a project within the Solution Explorer as the destination of your deployment. The latter allows you to select a component by browsing through your directories.

Selecting the project properties will reveal the following dialog box:

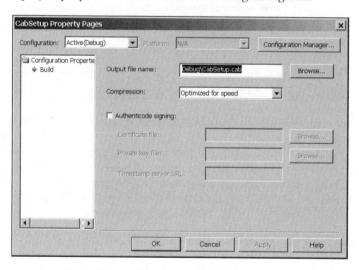

By using the Compression: combobox you can choose the compression level of your final CAB file.

❑   Optimized for speed: Generates a CAB file with lower compression that will allow a fast installation.

❏ **Optimized for size**: Generates a CAB file with greater compression that will allow fast download but slower installation.

❏ **None**: Generates a CAB file without compression.

Moreover, checking the Authenticode signing: checkbox will allow you to specify a valid certificate and private key file that signs your component.

Once the final CAB file has been built (selecting Build Solution from the Build menu) you can add it to your Web Application project. Putting the component in your web form, you can set the codebase property within the Properties window to specify the CAB previously created. In that way you will start the deployment automatically when a user requires the web page.

XCopy and Other Methods

The .NET Framework introduces a new entity: the assembly. Information is stored in the assembly that allows the CLR to dynamically load external libraries and other assemblies. This kind of metadata allows developers to avoid the registration of components in the system registry. So, when the application doesn't require COM+ components, database creation, and other advanced features it can be deployed by simply using the XCopy command or FTP.

XCopy copies files and directory trees into a specified destination path. You can see the various XCopy options by typing xcopy /? at the command prompt. Using the /s switch is common as it recursively copies all subdirectories to the target location as well.

```
Command Prompt                                                    _ □ x

C:\>xcopy /?
Copies files and directory trees.

XCOPY source [destination] [/A | /M] [/D[:date]] [/P] [/S [/E]] [/V] [/W]
                           [/C] [/I] [/Q] [/F] [/L] [/H] [/R] [/T] [/U]
                           [/K] [/N] [/O] [/X] [/Y] [/-Y] [/Z]
                           [/EXCLUDE:file1[+file2][+file3]...]

  source       Specifies the file(s) to copy.
  destination  Specifies the location and/or name of new files.
  /A           Copies only files with the archive attribute set,
               doesn't change the attribute.
  /M           Copies only files with the archive attribute set,
               turns off the archive attribute.
  /D:m-d-y     Copies files changed on or after the specified date.
               If no date is given, copies only those files whose
               source time is newer than the destination time.
  /EXCLUDE:file1[+file2][+file3]...
               Specifies a list of files containing strings. When any of the
               strings match any part of the absolute path of the file to be
               copied, that file will be excluded from being copied. For
               example, specifying a string like \obj\ or .obj will exclude
               all files underneath the directory obj or all files with the
               .obj extension respectively.
  /P           Prompts you before creating each destination file.
```

In order to deploy a simple web application you can follow these simple steps:

1. XCopy .aspx files, images, XML files, bin directory, and so on, into the destination folder.

2. Launch the Internet Services Manager tool creating a new virtual directory pointing to the destination folder created in Step 1.

Visual Studio .NET offers an easier way to copy a web application to a remote web server. From the Project menu, select the Copy Project... menu and the following dialog box will be displayed:

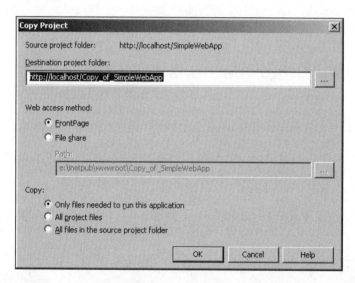

In the Destination project folder: textbox, you can specify the remote web server address and the virtual directory that will be created during the copy. Then you can select two different access methods to the web server: FrontPage and File share. The former uses FrontPage server extensions to contact the remote server and create the new web site (both servers have to have FrontPage server extensions installed). The latter uses Microsoft network directory sharing to deploy the files. Finally, using the Copy: radio button you can select the type of deployment: copy only files needed to run the application, copy all the files within the project, or copy all files in the source project folder.

Third-Party Products

Despite the quality of the Setup and Deployment options available with Visual Studio .NET, there may be times when we could benefit from products supplied by other companies that have decided to distribute their own tools. There are several on the market, such as InstallShield, and in this final section, we look at one such tool, Wise for Visual Studio .NET.

Wise for Visual Studio .NET

Wise Solutions has been always an active company in the installation scene. Over the years it has released new versions of the Wise deployment tool to offer even better installation solutions and assist developers during deployment phase. Now that many developers' attention seem to be pointed to the Microsoft .NET solutions, Wise has created a new installation tool that is fully integrated in Visual Studio .NET: Wise for Visual Studio .NET (you can download a trial version of this tool at http://www.wise.com/download.asp?filter=DEMO).

Once you have installed the product, you will see an additional icon on the Visual Studio .NET splash screen and a new template section in the New Project... dialog box.

Once you have completed your application, you can add a new project in the same solution, choosing to create a Wise installation project from the New Project... dialog box.

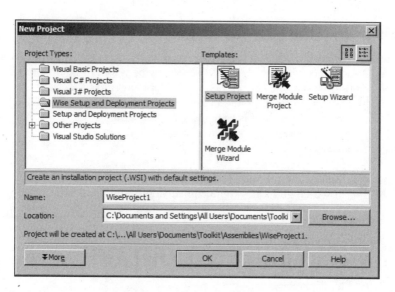

You need to choose a name and a location for the project as before, and then the new files will be added to the solution.

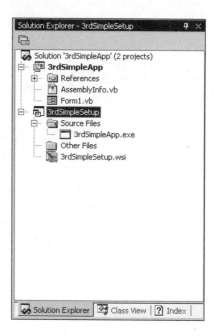

The output of the main project will be added to the Source Files folder automatically along with a .wsi file that contains all the Windows Installer information. By double-clicking the .wsi file, a graphic interface will be displayed within Visual Studio .NET's main window.

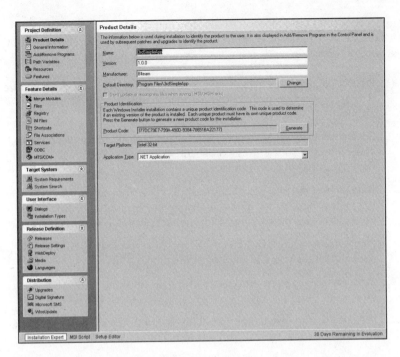

At the bottom side of the main window you will find three tabs that let you switch between Installation Expert, MSI Script, and Setup Editor. The first tab points to a graphical editor that allows you to customize every single aspect of your installation package. The second tab points to an editor that allows you to customize the actions making up your installation. Finally, the third tab allows you to have an in-depth view of your setup information. Moreover, you can change text on installation dialogs, build complex conditions that must be met to go with the installation, and edit Windows Installer installation database information.

In the left pane of the Installation Expert are grouped all the categories that characterize the installation's behavior. Let's examine each group in detail.

Project Definition

In this group you will find all the necessary information to customize your product by adding details such as author and application version, by changing icons, and by adding general information, and so on. Let's examine the function of each item:

❑ Product Details: Adds information, such as Name, Version, Manufacturer, the default destination path, and the application type (Win32 classic application, .NET application, or both).

❑ General Information: Adds general information to your application, such as Title, Subject, Author, Keywords, and Comments. Users will see them when they ask for application properties.

❑ Add/Remove Programs: Modifies the application appearance in the Add/Remove Programs control panel. You can change the application icon and add support information, such as support URL, contact person, phone number, and so on.

❑ Path variables: Defines variables to replace commonly used directory paths for source files you add to your installation.

❑ Resources: Manage resources used by your application by adding them to your installation package.

❑ Features: Create installation "modules" for your package. For example, you can add minimal, typical, and full installation features.

Feature Details

In this group you can specify the merge modules, files, registry keys, and so on that are included in your application's installation package. A combobox allows you to specify the target feature. For example, using this combobox you can decide which files a typical installation, and which files a minimal installation will contain.

Let's see them in detail:

❑ Merge Modules: Add merge modules to your installation package.

❑ Files: Add directories and files to your installation package.

- Registry: Specify new registry keys manually or select a `.reg` file to create them automatically.

- INI Files: Add an existing `.ini` file to your installation package or create a new one on the fly.

- Shortcuts: Add shortcuts, help files, Readme files, and so on to your application.

- File Associations: Define an extension that will be associated to your application.

- Services: If you have created a Windows Service application, you can use this to deploy and control the initial status.

- ODBC: Add ODBC information that will be created during application installation.

- MTS/COM+: Add an MTS or COM+ package that will be installed together with your application.

All Other Groups

Using the other groups you can define requirements on the target system, the user interface to show during the installation, the installation distribution media, and distribution mechanism. Let's see the groups in detail:

❑ Target System: You can define requirements on the target system by choosing the minimum operating system requirements. Moreover, you can search for a file, .ini file, Registry key, or components before starting to install the application. You can display a message when some requirements are not met canceling the installation.

❑ User Interface: You can define which kind of dialog box will be shown during the installation. Moreover, you can associate features to installation types, such as Typical, Custom, and Complete installations.

❑ Release Definition: You can customize installation package characteristics, such as generating multiple installation packages or web deployment packages. Moreover, you can customize languages for your final installation package.

❑ Distribution: You can create installation packages that upgrade existing versions of your application. Also, you can add a digital signature to your application and choose to deploy your application using the Microsoft SMS tool.

Building and Installing a Wise Installation Package

Since Wise for Visual Studio .NET is fully integrated in the development environment, you can build the installation package by simply building the solution. This is accomplished by selecting the Build | Build Solution... menu from Visual Studio .NET (you can press *Ctrl+Shift+B* as well).

At the end of the build process a new MSI file will be produced. Just launch this file to start the installation.

For more details you can refer to the official documentation that is integrated in the Visual Studio .NET help. You can also follow the tutorial PDF installed with Wise that shows you the typical steps to implement a full working installation package.

Summary

In this chapter you have been provided with an overview of the solutions available to Visual Studio .NET developers wanting to deploy their applications. You have seen how Visual Studio .NET facilitates the deployment of Windows applications by providing powerful editors. The same editors are useful to manage Web Setup projects.

You have additionally seen that Merge Modules could be a great solution when you have to deploy part of an application used in more than one project. Then we analyzed CAB projects that allow you to deploy components declaring them directly into a web page. Finally, you saw a third-party tool, Wise for Visual Studio .NET. It offers a user-friendly interface that allows you to create Windows Installer packages easily.

In the next chapter you will see some of the more advanced features of the Windows Installer.

VB.NET

Deployment

Handbook

3

Windows Installer Features

In the last chapter we introduced the possible methods for deploying a .NET application to a target computer. We saw that Visual Studio .NET offers project templates to assist in the creation Windows application setups, Web application setups, CAB files, and more. In this chapter we will see how to use the Visual Studio .NET setup editors to create an advanced installer package.

In this chapter, we'll look at the following tools:

❑ **File System Editor**: This editor allows us to select files for inclusion in our setups, create the directories to which we will deploy our application, and much more.

❑ **Registry Editor**: This editor allows us to insert new keys and values in the system registry of the target machine.

❑ **Files Types Editor**: This editor is used to associate a file extension with our application in the target operating system.

❑ **User Interface Editor**: This editor allows us to customize the user interface showing dialog boxes during the installation. For example, using this editor we could show a dialog box asking for a serial number before starting to install the application.

❑ **Custom Action Editor**: This editor allows us to add custom actions to our installers. Custom actions are external programs such as DLLs or EXEs that accomplish a particular task. We will use it to create a database before starting to deploy application files.

❏ **Launch Conditions Editor**: This editor allows us to specify particular
conditions that have to be satisfied in order to continue with the
installation. For example, we will see how check for the .NET Framework
installation on the target system before starting to deploy the application.

We will finish the chapter with an in-depth example that uses these editors to create an
installer, which will deploy an application that uses a database, registry keys, and the
other more advanced features.

Visual Studio .NET Editors

Visual Studio .NET introduces new setup project templates that enable developers to
deploy their applications. You saw in Chapter 2 that Windows application setup, Web
application setup, and Merge modules are managed by specific editors that are included
in the Visual Studio .NET IDE. In this section, we will examine each editor in detail.

File System Editor

You can view the File System Editor by selecting View | Editor | File System.

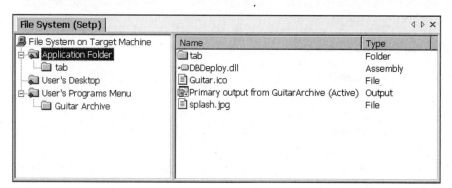

The File System editor is the main tool for the setup project. It allows the developer to
specify the directories and files that make up an application, and choose where to
deploy it on a target machine. In the screenshot above you can see the File System
editor for the Windows application that you will be building at the end of this chapter.
In the left pane there is a tree view that contains both the system and custom folders
where files and shortcuts will be deployed. In the right pane the selected folder's
content is displayed. By default, the File System editor contains several target machine
system folders (see Chapter 2 for more details) but we can always add other system
folders. Right-clicking on the File System on Target Machine root node in the tree view
will produce the following context menu:

In the following table you can find explanations for each option in the Add Special Folder menu.

Menu	Description
Common Files Folder	Files within this folder will be deployed to the x:\Program Files\Common Files folder (where x is the generic drive letter for the target operating system).
Fonts Folder	Files within this folder will be deployed to the x:\%SystemRoot%\Font. For example, C:\Winnt\Font by default for Windows NT and 2000 and C:\Windows\Font by default for Win9x and Me.
Program Files Folder	Files within this folder will be deployed to the x:\Program Files folder.
System Folder	Files within this folder will be deployed to the x:\%SystemRoot%\System32 folder. You should keep in mind that this folder can be secured. It could be dangerous for the final user to deploy files to this folder. You could overwrite DLLs, which may be COM+ components – creating the infamous DLL hell.

Table continued on following page

Menu	Description
User's Application Data Folder	Files within this folder will be deployed to the x:\Documents and Settings*Username*\Application Data folder (where *Username* is the current logged on user).
User's Favorites Folder	Files within this folder will be deployed to the x:\Documents and Settings*Username*\Favorites folder. You can use this folder to add online documentation for your application, as well as company links via Internet Explorer.
User's Personal Data Folder	Files within this folder will be deployed to the x:\Documents and Settings*Username*\My Documents folder.
User's Send To Menu	Files within this folder will be deployed to the x:\Documents and Settings*Username*\SendTo Menu.
User's Start Menu	Files within this folder will be deployed to the x:\Documents and Settings*Username*\Start Menu.
User's Startup Folder	Files within this folder will be deployed to the x:\Documents and Settings*Username*\Start Menu\Programs\Startup folder.
User's Template Folder	Files within this folder will be deployed to the x:\Documents and Settings*Username*\Template folder.
Windows Folder	Files within this folder will be deployed to the x:\%SystemRoot% folder.
Global Assembly Cache Folder	Files within this folder will be deployed to the x:\%SystemRoot%\assembly folder. This is important for deploying shared assemblies (see Chapter 5).
Custom Folder	By selecting this option, you can add a custom folder that is not included in the system folders.

File System Properties in a Windows Application Setup

Once you have finished adding system and custom folders you can set their properties using the Properties window.

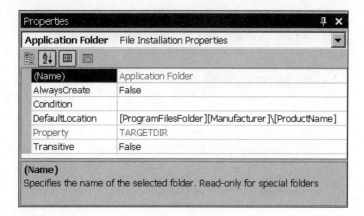

In the following table you can find descriptions for each property:

Property	Description
(Name)	You can specify the name of a custom folder. Read-only value for system folders.
AlwaysCreate	This Boolean value indicates whether to always create the specified folder, when the installer doesn't find it on the target computer.
Condition	You can specify a condition that has to be satisfied in order to deploy the content of the folder.
DefaultLocation	This specifies the default location that will be prompted to the user during installation. You can use attributes to indicate system folders. For example, by specifying: [ProgramFilesFolder][Manufacturer]\[ProductName] the user will be prompted with x:\Program Files\Wrox\GuitarArchive in the example later in this chapter.
Property	This is a property that can be accessed at installation time to override the path of a custom folder. It is a read-only value for system folders.
Transitive	This is a Boolean value that indicates whether the installer has to re-evaluate the specified condition each time that the installation or un-installation is performed (True) or just the first time (False).

File System Properties in a Web Application Setup

In a web application setup the File System on Target Machine folder is different from the Windows application setup version, so that it can allow developers to set Internet Information Services properties.

In the following table you will see descriptions for each property that has not already been described in the previous table:

Property	Description
(Name)	You can specify the name of the custom folder. If you specify a special folder, such as one added from the context menu, this value will be read-only.
AllowDirectoryBrowsing	This is a Boolean value that specifies whether the Internet Information Services (IIS) Directory browsing property for the site has to be set to True or False. True permits users to browse through the site directories using an Internet browser.
AllowReadAccess	This is a Boolean value that specifies whether the IIS Read access property for the site has to be set to True or False. True allows IIS to read the content of your files.

Property	Description
AllowScriptSourceAccess	This is a Boolean value that specifies whether the IIS Script source access property for the site has to be set to True or False. True allows users access to the script files (either Read or Write permission must be set).
AllowWriteAccess	This is a Boolean value that specifies whether the IIS Write access property for the site has to be set to True or False. True allows IIS to write into the application folder.
ApplicationProtection	This property indicates the IIS Application Protection level for your application. Possible values are: vsdapLow so your application will run in the same memory process as Web Services, vsdapMedium so your application will run in an isolated process pool along with other applications, and vsdapHigh so your application will run in a dedicated memory process.
AppMappings	This property indicates the IIS Application Mappings information for your application. Using this property you can map file extensions to executable files on the server.
DefaultDocument	This property indicates the default page that has to be displayed when the user contacts your site.
ExecutePermission	This property indicates the IIS Execution Permission level for your application. Possible values are: vsdepNone so only secure files will be executed (static HTML file, images, and so on), vsdepScriptsOnly so only script files will be run, and vsdepScriptsAndExecutables so all file types can be executed.
Index	This is a Boolean value that indicates whether the site will be indexed in the Microsoft Indexing Services (True) or not (False).
IsApplication	This is a Boolean value that indicates whether an IIS application root will be created for the selected folder (True) or not (False).
LogVisits	This is a Boolean value that indicates whether the IIS Log visits property has to be set to True or False. True indicates that visits to the selected folder will be inserted in a log file.
Port	This property indicates the port that will be assigned to the site. The default is 80.
VirtualDirectory	This property specifies the virtual directory where the application will be deployed to by the installer.

File System Content Properties

You saw in Chapter 2 how you could add a project output, file, assembly, or new folder to the selected folder in the tree view on the left pane of the File System editor. Once you have added an output to the file system you can select it and specify its properties:

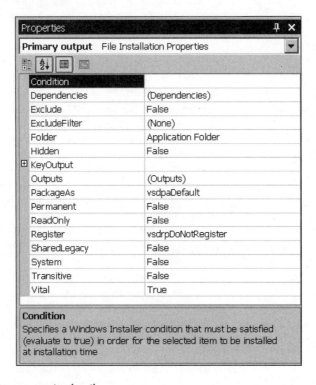

Let's see each property in detail:

Property	Description
Condition	You can specify a condition that has to be satisfied in order to deploy the content of the folder.
Dependencies	Displays a dialog box with a list of the dependencies of the output.
Exclude	Defines any specified output that has to be excluded from the project.
ExcludeFilter	Displays a dialog box that allows developers to specify a filter to the file extensions (wildcards are permitted) to exclude a group of files from the project.

Property	Description
Folder	Specifies the folder where the selected output will be deployed.
Hidden	This is a Boolean value that indicates whether the selected output will be deployed as hidden output (the hidden property will be set on the file).
KeyOutput	This is a node property that contains a summary of read-only properties, such as file version, public key, and so on.
Outputs	This is a property for project output that shows a dialog box with a list of output files.
PackageAs	This property overrides the one specified in the Package files: combobox in the Properties Pages dialog box. You can choose between two values: vsdpaDefault so you don't override settings specified by the Package files: combobox, and vsdpaLoose so you will override settings specifying to use uncompressed files in the installation package.
Permanent	This is a Boolean value indicating whether the specified file has to be removed by the uninstaller (False) or has to be permanent (True).
ReadOnly	This Boolean value indicates whether the selected output will be deployed as read-only (the file's read-only property will be added to the file). Typical files that should be deployed read-only are application's configuration files.
Register	Specifies if the selected output has to be registered during the installation. This property can assume one of the following values: vsdrpDoNotRegister means the output will not be selected, vsdrpCOM means your output will be registered as a COM object, vsdrpCOMRelativePath means your output will be registered as an isolated COM component, vsdrpCOMSelfReg means your output will be registered as a self-register COM component, and vsdrpFont means your component will be registered as a font.
SharedLegacy	This is a Boolean value that specifies whether the selected output has to be considered a shared legacy output. This value is used by Windows Installer to maintain a counter on every shared file installed in the target machine. During the uninstallation step, the installer checks the counter and decides whether or not to remove the shared file. This is accomplished when no application is still using the file.

Table continued on following page

Property	Description
System	This is a Boolean value that indicates whether the selected output will be deployed as system output (the system property will be set on the file).
Transitive	This is a Boolean value that indicates whether the installer has to re-evaluate the specified condition each time installation or uninstallation is performed (True), or just the first time (False).
Vital	This is a Boolean value that indicates whether the file is vital for the installation. When this property is set to True and the installation fails to deploy the file then the entire installation will fail.

Registry Editor

You can view the Registry Editor by selecting the View | Editor | Registry menu item.

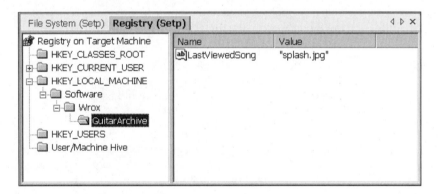

The Registry editor is the tool that allows developers to manage system registry keys. Normally you store data such as connection strings, most recently used files, and so on in the registry. In the screenshot above you can see the Registry Editor in action. In the left pane there is a representation of the registry hierarchy keys, and in the right pane is displayed the selected registry key's content.

By right-clicking on the Registry on Target Machine root node, you can select the Import... menu, which allows developers to specify a .reg containing system registry keys to create in the registry of the target system. You can export registry keys directly from the system registry. By launching the regedit.exe tool from the command prompt the following window will be displayed:

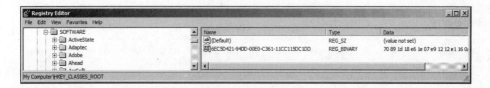

By right-clicking on the node you want to export, you can select the Export item contained in the related context menu. A file dialog box appears, allowing you to browse your computer's folders before choosing a path to store the final .reg file once deployed.

Also, you can manually insert new keys and values by right-clicking on the registry key and selecting the New Key item in the related context menu. Selecting the new key you can set its properties using the Properties window:

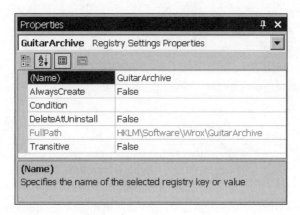

Let's examine each property in detail:

Property	Description
(Name)	The name of the registry key.
AlwaysCreate	A Boolean value indicating whether to always create the specified registry key even when its content is empty (True).
Condition	A condition that has to be satisfied in order to create the selected registry key.
DeleteAtUninstall	A Boolean value indicating whether to remove the selected registry key and all sub-keys during an uninstallation (True).

Table continued on following page

Property	Description
FullPath	A read-only value containing the selected registry key's full path.
Transitive	A Boolean value indicating whether the installer has to re-evaluate the specified condition each time the installation or uninstallation is performed (True) or just the first time (False).

As you can see, you have no way to set the value of the new key from those properties. You have to right-click on the right pane and choose one of the following menus:

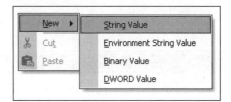

In the following table, you can see a description for the registry's values shown above.

Value	Description
String	Permits a string value to be added to the selected registry key. A typical example is the connection string used by the application to connect to the database.
Environment String	Permits a string value that contains an environment variable (%PATH%, for instance) and this will be expanded with the related value.
Binary	Permits a binary value to be added to the selected registry key.
DWORD	Permits a DWORD value to be added to the selected registry key.

> **The Registry editor doesn't allow multi-line string values (REG_MULTI_SZ). Moreover, when you import a registry file containing multi-line string values, they will be transformed into binary values.**

Once you have added a new key, you can either leave it empty, or specify a value using the related Value property in the Properties window.

File Types Editor

You can view the File Types Editor by selecting the View | Editor | File Types menu item.

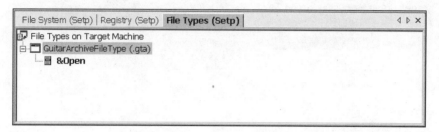

The File Types editor allows developers to associate an action undertaken by the application with a file extension. Usually, we will use this editor to associate the file extension representing our application's document with the Open action. When the user double-clicks on the application document file, the application will be opened and the file will be displayed in the application. For instance, if you double-click on a .doc file, then Microsoft Word will open the file (if it is installed).

By right-clicking on the File Types on Target Machine root node, you can select the Add File Type menu from the related context menu. Two new nodes will be added to the tree view:

- ❏ New Document Type #1 (no extensions) is a description for your new file type.

- ❏ &Open is the action that will be undertaken by the application when the user launches a file with that file extension.

You can add new actions to the file extension and sort them with the order you prefer. By right-clicking on the description node you can select the Add Action item from the related context menu.

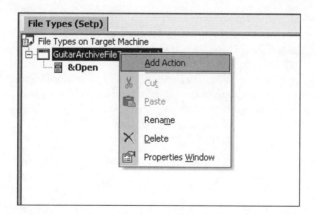

You can view the properties for the description node in the **Properties** window:

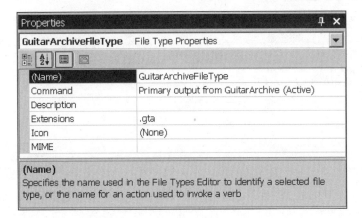

Let's examine the properties for the description node:

Property	Description
(Name)	The description used by the File Types Editor to identify a file type.
Command	Specifies the executable file that will be launched when the user double-clicks on the new file type.
Description	Represents a file type description that will be inserted in the File Types column of the Windows Folders Options dialog box, and in the ToolTip within the Windows Explorer.
Extensions	Specifies one or more file extensions (separated by semi-colon characters) associated to the file type.
Icon	Specifies the icon that will be displayed in Windows Explorer for the file type.
MIME	Specifies one or more Multipurpose Internet Mail Extension (MIME) extensions (separated by a semi-colon character) to be associated with the file type. It takes the application/type form where application is the application name or the application class such as image and type is the MIME type. For example, you can add a MIME for your application in order to let both Internet Explorer and Outlook applications manage your files.

Selecting the action contained in the file type description node populates the **Properties** window with its properties.

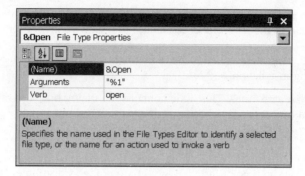

Let's examine the properties for the action node:

Property	Description
(Name)	Specifies the name of the action. By using an ampersand character, you can specify a shortcut key to the action as well.
Arguments	Specifies the arguments that will be passed to the application when the user double-clicks on the file type. A typical example is the file name that will be shown when the application starts.
Verb	Specifies the verb used to invoke a selected action for a file type. A typical verb is Open, and this is used to open the file specified in the argument.

User Interface Editor

You can view the User Interface Editor by selecting View | Editor | User Interface.

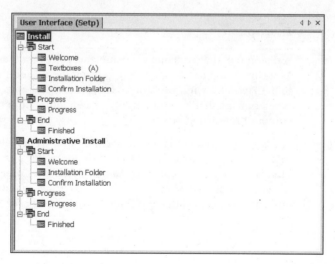

The User Interface Editor allows developers to manage the dialog boxes that are shown during the installation process. The User Interface tree view has two root nodes:

❑   Install: This node contains the dialog boxes to be displayed to the end user during installation

❑   Administrative Install: This node contains the dialog boxes to be displayed when a system administrator uploads the Windows Installer package to a network folder.

Both nodes contain the same set of dialog boxes. You have to customize the right node depending on the type of installation you are going to distribute. For example, you will customize the Install node if you plan to distribute your application directly to the end user using a media such as CDROM.

Dialog boxes are divided into three categories:

❑   Start: These dialog boxes are shown before the installation starts. They allow users to select a destination folder, examine the application's required disk space, and so on.

❑   Progress: These dialog boxes are shown during installation. They represent installation progress and show detailed information about what is going to be installed on the target machine.

❑   End: These dialog boxes are shown at the end of the installation process. They contain information about the installation's outcome.

The dialog boxes automatically inserted by the setup project template are described in the following table:

Dialog Box	Description
Welcome	A dialog box that contains welcome and copyright messages. You can customize these messages using the related properties in the Properties window. Moreover, you can customize the banner image that is automatically placed in the upper right corner of the dialog box.
Installation Folder	A dialog box containing the Browse... button, which allows users to select an alternative folder to deploy the application. Moreover, there is a Disk Cost... button that allows users to check the application disk space required, and two radio buttons that allow users to install the application for Just me or for Everyone.

Dialog Box	Description
Confirm Installation	This dialog box is a prompt to users before starting to deploy the application. This is useful because it allows users to refine their choices by going back to previous steps before starting the installation.
Progress	A dialog box that shows the installation progress.
Finished	A dialog box that reports the installation outcome.

You can add other dialog boxes, such as a splash screen, and you can drag dialog boxes between tree nodes to decide the display order. The editor will be flexible – allowing you to place dialog boxes where you prefer. However, the editor will check for position congruency. For example, the splash screen cannot be placed during the installation progress phase. You will receive an error message during the build.

You can add a dialog box by right-clicking on one of the three categories nodes and selecting the Add Dialog menu from the related context menu.

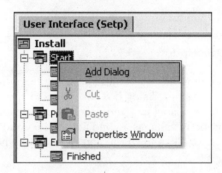

The Add Dialog dialog box will be shown:

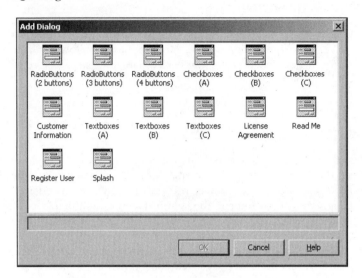

Below is a description of each dialog box:

Dialog Box	Description
RadioButtons (2, 3, 4 buttons)	A dialog box that contains two, three, or four radio buttons. You can set dialog box properties to specify each radio button's label text and value. Using the `ButtonProperty` property value as a condition in the `Condition` property of a folder, file, and so on, you can decide whether to install it or not.
CheckBoxes (A, B, C)	A dialog box that contains up to four checkboxes. You can add up to three checkboxes dialog boxes in the User Interface editor. Each dialog box can be customized using the Properties window; you can change checkbox label text, value, and visibility. Using the `CheckboxProperty` property value as a condition in the `Condition` property of a folder, file, and so on, you can decide whether to install it or not.
Customer Information	A dialog box that contains textboxes to retrieve the user's information such as name, company, and so on. Moreover, using the Properties window you can decide to ask the user for a serial number. In this case, you have to specify a Serial Number template that will be used to check the serial number inserted by the user.

Dialog Box	Description
TextBoxes (A, B, C)	A dialog box that contains up to four textboxes. You can add up to three textbox dialog boxes in the User Interface editor. Each dialog box can be customized using the Properties window; you can change textbox label `Text`, `Value`, and `Visibility`. Using the `EditProperty` property value as a condition in the `Condition` property of a folder, file, and so on, you can decide whether to install it or not.
License Agreement	A dialog box that shows a license agreement document in rich text format (`.rtf` file). You can use the Properties window to specify the file that contains the document and whether to use a 3D effect (sunken) for the textbox that will contain it.
Read Me	A dialog box that shows a read-me document in rich text format (`.rtf` file). You can use the Properties window to specify the file that contains the document and whether to use a 3D effect (sunken) for the textbox that will contain it.
Register User	A dialog box that allows users to register themselves. The user information will be submitted to an executable specified in the related property within the Properties window.
Splash	A dialog box that contains an image, such as the application's logo. You can specify the image using the `SplashBitmap` property in the Properties window. You should create a bitmap of 480 pixels in width and 320 pixels in height so that the installer doesn't resize it.

Custom Actions Editor

We can view the Custom Actions Editor by selecting View | Editor | Custom Actions.

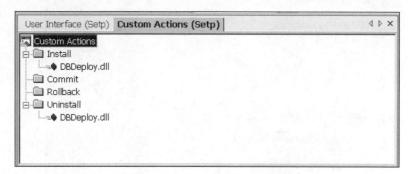

The Custom Actions Editor allows developers to specify a custom action that will be executed during the installation process. Custom actions are external DLLs or executables executed at the end of the installation. For example, if your application needs to manage data in a Microsoft SQL Server database, you can add a custom action that creates the database and its structure.

The tree view in the left pane of the Custom Actions Editor contains four predefined nodes that correspond to installation phases. By adding a custom action to the Install node, an executable will be launched during the installation. Commit adds actions to the commit phase. You can add a custom action to the Rollback node for rolling back the custom action if something went wrong. Finally, by adding a custom action to the Uninstall node, an executable will be launched when the user uninstalls your application.

You can add custom actions by right-clicking on the tree node and selecting the Add Custom Action... menu from the related context menu:

This operation will display a dialog box that allows developers to choose for an executable, DLL, script, or assembly containing the custom action, which must have been included in the File System editor.

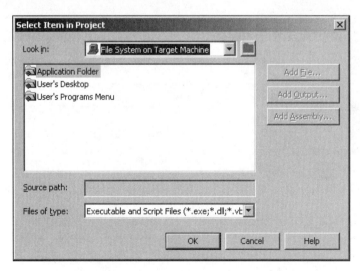

Launch Conditions Editor

You can view the Launch Conditions Editor by selecting View | Editor | Launch Conditions.

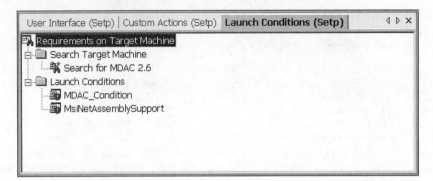

The Launch Conditions Editor allows developers to add conditions that must to be satisfied in order to proceed with the installation. The Windows Installer will check every launch condition in the order specified in the editor (use drag and drop to sort them) before showing the Confirm Installation dialog box. The editor contains a tree view in the left pane that shows two nodes: Search Target Machine and Launch Conditions. The former allows developers to add searches on the target machine for files, registry keys, and Windows Installer components. The latter allows developers to specify a condition that can be custom or provided by the editor, such as the presence of the .NET Framework.

Adding Predefined Launch Conditions

By right-clicking on the Requirements on Target Machine root node, you will see a context menu that lists all the predefined launch condition categories:

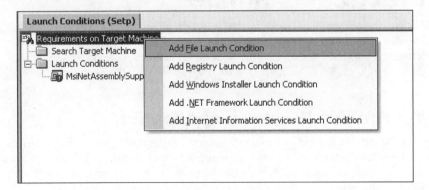

Below we discuss each menu item in detail:

❑ Add File Launch Condition: This adds a condition based on the presence of the specified file on the target machine. Using the Properties window you can refine condition properties by selecting the filename to search for, the folder in which to search for it, the file's creation date, levels of subdirectories to search for the file, and so on.

❑ Add Registry Launch Condition: This adds a condition based on the presence and the value of a registry key. Using the Properties window you can specify which registry key to search for and what its value should be.

❑ Add Windows Installer Launch Condition: This adds a condition based on the presence of a component in the target machine. Using the Properties window you specify the ComponentId GUID value of the component you want to search for. You can retrieve the ComponentId for a component by using specific tools, such as the MSI Spy tool.

❑ Add .NET Framework Launch Condition: This adds a predefined MsiNetAssemblySupport condition that checks for the .NET Framework on the target machine (this condition is added by default by the setup project template). When the .NET Framework is not found the Message property is used to display the error message. The installation will be stopped.

❑ Add Internet Information Services Launch Condition: This adds a predefined condition that checks for the presence of IIS on the target computer. This check is performed by searching for the SYSTEM\CurrentControlSet\Services\W3SVC\Parameters key in the HKEY_LOCAL_MACHINE root key of the registry on the target machine.

A Practical Example

So far in the chapter you have seen much theory examining all of the editors provided by Visual Studio .NET. In this section, you will see a practical example that includes most of these editors. We'll start by analyzing the application features that you have to replicate on a target computer. Then, we'll analyze each step necessary to create the installer.

Guitar Archive Windows Application

In order to demonstrate how to create advanced installer features this application has been created that allows users to search for guitar tablatures (a musical notation) stored in a database – displaying them in the main form of the application. You can recreate the following example by downloading the source code from the Wrox site.

Let's see the features of this application:

- ❏ It uses a Microsoft SQL Server 2000 database in order to store tablature information, such as author and title.

- ❏ It uses registry keys in order to display the last viewed song when the application starts, or a splash screen if no tablatures has been selected since the application was installed.

The installer has to recreate the application features on the target computer. This means the installer has to accomplish these tasks:

- ❏ Since all .NET applications require the .NET Framework, the installer has to check for its presence before starting deployment.

- ❏ Since the Windows application uses the Microsoft SQL Server 2000 database package, the installer has to display a custom dialog box for the user to enter database information, such as a database server, username, and password (with write access). After retrieving them, the installer has to create the database, adding tables and data.

- ❏ Since the Windows application uses database access classes, the installer has to check for the presence of MDAC 2.6 or greater on the target system.

- ❏ Since the Windows application uses the Registry to store information, the installer has to recreate the hierarchy of tree nodes and insert the right values during the installation.

With the Guitar Archive application complete, you would add a new Windows Installer project, called Setp in this case, and add a dependency to the Project Output to get this installer project started.

Using Visual Studio .NET to Redistribute .NET Framework

The Setup project template automatically adds a Launch Condition that checks for the existence of the .NET Framework on the target machine. If the Framework is not found, a standard message is displayed:

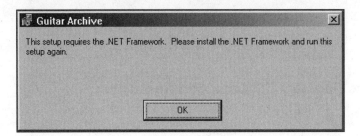

We have three possible choices to customize this default installer behavior:

1. Using a tool such as Microsoft SMS to deploy the .NET Framework redistributable on each computer on your LAN.

2. Using a custom message that informs the user that they need to install the .NET Framework, launching the dotnetfx.exe file provided alongside the installer on the distribution media.

3. Changing the setup.exe installer file with a new executable that launches dotnetfx.exe silently. You can find the executable and all the information on using it at http://msdn.microsoft.com/downloads/sample.asp?url=/msdn-files/027/001/830/msdncompositedoc.xml.

For this example, we will implement solution number two. Expanding the Launch Conditions editor toolbar button from the Design window, you can select the MsiNetAssemblySupport tree node.

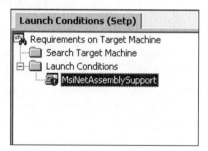

In the Properties window change the Message property value to "This setup requires the .NET Framework. Please install the .NET Framework by running the file Dotnetfx.exe, which can be found in the CD, and then run this setup again".

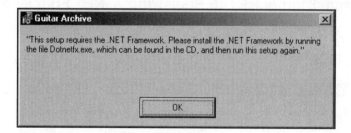

Using the Registry Editor to Add New Keys

The installer has to add registry keys in order to allow the application to display the last viewed song or a splash screen when no tablatures have been viewed by the user. The Registry editor within Visual Studio .NET is the right tool to accomplish this task.

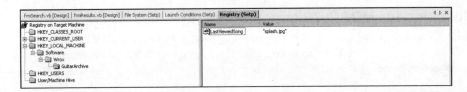

By expanding the HKEY_LOCAL_MACHINE node, we can right-click over the Software node and choose to create a new key called Wrox (usually under the Software key we will find the manufacturer). Perform the same operation on the new node to create a new key called GuitarArchive.

By right-clicking on the right pane with the GuitarArchive key selected we can add a new String value called LastViewedSong. From the Properties window set the Value property to splash.jpg.

Let's see the code in the Windows application that looks for this registry structure. The frmMain form is the main application form that is shown after the application execution. In order to show the last viewed song or a welcome splash screen we have to use the Load event handler that is fired just before the form is shown:

```
Private Sub frmMain_Load(ByVal sender As Object, _
              ByVal e As System.EventArgs) Handles MyBase.Load

    ' Retrieve last viewed song
    Dim key As RegistryKey = Registry.LocalMachine.OpenSubKey( _
                       "SOFTWARE\Wrox\GuitarArchive", False)

    If Not key Is Nothing Then
        Dim strFile As String = key.GetValue("LastViewedSong")
        If strFile <> "" Then
            ' pbTab is a picture box placed over the frmMain form.
            pbTab.Image = Image.FromFile(strFile)
            key.Close()
        End If
    End If

End Sub
```

During the form Load event, the code opens the registry's local machine root key looking for the path specified in the OpenSubKey() method. If the key is retrieved with no errors, then the GetValue() method is used to retrieve the LastViewedSong value that will be passed to the FromFile() method in order to display it in the picture box on the form. The registry key will contain the image path that will be loaded into the picture box using its own Image property.

Checking for MDAC Presence During Installation

Since applications that use database access (like Guitar Archive) need the MDAC 2.6 libraries (or greater), we have to instruct the installer to check for MDAC presence on the target machine. We have two possible choices:

❑   Inform users that their operating system doesn't include an installation of the MDAC 2.6 or greater library.

❑   Use a sample setup executable that you can download at http://www.microsoft.com/data/download_26sp1.htm that installs MDAC and DCOM libraries automatically.

Let's examine the first case. Open the Launch Conditions editor and add a new registry key launch condition by right-clicking on the root node. This creates new nodes called Search for RegistryEntry1 and Condition1. Select the new Registry Search Node and use the Properties window to specify the following registry key characteristics:

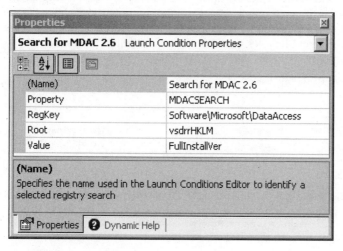

As you can see from the screenshot above, the application searches for the DataAccess registry key within the HKEY_LOCAL_MACHINE root key. That key contains the values for the MDAC library versions; so you can add a simple condition to the Condition property of Condition1 of MDACSEARCH>="2.6". The launch condition, at the beginning of the installation, will search for the specified registry key checking for the specified condition. Using the Message property we can set the error message that will be displayed when the condition is not satisfied:

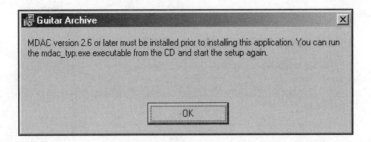

Creating a Database During an Installation

The last and most complex step is creating the database used by the Windows application during the installation. We have to divide our work in two groups:

1. Creating a class library component that is used to retrieve information from the installer (such as database server name, username, and password) and creating the database, tables, and so on

2. Including the component in the Custom Action Editor in order to execute the database creation during the installation

Step 1

Firstly, you have to add a User Interface dialog box that will be used to retrieve database information. From the User Interface editor add a new Textboxes (A) dialog box by right-clicking on the Start tree node and selecting the Add Dialog menu:

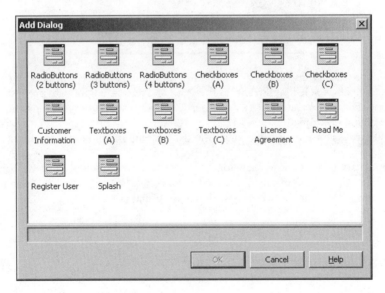

Using the Properties window set the dialog box's properties:

We need to retrieve three values, Server name, username, and password, so we can hide the last textbox selecting `False` in the `Edit4Visible` combobox property. The other properties are used to specify a banner text and description informing the user about the dialog box functionality. The three "EditProperty" properties will be used in the class library because they will contain the database information inserted by the user.

The Class Library project allows developers to create a DLL assembly that will be run by the installer during the installation process. From the Visual Studio .NET File menu, select the New Project... menu to show the following dialog box:

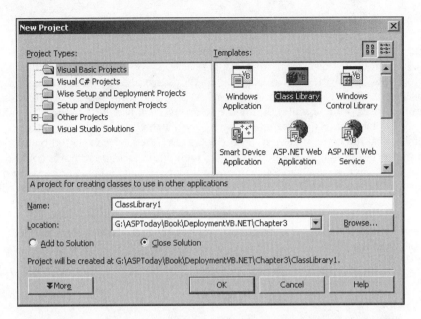

Once the project's name and location have been chosen, the project template will create an empty `class1.vb` module. Remove this. From the Project main menu select the Add New Item... option, which will show the following dialog box:

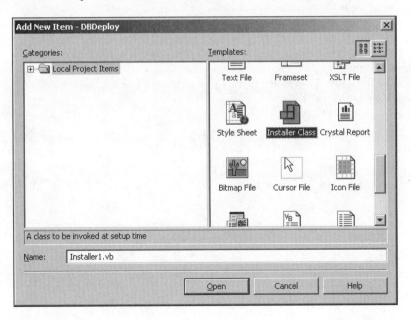

In the Add New Item dialog box there is a template useful when creating an Installer Class. This kind of class is derived from the System.Configuration.Install.Installer class and is invoked during the installation process. This class represents the base class for each custom installer you want to create. It provides four overridable methods that are called automatically by the installer: Install(), Commit(), Uninstall(), and Rollback(). These methods represent phases of the installer during the setup. We will use the Install() and Uninstall() methods for database creation and database removal, respectively. Remember that the code written in the Uninstall() method is executed by a different process from that of the Install() method. In fact, the removal could occur many months later, so you cannot share memory-based content between these two methods, and that's why the Uninstall() method will retrieve the connection string from the registry.

Let's see the code found in the DBDeploy project contained in the source zip file available from the Wrox site:

```
Public Overrides Sub Install( _
                ByVal stateSaver As System.Collections.IDictionary)
    MyBase.Install(stateSaver)

    ' Retrieve database information from the installer dialog box
    Dim ServerName = Me.Context.Parameters.Item("SERVERNAME")
    Dim Username = Me.Context.Parameters.Item("USERNAME")
    Dim Password = Me.Context.Parameters.Item("PASSWORD")
```

The Installer class provides the Context property created from the InstallContext class that contains all the information specified during the installation. In this case, we use this collection to retrieve database information provided by the user. We will see that item names have been specified in the User Interface editor using a particular syntax:

```
    Connection = "server=" & ServerName _
                & ";database=master;uid=" _
                & Username & ";pwd=" & Password

    CreateDB("GuitarArchiveDB")

    Try
        Dim key As RegistryKey = Registry.LocalMachine.OpenSubKey( _
                            "SOFTWARE\Wrox\GuitarArchive", True)

        If Not key Is Nothing Then
            key.SetValue("DBConnectionString", "server=" & ServerName _
                    & ";database=GuitarArchiveDB;uid=" _
                    & Username & ";pwd=" & Password)
            key.Close()
        End If
```

```
    Catch ex As Exception
        ' Report any errors and abort.
        MsgBox("Install: " & ex.Message)
        Throw ex
    End Try
End Sub
```

In the rest of the code, you will find that the application will add a new registry key to store the database connection string used by the Windows application. The `CreateDB()` method needs to know the name of the database it creates. In the method's body there is a call to the `ReadSql()` method explained below.

```
Public Overrides Sub Uninstall(ByVal savedState As IDictionary)
    MyBase.Uninstall(savedState)

    Dim key As RegistryKey = Registry.LocalMachine.OpenSubKey( _
                        "SOFTWARE\Wrox\GuitarArchive", False)

    If Not key Is Nothing Then
        Connection = key.GetValue("DBConnectionString")
        Connection.Replace("GuitarArchiveDB", "master")
        key.Close()
    End If

    ExecuteSql("master", "DROP DATABASE GuitarArchiveDB")
End Sub
```

During the uninstall process the `Uninstall()` method will be called. The code retrieves the database connection string from the registry and executes the DROP SQL command to remove the database from the database server using the `ExecuteSql()` method. This method accepts two parameters; the first is the database's name, against which the SQL command specified in the second parameter is executed.

In order to create the database we could code many `ExecuteSql()` method calls, specifying the SQL instruction to execute each time. However, there is a more elegant way to specify SQL commands for the database creation. We can add to the project an empty text file that we will fill with all the SQL instructions that we want to execute. This is what our text file will contain:

```
CREATE TABLE [dbo].[tabAuthor] (
    [ID_AUTHOR] [int] IDENTITY (1, 1) NOT NULL ,
    [Name] [varchar] (50) COLLATE SQL_Latin1_General_CP1_CI_AS NOT NULL
) ON [PRIMARY]

CREATE TABLE [dbo].[tabSong] (
    [ID_SONG] [int] IDENTITY (1, 1) NOT NULL ,
    [ID_AUTHOR] [int] NOT NULL ,
```

```
    [Title] [varchar] (255) COLLATE SQL_Latin1_General_CP1_CI_AS
                      NOT NULL ,
    [Path] [varchar] (255) COLLATE SQL_Latin1_General_CP1_CI_AS NOT NULL
) ON [PRIMARY]

ALTER TABLE [dbo].[tabAuthor] WITH NOCHECK ADD
  CONSTRAINT [PK_tabAuthor] PRIMARY KEY  CLUSTERED
  (
    [ID_AUTHOR]
  )  ON [PRIMARY]

ALTER TABLE [dbo].[tabSong] WITH NOCHECK ADD
  CONSTRAINT [PK_tabSong] PRIMARY KEY  CLUSTERED
  (
    [ID_SONG]
  )  ON [PRIMARY]

INSERT INTO [dbo].[tabAuthor] ([Name]) VALUES ('Metallica')
INSERT INTO [dbo].[tabSong] ([ID_AUTHOR], [Title], [Path]) VALUES
(1,'Enter Sandman', '\tab\00000001.bmp')
```

If we select the Embedded Resource value for the Build Action property of the
new text file, the compiler will insert the file into the final executable as a resource.

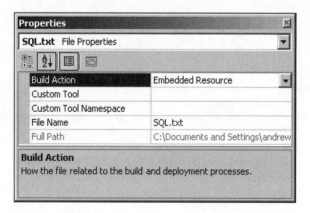

This is useful because you don't have to deploy the text file together with the assembly.
Let's see the code that allows us to retrieve the content from the embedded text file:

```
Private Function ReadSql(ByVal name As String) As String
  Try
    ' Get the current assembly.
    Dim Asm As [Assembly] = [Assembly].GetExecutingAssembly ()

    ' Resources are named using a fully qualified name.
    Dim strm As Stream = _
      Asm.GetManifestResourceStream(Asm.GetName().Name & "." & name)
```

```
      ' Read the contents of the embedded file.
      Dim reader As StreamReader = New StreamReader(strm)
      Return reader.ReadToEnd()
    Catch ex As Exception
      MsgBox("ReadSQL: " & ex.Message)
      Throw ex
    End Try
  End Function
```

Using the `System.Reflection` namespace, you can retrieve assembly information at run time. With the `GetExecutingAssembly()` shared method, you can retrieve a reference to the running assembly as an object. The `GetManifestResourceStream()` method of the provided `Assembly` object will return a `Stream` object that points to the embedded file. Now we can read the stream content using the `ReadToEnd()` method.

We can build the project and so create the component assembly.

Step 2

Now you have to add the component created in the previous step to the setup project of the `GuitarArchive` Windows application. From the File System editor you can add the file into the Application Folder system folder:

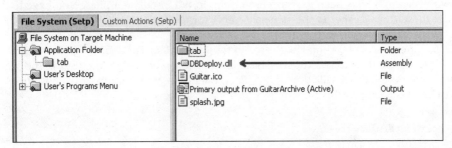

Now you can add a custom action that will execute the code contained in the assembly and will pass the database information retrieved from the user interface added in Step 1. From the View menu we have to select the Custom Actions editor:

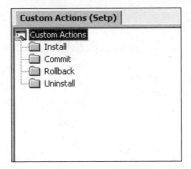

By right-clicking on the Install tree node, you can select the Add Custom Action... option from the context menu. A dialog box allows browsing of the files within the setup project, allowing you to select the DBDeploy assembly.

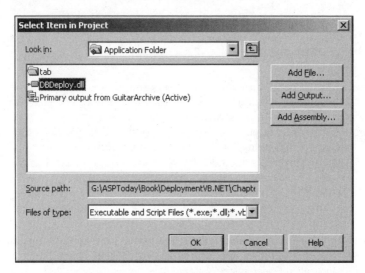

Now the assembly has been associated with the Install installation phase you have to repeat these steps to specify the same assembly for the Uninstall and other phases.

The last operation to be completed is to set the CustomActionData property within the Properties window to pass the database information provided by the user in the dialog box during the installation phase. Each parameter you want to provide to the assembly has to follow this rule:

```
/parametername=[property]
```

The parametername must be the same as that declared in the Context collection's Item property. The [property] parameter must contain a value defined in the Textboxes (A) User Interface editor's EditProperty property.

In this case, the property will be set to:

```
/SERVERNAME=[SERVER] /USERNAME=[USERNAME] /PASSWORD=[PASSWORD]
```

As you can see, like all other command-line arguments, you can pass more than one parameter by separating them with a space.

Summary

In this chapter you have learned about each editor provided by Visual Studio .NET to allow developers to implement a Windows Installer installation package. You created a Windows application setup example in order to show how to implement all the advanced features analyzed in the first part of the chapter.

You have seen how to deploy the .NET Framework using Visual Studio .NET, and we analyzed the class library project that allows developers to create an assembly that is called by the installer during the installation. You have seen how to create a database, tables, and data during the installation by adding a custom action.

Remember that you can download the complete code and the final installer from the Wrox site at: http://www.wrox.com/.

VB.NET

Deployment

Handbook

4

Configuring and Securing Applications

In this chapter we will examine how to configure and secure our applications. To get started, we will first examine the building blocks of .NET applications: Assemblies. We will examine what they are, what their features are, as well as their structure.

Once we have established an understanding of assemblies, we will begin examining how we can configure our applications. This topic will introduce us to the use of configuration files in .NET and how we can manipulate our applications at run time by saving information to configuration files.

When we build our applications, it is important that we ensure that our code is safe. Not only safe from improper use by other parties, but also safe in that it will be able to access the resources that it requires when it is executing. In addition, we will have to ensure that users of our code have the privileges to be running that code. In the section on security, we will cover a variety of topics including Code Access Security, Security Configuration files, Code Groups, and Permission Sets.

Let's get started by discussing assemblies.

Assemblies

If you plan to use the .NET Framework effectively then you need to understand assemblies. In this section, we'll discuss what assemblies are and what they contain. We'll look at their structure and how to create them using both the Visual Basic .NET command-line compiler and Visual Studio .NET.

What are Assemblies?

Assemblies are the basis of all .NET applications and every application must consist of at least one assembly in addition to the base assemblies in the .NET Framework. Although we can create assemblies with code that may or may not be related, a good design will usually consist of assemblies that are logical units of classes, types, structures, etc., organized together. By logical unit we mean that each assembly should contain definitions that are all related to a similar functionality. For example, System.Drawing.dll is an assembly that ships with the .NET Framework that provides functionality for working with bitmaps, GDI+, as well as various drawing classes.

Assemblies answer one of the more serious problems that we frequently encountered in component based applications (COM). The main problem, infamously known as 'DLL Hell', has been addressed with the .NET assembly's feature of being self-describing. This feature and other key features of assemblies will be discussed in the following section.

Assembly Features

Assemblies provide a variety of features that make them easier to work with than DLLs built with COM technology. These features include the following items:

- ❑ Versioning dependencies and policies
- ❑ Self-description
- ❑ Isolation
- ❑ Side-by-side execution

Each of these will be discussed in detail.

Version Dependency and Policies

For the Common Language Runtime (CLR) to uniquely identify an assembly, it will use various pieces of information, such as the assembly's name, public key token, and, of course, its version. The assembly version is in a four part format: major, minor, build, and revision (for example, 4.0.0.2). All assemblies with the same major and minor version numbers are recognized by the CLR as the same version and the latest one will be used unless otherwise specified in the assemblies policy (see Chapter 5 for more information about defining the version policies). So, version 4.0.0.2 and version 4.0.0.3 are, at least according to the CLR, the same version.

However, if you increased the major and/or minor version the CLR would recognize the two assemblies as different versions. As such, these two versions would be able to run concurrently on the same machine without any confusion to the runtime. For example, one application could be running with version 4.0.0.2 and another application could be running with 4.1.0.3 at the same time.

The client applications that reference assemblies define in their own configuration the version dependency policies they will follow.

Self-Describing

In the COM world, components were dependent on the registry in order to enable client applications to locate them on the physical disk. You may be all too familiar with the `regsvr32.exe` utility that is used to register and unregister DLLs with the system registry in order for applications to be able to use them. If your COM component did not break backwards compatibility (by changing the public interface in any way), you could usually get away with just overwriting the old component with the new. But, what happens if the interface did change? What if these changes are required for a new application that is being deployed, but will break pre-existing applications? We are only able to have one instance of a component registered with the registry at one time. Sure, there are ways to get around this. However, the point is that the more you have to do to make all your applications live happily together, the more likely it is that something will go wrong.

The answer to this problem comes with assemblies that are fully self-describing. By using reflection, the assemblies are able to interrogate themselves and provide a description to the runtime. Based on this description, the CLR will determine if it is the appropriate assembly to use. The assemblies contain all the important information, such as version, that the CLR requires to be able to run and so have eliminated any dependencies on the registry.

Isolation

Assembly isolation is one solution to the problems imposed by the COM-based implementation of versioning. Isolation implies that each application that references a particular assembly will have its own local copy of that assembly that no other application will be referencing. If you were to create an assembly that contained some data access code, and you had three applications that referenced it, each of the three applications would be deployed with its own copy of that assembly. In the future, if any changes are made to the assembly for any one of the three applications, you are guaranteed that the updated version will be exposed to the application that requires it. Since each copy of the assembly is self-describing and there is no dependency on the registry, these three copies of the assembly can co-exist happily on the same computer. This greatly simplifies deployment as each application is shipped with its own copy the assembly.

In addition, issues surrounding maintenance are resolved (such as having to worry about backwards compatibility) in that when an assembly is updated it is copied into the directory for the application that is being updated. Also, when the application is uninstalled, the assemblies are completely removed without any trace left behind (such as dangling registry entries).

In contrast to the concept of isolation, there is also the **Global Assembly Cache** (GAC) that acts as a repository for assemblies to be available, as the name implies, globally to all applications. We will discuss the GAC in detail in Chapter 5.

Side-by-Side Execution

For some assemblies, such as the data access assembly referred to in the previous section, isolation may not be desirable. In this case, the assembly may be generic code so that we may prefer to have one copy of the assembly available to all applications on the machine; most likely in the GAC. That way, multiple applications would be able to use the same assembly registered into the GAC. However, when you register multiple versions of the same assembly into the GAC, you get side-by-side execution. Side-by-side execution is the ability to have different versions of the same assembly running concurrently, just as the title implies, side-by-side.

This concept helps to battle the problems of backwards compatibility in COM-based applications where only one instance of the component could be registered and run on the same machine at one time. This is achieved because each assembly describes itself fully including its own version and strong name that is used to uniquely identify the assembly. Each application defines in itself what version of the referenced assemblies it is looking for. Versioning policies will be covered in more detail in their own section a little later; however, the important concept here is that an updated version of an assembly can be installed onto a machine that has an older version and it will not interfere with any applications referencing the older version. Essentially, backwards compatibility becomes an obsolete issue.

There are two types of side-by-side execution. Firstly, the assemblies can be running in the same process on the same machine and, secondly, they can be running in their own processes on the same machine. In either case, as side-by-side execution can be very convenient, care must be taken when writing code for assemblies that will be running side-by-side. This is especially true if the assemblies are both dependent on external resources at fixed locations (file I/O operations, for example).

Application Domains

Application domains are how multiple applications running concurrently are separated. Typically, each application is allocated its own process space so as not to interfere in any way with the execution of other applications. This process space can contain multiple application domains, which helps to alleviate the overhead of marshaling data from one application to another. When an application is loaded into its own application domain, any assemblies that it references are also loaded into the same application domain. The result is that the data being used by the assembly in each application domain is protected from all other instances of the assembly loaded in other application domains.

Assembly Structure

An assembly is structured in such a way that it may consist of one or multiple files. Typically, the assembly will have one of the following structures:

Figure 1

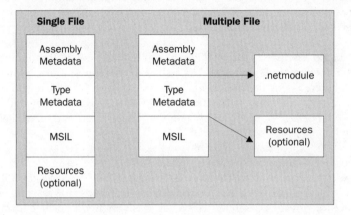

The assembly may optionally be divided across multiple files. For example, resources may be in files external to the assembly.

Assembly Manifests

The assembly manifest is the portion of the assembly that enables the assembly to be self-describing. This aspect of an assembly contains all the critical information about the assembly and how all the pieces of the assembly relate to each other. An assembly cannot exist without a manifest.

The manifest provides us with the following four sections of information:

- ❑ Identity

- ❑ File List

- ❑ References

- ❑ Custom Attributes

The identity section provides the name, version, culture (if specified), and strong name (if specified). It is the identity section that is interrogated by the CLR in order to ensure that it loads the correct assembly for any applications that are requesting the assembly. The CLR will also check the file list to ensure that required files are available and the references section to ensure that all dependent assemblies can be found. If any of these checks fails, an exception will be thrown and the assembly will not be loaded.

We will examine the manifest if more detail later when we discuss the Intermediate Language Disassembler utility, ildasm.exe.

Private and Shared Assemblies

Assemblies can fall into two distinct categories. They can be either **Private** or **Shared**. A private assembly is one that is only used by a single application on the computer and is isolated from any other applications. Private assemblies are generally stored in the bin directory for the application itself.

In contrast, shared assemblies are available globally on the computer to multiple applications. For example, System.dll is a shared assembly shipped with the .NET Framework. Shared assemblies are normally stored in the GAC, which is located in the %System% directory in the Assembly folder (C:\WINNT\Assembly by default for Windows 2000). For assemblies to be shared, they must be given a **Strong Name** (again, this will be discussed in Chapter 5).

There isn't really a difference between a private and a shared assembly. They are created in exactly the same way. The only difference is their availability on the machine to which they are installed. A strong name is required for assemblies that are shared but not for private assemblies. However, it is very good practice to strong-name all of our assemblies to add more protection to our code.

Viewing Assemblies

When assemblies are compiled into .dll or .exe files, they are compiled to the **Microsoft Intermediate Language** (MSIL). Since the files are not yet compiled to native code, they can be viewed using the Intermediate Language Disassembler, ildasm.exe. The utility can be found under Program Files at the following location <install directory>\FrameworkSDK\Bin.

> **The fact that we can view assemblies with tools such as ildasm.exe presents some security issues in that anyone can view our assemblies once they have been deployed. This issue is discussed in Chapter 7.**

In order to view an assembly, run the utility, and select File | Open, or use the following command line code:

```
> ildasm.exe AssemblyName.dll
```

When you open an assembly with the `ildasm.exe` utility, you are provided with a tree-view in the top pane that outlines the structure and interfaces provided by the assembly, as well as a description in the bottom pane. We also get access to the assembly's manifest. The following screenshot shows the `ElementaryMath.dll` assembly that we will be developing shortly.

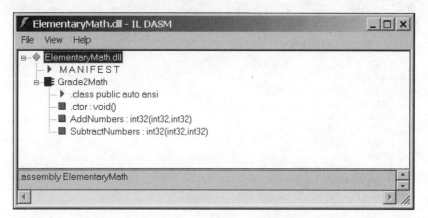

Of particular interest in this view, is the manifest. By double-clicking the MANIFEST node in the tree view in the top pane, you will be able to examine the assembly's manifest.

```
MANIFEST                                          _ □ x
.module extern Grade3Math.netmodule
.assembly extern mscorlib
{
  .publickeytoken = (B7 7A 5C 56 19 34 E0 89 )
  .ver 1:0:3300:0
}
.assembly extern Microsoft.VisualBasic
{
  .publickeytoken = (B0 3F 5F 7F 11 D5 0A 3A )
  .ver 7:0:3300:0
}
.assembly ElementaryMath
{
  .hash algorithm 0x00008004
  .ver 0:0:0:0
}
.file Grade3Math.netmodule
      .hash = (27 5C 8B 2E 7E 70 6B BD F7 49 82 06 83 15 10 83
               1B 92 D3 69 )
```

It's beyond the scope of this book to explain in detail the information exposed by ildasm.exe, but you can see the other assemblies that this assembly is dependent on. Likewise, if you double-click on one of the methods exposed, you can examine the MSIL created by the compiler.

```
Grade2Math::AddNumbers : int32(int32,int32)                        _ □ ×
.method public instance int32  AddNumbers(int32 Num1,
                                          int32 Num2) cil man
{
  // Code size        8 (0x8)
  .maxstack  2
  .locals init (int32 V_0)
  IL_0000:  ldarg.1
  IL_0001:  ldarg.2
  IL_0002:  add.ovf
  IL_0003:  stloc.0
  IL_0004:  br.s          IL_0006
  IL_0006:  ldloc.0
  IL_0007:  ret
} // end of method Grade2Math::AddNumbers
```

Now that you have an understanding of what assemblies are, let's look at how we can create assemblies.

Building Assemblies

Building assemblies is rather simple. All you need is some source code and a compiler. As mentioned earlier, we can create assemblies from multiple files. Using Visual Studio .NET, creating assemblies is seamless since the IDE will create all required assemblies and build their manifests automatically. However, in order to get a better understanding of what is happening under the hood, we will first create some assemblies using NotePad and the Visual Basic .NET compiler, vbc.exe, at the command prompt.

Command Line Modules and Assemblies

In order to build assemblies on the command line, you must have an understanding of the options available to you. First, create your Visual basic source files. So, using NotePad (of course, use whichever editor you prefer), let's create two visual basic files.

Firstly, create `Grade2Math.vb`:

```vb
Imports System

Public Class Grade2Math

    Public Function AddNumbers(ByVal Num1 as Integer, _
                               ByVal Num2 as Integer) as Integer
        Return Num1 + Num2
    End Function

    Public Function SubtractNumbers(ByVal Num1 as Integer, _
                                    ByVal Num2 as Integer) as Integer
        Return Num1 - Num2
    End Function
End Class
```

Next create `Grade3Math.vb`:

```vb
Imports System

Public Class Grade3Math

    Public Function MultiplyNumbers(ByVal Num1 as Integer, _
                                    ByVal Num2 as Integer) as Integer
        Return Num1 * Num2
    End Function

    Public Function DivideNumbers(ByVal Num1 as Integer, _
                                  ByVal Num2 as Integer) as Integer
        If Num2 = 0 then
            Return 0
        End if
        Return Num1 / Num2
    End Function
End Class
```

As was briefly mentioned earlier, assemblies may comprise multiple files or just one file. One of the options provided is to build .NET modules. You specify to the compiler that you would like the output to be a module by specifying the `/target:module` flag on the command line. Let's create modules for each of our visual basic source files using the `vbc.exe` with the `/target:module` switch:

```
> vbc.exe /target:module Grade2Math.vb
> vbc.exe /target:module Grade3Math.vb
```

You can see here that the commands created two files, one for each .vb file. Both have the same name as the original source file, but with an extension of .netmodule. This is the extension for modules created by the .NET compilers. Next, you can create a multifile assembly by compiling the Grade2Math.vb file into an assembly and adding the Grade3Math.netmodule into the assembly with the following command, which will produce ElementaryMath.dll as output:

```
> vbc.exe /target:library /addmodule:Grade3Math.netmodule
          Grade2Math.vb /out:ElementaryMath.dll
```

You can add as many modules as you require using the /addmodule: switch. Of course, this example is over simplified. We do not require that a module be created. You could compile both .vb files as input into a single DLL file. Also, as occured in the previous section, you can use the ildasm.exe utility to view the DLL and .netmodule files.

Visual Studio .NET Assemblies

You can also (and normally would) create assemblies using Visual Studio .NET. The Visual Studio .NET IDE makes it much easier to create assemblies and to configure them using the AssemblyInfo.vb file that is added automatically to each project. Though it is possible to create an AssemblyInfo.vb file manually and add it into a command-line compile, the IDE provides us with a shell to work with and requires us to simply fill in the blanks. More advanced configuration options, such as specifying a COM+ application name, must be added manually as they are less commonly used.

The AssemblyInfo.vb file provides a list of attributes in XML format that you can define explicitly in order to set up the assembly's identity, such as versioning, copyright, author details, trademark, product, and a description (for advanced versioning and signing of assemblies refer to Chapter 5).

Let's fire up Visual Studio .NET, create an assembly, and specify the identity information in the AssemblyInfo.vb file. You can use the class from the previous section, Grade2Math.vb. Add the following entries to the AssemblyInfo.vb file:

```
<Assembly: AssemblyTitle("ElementaryMath")>
<Assembly: AssemblyDescription("Implementation of various
computational functions")>
<Assembly: AssemblyCompany("Wrox Press")>
<Assembly: AssemblyProduct("Mathematical Library")>
<Assembly: AssemblyCopyright("Wrox Press")>
<Assembly: AssemblyTrademark("")>
<Assembly: CLSCompliant(True)>

<Assembly: AssemblyVersion("1.0.*")>
```

Now, build the project so that the assembly .dll is created. Navigate to the file, right-click the assembly, and select Properties. Then on the Version tab, you will be able to examine all the properties that you defined in the AssemblyInfo.vb file.

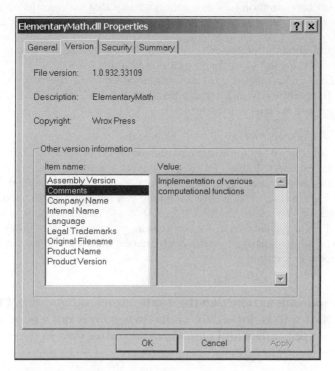

Configuration Files

Configuration files are standard XML files that can be used to save and modify application settings in such a way that modifying the settings can affect the behavior of the application without having to recompile the application with the new settings. The configuration file provides a very easy method to configure and control applications. Alternatives used in the past have been .ini files and the registry. Application configuration files are saved in pure XML format, meaning that in order for the file to be read by the application, the XML must be well-formed (for example, all closing tags must be present).

There are three types of configuration files:

- ❑ Machine
- ❑ Application
- ❑ Security

The machine configuration file is called `machine.config` and can be found on any system that has the .NET Framework installed, usually at `C:\WINNT\Microsoft.NET\Framework\<runtime version>\Config`. Any application-level configuration files that define settings that are also defined in the `machine.config` file will be ignored and the `machine.config` settings will prevail.

The security configuration file (`security.config`) is where the default security policies are defined for the CLR. This file can be found at `C:\WINNT\Microsoft.NET\<runtime version>\Config`. The security configuration file will be covered in more detail later in the chapter as it is also used for applying security settings at the user level.

Application configuration files are used to control the various settings of a particular application. The name of an application configuration file is the name of the application's executable with the `.config` extension appended to it. For example, an application called `MathTutor.exe` would have a configuration file called `MathTutor.exe.config`. This configuration file can be used to apply global settings for your application. For example, the configuration file is a convenient way to store a connection string for a database. If, for any reason, your connection information should change, you can simply change it in the configuration file. The application will use the new string once it is restarted.

> **It is important to note that the application configuration file is plain XML and is not secure on its own, so it is not a good idea to store user names and passwords to secure data in there.**

Categories and Settings

Application configuration files have a wide variety of settings, from user preference settings to file locations, which can be saved and used by an application. Settings are defined using XML attribute name-value pair syntax. The root element of all configuration files is `<configuration>`, which contains startup settings, runtime settings, security settings, user info, and versioning settings to name a few. A brief explanation of the more commonly used sections will be provided here. For a complete reference, refer to the .NET Framework documentation (at the time of writing, this could be found at: ms-help://MS.VSCC/MS.MSDNVS/cpgenref/html/gngrfconfiguration.htm).

Startup Settings

The `<requiredRuntime>` element within the startup settings specifies which version of the CLR should be used to run the application. This setting can be handy since multiple versions of the CLR can co-exist on the same machine. To specify the required run-time version of the CLR, the entry in the configuration file would like the following:

```
<configuration>
  <startup>
    <requiredRuntime version="v1.0.3705" />
  </startup>
</configuration>
```

The version string must match the name of the directory where the runtime is installed.

Runtime Settings

The runtime settings specify how the CLR should handle garbage collection and the version of an assembly to use. One of the top-level settings in the runtime setting section is the <assemblyBinding> element. Within this element there are three sub-elements: <probing>, <publisherPolicy>, and <dependentAssembly>. The following table contains a list of the most common settings (refer to the .NET documentation for a complete list). These settings are discussed in more detail in the *Redirecting Clients* section of Chapter 5.

Element	Purpose
<assemblyBinding>	This child node of the <runtime> element allows you to specify redirection to other assemblies and versioning information as well as where assemblies are located.
<probing>	This child node of the <assemblyBinding> element specifies where in the file system the CLR will search for referenced assemblies.
<publisherPolicy>	This specifies whether an application should use the newest version of an assembly. To apply at an assembly level, put this tag in the <dependentAssembly>, or if applying to an entire application, place under the <assemblyBinding> element.
<dependentAssembly>	This child node of the <assemblyBinding> element specifies the location of each referenced assembly. One entry per referenced assembly.
<bindingRedirect>	This child node of the <dependentAssembly> element allows you to specify to the CLR to load a different assembly from that specified by the manifest.
<gcConcurrent>	This child node of the <assemblyBinding> element specifies whether the CLR will run the garbage collector concurrently.

Remoting Settings

The root element of the Remoting settings is `<System.Runtime.Remoting>`. With this element you can define information about remote objects that the application consumes, channels used for communication, and sinks used to process remote requests. In addition within the root element, you can specify client or server activation of remote objects consumed by a client, and you can specify client or server activation of objects provided to clients.

Using Configuration Files

Now that you have been hearing about how easy it is to use configuration files to control the behavior of applications, let's build a small application and try this out. The application will be very simple yet effective. Let's begin by opening Visual Studio .NET and creating a new Windows application called `ConfigurationFileTest`. Then right-click of the project file in the solution exploring and select Add | Add New Item. From the list of files to add, add an Application Configuration file. Rename the file to `ConfigurationTest.exe.config`. If you examine the configuration file before running the application, you will see this: (the `<appSettings>` tags may not be present; if not make sure to add them):

```
<?xml version="1.0" encoding="utf-8"?>
<configuration>
  <appSettings>
  </appSettings>
</configuration>
```

The application will search in its `bin` directory for this file, so you then need to move it to that location.

In the test application we will allow the user to specify the color they prefer their form to be. We will accomplish this by providing them with a combobox of colors to choose from, and then when the application closes, save the color to the application's `config` file where it will be read from the next time the application starts. Create your UI so it looks like the following:

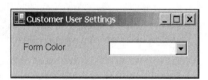

Next, add in the code below:

```
Imports System.Drawing
Imports System.Configuration
```

```
Imports System.Reflection
Imports System.Xml
Imports System.IO

Public Class CustomSettingsForm
  Inherits System.Windows.Forms.Form

  Dim colors() As String = {KnownColor.Aquamarine.ToString, _
                            KnownColor.BurlyWood.ToString, _
                            KnownColor.CadetBlue.ToString, _
                            KnownColor.Chartreuse.ToString}

  Private Sub CustomSettingsForm_Load(ByVal sender As System.Object, _
          ByVal e As System.EventArgs) Handles MyBase.Load

    cboFormColor.Items.AddRange(colors)
  End Sub

  Private Sub cboFormColor_SelectedIndexChanged( _
          ByVal sender As Object, ByVal e As System.EventArgs) _
          Handles cboFormColor.SelectedIndexChanged

    BackColor = System.Drawing.Color.FromName(cboFormColor.Text)
  End Sub
```

The first thing you need to do is import the namespaces you need. Next, create an array called colors and give it a set of values representing colors (feel free to use your favorites).

In the Load event of our form, populate the combobox so that the users can choose their favorite color. In the SelectedIndexChanged event of the combobox set the BackColor property to the user's selection. If you run your application now, you can change the form's color but it will not be saved, so next time you run the application, you will get the default color.

In order to save your favorite form color to the configuration file, add the following code to the form's Closing event:

```
Private Sub CustomSettingsForm_Closing(ByVal sender As Object, _
        ByVal e As System.ComponentModel.CancelEventArgs) _
        Handles MyBase.Closing

  Dim MyAssembly As [Assembly] = [Assembly].GetExecutingAssembly
  Dim ConfigLoc As String
  ConfigLoc = MyAssembly.Location

  Dim TempString As String
  TempString = Path.GetDirectoryName(ConfigLoc)
```

```
Dim XmlDoc As New XmlDocument()
XmlDoc.Load(TempString & "\ConfigurationFileTest.exe.config")

Dim Node As XmlNode
Dim Found As Boolean = False
For Each Node In XmlDoc.Item("configuration").Item("appSettings")
  If Node.Name = "add" Then
    If Node.Attributes.GetNamedItem("key").Value = _
        "CustomSettingsForm.BackColor" Then
      Node.Attributes.GetNamedItem("value").Value = _
          BackColor.ToKnownColor.ToString
      Found = True
    End If
  End If
Next Node

If Not Found Then
  XmlDoc.Item("configuration").Item("appSettings").InnerXml = _
      "<add key='CustomSettingsForm.BackColor' value='" & _
      cboFormColor.Text & "' />"
End If

XmlDoc.Save(TempString & "\ConfigurationFileTest.exe.config")
  End Sub
End Class
```

Your first task is to get the location of the configuration file. As you know, this must be in the same folder as the .exe file, so you can use reflection to determine this. Next, load the configuration file into an XmlDocument object so that you can manipulate it easily. The code tries to locate <add> nodes and, if it finds any, it looks for the add key with the value CustomSettingsForm.BackColor. If it finds it, it sets its value property to the BackColor of the form.

If the add key does not exist, which will be the case the first time the application is run, the code creates the key and sets its value. Then it saves the configuration file to disk.

The final task is to amend the form's Load event to read the information from the configuration file, and set the BackColor as appropriate:

```
Private Sub CustomSettingsForm_Load(ByVal sender As System.Object, _
            ByVal e As System.EventArgs) Handles MyBase.Load

    cboFormColor.Items.AddRange(colors)
    Dim ColorName As String

    Try
      ColorName = ConfigurationSettings.AppSettings.Get( _
                  "CustomSettingsForm.BackColor")
      BackColor = Color.FromName(ColorName)
```

```
      Catch ex As Exception
          BackColor = Color.FromKnownColor(KnownColor.LightGray)
      End Try
   End Sub
```

It's important to notice the Catch block, which will set the form's BackColor property to a default if an exception occurs. If you run the application and change the color, when the form closes the Closing event will fire and save the selected color to the configuration file. Also, Visual Studio .NET will display a message box telling you that one of the files in the project has been amended. This is fine, as it happened in the Closing event, so click Yes.

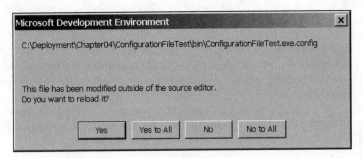

Navigate to the application's bin folder and examine the configuration file. Here is a view of the configuration file after changing the color to BurlyWood:

```
<?xml version="1.0" encoding="utf-8"?>
<configuration>
  <appSettings>
     <add key="CustomSettingsForm.BackColor" value="BurlyWood" />
  </appSettings>
</configuration>
```

Try changing the value property to another color manually and starting the application again (by double-clicking on the .exe file in the bin folder, not using Visual Studio .NET as that would recompile the project). You should see the form with the new color you specified, or light gray if you typed something wrong.

This model is completely extensible for any properties and/or data that you may want to save and alter dynamically at run time.

Security in .NET

Security is always an important topic when discussing application architecture. More often than not, it is the portion of an application that is designed without much thought, but then implemented haphazardly. In this section, we will discuss some of the key issues surrounding security and how the .NET Framework provides solutions to these issues. We begin by discussing Code Access Security.

Code Access Security

Code Access Security is used to determine whether an application has enough rights to access certain secured resources and operations on a computer. Code access security is designed to ensure that any code executing on a system is not malicious and has the right to be there. We see many examples of this level of security on the World Wide Web when we access web pages with objects, such as ActiveX controls, or on corporate intranets when prompted for credentials when accessing various resources. The CLR imposes a security model on any code that it processes and in order for the code to execute, it must meet the requirements imposed on it by the security model. Ultimately, it is the responsibility of developers to make sure that their code has sufficient privileges to do what it has to on the machines that it will be running on.

Each and every assembly loaded by the CLR is examined to ensure that it has the power to do what it is trying to do. This step of execution is called gathering the **Evidence**. For a more elaborate discussion, refer to the Wrox title *Visual Basic .NET Code Security Handbook* (ISBN: 1-86100-747-7).

Evidence

Evidence is collected when the CLR interrogates the calling assembly for information about its identity. The evidence gathered provides the runtime with enough information about the assembly in order to determine whether or not the code is from a trusted source. The types of evidence collected are attributes such as:

- ❏ **Zone** – Internet Zone, Intranet Zone, My Computer Zone, Restricted Zone, Trusted Zone

- ❏ **Publisher** – a software signature (Authenticode).

- ❏ **Site** – the site the assembly is from. For example, http://www.wrox.com.

- ❏ **Application Directory** – the directory where the application is installed.

- ❏ **URL** – the URL of the assembly. For example: http://www.wrox.com/myassembly.dll

It is important to note the key difference between the URL and the Site. The URL specifies a fully qualified path to a specific assembly, whereas the site refers to all assemblies downloaded from that particular site.

As seen in the following example, not all assemblies provide all types of evidence. Here is the evidence discovered for the `System.data.dll` assembly (this information was acquired by using reflection. For more information about reflection, refer to the Wrox title *Visual Basic .NET Reflection Handbook*, ISBN: 1-86100-759-0):

```
<evidence>
  <System.Security.Policy.Zone version="1">
    <Zone>MyComputer</Zone>
  </System.Security.Policy.Zone>
  <System.Security.Policy.Url version="1">
<Url>file://C:/winnt/assembly/gac/system.data/1.0.3300.0__b77a5c561934
e089/system.data.dll</Url>
  </System.Security.Policy.Url>
  <StrongName version="1" Key="00000000000000000400000000000000"
            Name="System.Data" Version="1.0.3300.0" />
  <System.Security.Policy.Hash version="1">
```

In this listing, you can see the Zone is my local computer and the URL is a file-based URL to the GAC where the assembly was installed. The information gathered from the evidence of the assembly will then be compared against a code group to determine what access rights the code has, if any (for example, File I/O, Registry, Environment variables). This will be seen in more detail when we discuss code groups in a later section. For now, let's take a moment to discuss another concept that can be used to secure aspects of you applications called Isolated Storage.

Isolated Storage

When an application must hold unique data for each instance of itself on a computer, it requires that some system be constructed to ensure that data from one instance of the application does not interfere with another and vice-versa. Isolated storage provides a mechanism where this type of maintenance is not required because the .NET Framework manages this for us. Otherwise this would be managed by hard-coding a physical path somewhere in the application, writing data to a file and saving the file to the physical disk. The inherent maintenance problems and lack of security make isolated storage a more desirable approach to file I/O.

Applications that use isolated storage store their data to unique compartments that are identified by both user and assembly and/or application domain. The compartment is an abstract entity called a store that consists of isolated storage files, isolated from all applications other than the one that the data pertains too. Access to the store is restricted to the user that created it. An important note is that the restrictions are given by the local system security settings, which may need to be configured.

Code Groups

Code groups are a way of defining a set of permissions, and then having the ability to assign assemblies the rights to perform actions based on the rights granted by this code group. Code groups work in much the same way the Active Directory user groups work in that you can define a group, assign the group access to various resources, and then assign individual users to the group. The users assigned to the group will be able to do no more than the group permits. In the same respect, an assembly will not be able to modify environment variables if the code group it is assigned to only grants the assembly read-only access to the variables.

Code groups can be configured using the **Code Access Security Policy Tool**, CasPol.exe, which ships with the .NET Framework. This utility can be found at %System%\Microsoft.NET\Framework\<version> where <version> is the version of the Framework that is installed. CasPol.exe is a command-line utility that allows you to configure policies at all three levels (Enterprise, Machine, and User – these will be covered later in the chapter).

By using CasPol.exe, you can view all of your currently configured security policies. The command to do this is:

```
> CasPol.exe -<level> -list
```

In the above code, <level> refers to a specified security level (Enterprise, Machine, or User). If an administrator is logged into the system, the default level is Machine. For all others, the default level is User. The level of –all may also be specified to avoid the filter based on level. The following output displays (a portion) the results of the –all command:

```
> CasPol.exe -all -list

Microsoft (R) .NET Framework CasPol 1.0.3705.0
Copyright (C) Microsoft Corporation 1998-2001. All rights reserved.

Security is ON
Execution checking is ON
Policy change prompt is ON

Level = Enterprise

Code Groups:

1.  All code: FullTrust

Named Permission Sets:
```

```
1. FullTrust (Allows full access to all resources) =
<PermissionSet class="System.Security.NamedPermissionSet"
              version="1"
              Unrestricted="true"
              Name="FullTrust"
              Description="Allows full access to all resources"/>

...

13.  System.DirectoryServices.resources 1.0.3300.0 =
StrongName -
00240000048000009400000006020000002400005253413100040000010001 0007D1FA
57C4AED9F0A32E84AA0FAEFD0DE9E8FD6AEC8F87FB03766C834C99921EB23BE79AD9D5
DCC1DD9AD236132102900B723CF980957FC4E177108FC607774F29E8320E92EA05ECE4
E821C0A5EFE8F1645C4C0C93C1AB99285D622CAA652C1DFAD63D745D6F2DE5F17E5EAF
0FC4963D261C8A12436518206DC093344D5AD293 name =
System.DirectoryServices.resources version = 1.0.3300.0
Success
```

Each security level policy comprises code groups. These code groups have conditions that must be met in order to determine membership. The conditions are defined and then tested against the evidence provided by an assembly. You can view all the code groups for a security level by executing the following command:

```
> CasPol.exe -machine -lg

...

Level = Machine

Code Groups:

1.  All code: Nothing
     1.1.  Zone - MyComputer: FullTrust
        1.1.1.  StrongName -
00240000048000009400000006020000002400005253413100040000010001 0007D1FA
57C4AED9F0A32E84AA0FAEFD0DE9E8FD6AEC8F87FB03766C834C99921EB23BE79AD9D5
DCC1DD9AD236132102900B723CF980957FC4E177108FC607774F29E8320E92EA05ECE4
E821C0A5EFE8F1645C4C0C93C1AB99285D622CAA652C1DFAD63D745D6F2DE5F17E5EAF
0FC4963D261C8A12436518206DC093344D5AD293: FullTrust
        1.1.2.  StrongName - 00000000000000000400000000000000: FullTrust
     1.2.  Zone - Intranet: LocalIntranet
        1.2.1.  All code: Same site Web.
        1.2.2.  All code: Same directory FileIO - Read, PathDiscovery
     1.3.  Zone - Internet: Nothing
     1.4.  Zone - Untrusted: Nothing
     1.5.  Zone - Trusted: Internet
        1.5.1.  All code: Same site Web.
Success
```

You can see what code groups are configured on my machine at the Machine level. Any code that doesn't match any of the permissions defined will be granted the ability to do nothing. But, if it does match a defined permission set, the code will be granted the access rights provided by that group. For example, if the code's evidence indicates that it is coming from a Trusted Internet site, it will be granted privileges on the computer by the definition of code group 1.5.

When the time comes to add your own assemblies to code groups, you can either add them to a code group that already exists, or create your own code groups. The safest route is to create new code groups. By adding them to existing code groups you are putting other applications at risk when your assembly requires some permission that is not already defined. The rule of thumb is to only expose as much functionality as is minimally required by your assembly. To create your own code group you will need to specify a membership condition, a permission set, and the name of the group to which you are adding the new code group. The syntax for this command is as follows:

```
> CasPol.exe -<policy level> -addgroup membership permissionset
```

Before demonstrating how to add a code group, let's see all the code groups at the User security policy level:

```
> CasPol.exe -user -lg

. . .

Level = User

Code Groups:

1.  All code: FullTrust
Success
```

Now execute the following command, which will add a new code group called MyNewGroup:

```
> CasPol.exe -user -addgroup 1 -zone Trusted LocalIntranet
  -name "MyNewGroup" -description "Test Adding new code group"
```

Here we have created a code group that gives the Local Intranet permission set to any code that provides evidence to satisfy this permission set. You can view your newly created group in two ways. Using the -listdescription attribute, you can display the name and description that was specified when creating the code group:

```
> CasPol.exe -user -listdescription

. . .
```

```
Level = User

Full Trust Assemblies:

1. All_Code: Code group grants all code full trust and forms the root
of the code group tree.
   1.1. MyNewGroup: Test Adding new code group
Success
```

Alternatively, you can use the -listgroups attribute to give a list of groups as follows:

> **CasPol.exe -user -listgroups**

```
...

Level = User

Code Groups:

1.  All code: FullTrust
    1.1.  Zone - Trusted: LocalIntranet
Success
```

You may also remove groups by using the following syntax:

> **CasPol.exe -<level> -rg <label|name>**

Later in the chapter we'll come back to code groups and examine in more detail how to manage code groups and permission. We will also use the graphical user interface provided by the .NET Framework Configuration tool.

Code Access Permissions and Permission Sets

Code Access Permissions and Permission Sets are the backbone of code access security on .NET. Essentially, they are the properties that are assigned to code groups in order to define what type of access a code group grants. You may have a code group called MyCompanyFinancials. In this code group you can specify the site on your local intranet where code should be granted access to the registry and local files. To accomplish this, you simply create a permission set that encompasses access to the registry and local files. This is an example of creating a custom permission set for specific needs. The .NET Framework also comes with a list of predefined permission sets:

❏   FullTrust – grants full access to all resources

❏   SkipVerification – allows code to bypass the evidence discovery and security verification phase

❏   Execution – grants permission for the code to run, but not to access protected resources

- ❑ Nothing – grants no access and the code cannot run
- ❑ LocalIntranet – default set of permissions for within the enterprise
- ❑ Internet – default set of permissions for unknown sites on the Internet
- ❑ Everything – all standard permissions

The above pre-defined permission sets include some (or all in the case of FullTrust) of the following most common code access permissions. These are also available when creating custom permission sets, and the following list is not exhaustive:

- ❑ Event Log – access to read/write to the event log
- ❑ File Dialog – access to files that user opens with the Open File dialog
- ❑ Printing – access to printers
- ❑ Registry – access to the registry

The above types of permissions are considered action permissions because they all have something to do with the code performing some type of action. You can see these permissions by using the .NET Framework Configuration Tool. Expand the Runtime Security Policy node, then either the User node (or the Enterprise or Machine node), and then the Permission Sets node. Select one of the permission sets and press the View Permissions link and you will see the following screenshot.

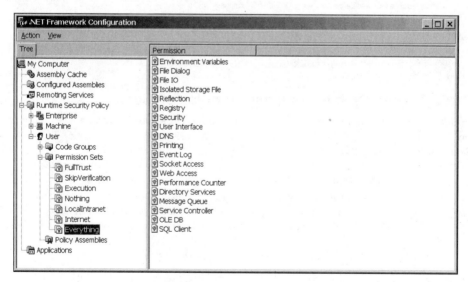

By right-clicking on any of the entries in the right-hand pane and selecting Properties, you will see a dialog box detailing the various permissions granted.

The .NET Framework also allows permissions to be established based on a user's Identity. When the CLR queries the assembly for evidence, it will look for the specified attribute that identifies the assembly as being trusted. Some of the attributes available for use as Identity permissions are: Zone, Strong Name, URL, and Site.

Policy Levels

The .NET Framework uses policy levels to determine what type of access rights should be granted to an assembly or application domain. There are four policies defined by the Framework:

- ❑ Enterprise
- ❑ Machine
- ❑ User
- ❑ Application Domain

These policies are structured hierarchically, starting with the Enterprise level, then to the Machine, then to the User, and finally to the Application Domain. The lower-level policies are restricted in the rights they can provide by any superceding higher-level policy. For example, OS-level security cannot be overtaken simply by providing the rights to code in the security.config file.

The Enterprise policy level provides access to all enterprise-level code as specified by the system administrator. The Enterprise policy affects all computers on the network and all users of the network. The Machine-level policy grants access to all code running in the runtime on the local computer and the User policy grants access to all code associated with the currently logged on user. Finally, the Application Domain-level policy is limited to code executing in the host's application domain.

.NET Framework Security

.NET has shipped with a very robust Framework for implementing security in our applications. Within that Framework is the ability to check the owner of the executing thread against a set of your own predefined rules, or to integrate your security model with Windows authentication. The details of how some of these tasks can be performed will be outlined in the next section, *Role-Based Security*. For the purposes of the section, we will discuss the Framework itself.

The Framework provides three key namespaces for working with security in your applications. Let's delve into each one of these a little before putting some of them to use. The three namespaces are:

- ❑ System.Security.Permissions
- ❑ System.Security.Policy

❑   System.Security.Principal

The System.Security.Permissions namespace provides a series of classes surrounding identities and principals. As you will see in the next section, identities are used to identify the user that the current code is executing under and the principal holds a reference to the identity and the groups that the identity belongs. Some of the more common classes in this namespace deal with code access security and role-based security. Such code access classes are:

❑   FileDialogPermission

❑   RegistryPermission

❑   FileIOPermission

These classes are used for imperative security checks (more on this later) where the objects are instantiated in code and checked against the currently executing principal. Each has a corresponding attribute class:

❑   FileDialogPermissionAttribute

❑   RegistryPermissionAttribute

❑   FileIOPermissionAttribute

These attributes are used for declarative security checks (again more on this later) where access to various methods and classes is defined with method and class attributes.

The key role-based security class in the System.Security.Permissions namespace is the PrincipalPermission class. This class is used to define a name and a role that is compared against the principal of the currently running thread in order to determine if the user has access to the code.

The System.Security.Principal namespace provides a series of classes that are used to define principal objects and identity objects. The use of these objects will be elaborated on in the next section. Essentially, as alluded to earlier, we'll create an Identity object to identify who the current user is. This information can be obtained via a UI prompt, or via Windows integrated security. The principal object is used to group the identity with a set of roles. The principal object is assigned to the principal of the currently executing thread to allow other segments of code to evaluate what level of access the current user has in the application.

The System.Security.Policy namespace provides you with a series of classes that were seen earlier in *Code Access Security*. These classes include Evidence, CodeGroup, and PolicyLevel.

Not only does the Framework provide the mechanisms for the CLR to interrogate and grant or refuse code to execute, it also provides a mechanism for code to request permissions to perform various functionalities. The requests are done declaratively using attributes. For example, if you had a method called `AddLineToTextFile()`, you'd want it to be able to open a file for write access and save the updated file. However, the system's security policy dictates how much access your code can have. The request only asks the CLR for permission; if there are no code groups that the assembly is granted access by, the request will be denied.

Role-Based Security

It is usually in an enterprise where access is granted to various resources based on the roles the individuals play in the organization. For example, in a bank, only select individuals (usually bank managers) would have the combination to the vault. Their role allows them access to that type of information. In the same manner, we use roles in our applications to determine whether or not a user has access to certain resources, such as the RDBMS (SQL Server for example) or file shares. .NET provides mechanisms to leverage Windows integrated security in your applications, or create custom security roles on the fly. Role-based security in the .NET Framework authenticates users based on their principal. All principals are provided in the security context in which the code is executing. Three types of principals are supported:

❑ Windows principals

❑ Generic principals

❑ Custom Principals

Windows principals are completely based on Windows user accounts whereas generic principals are completely independent of Windows accounts. In addition, we may define our own custom principal classes. A `Principal` object contains a reference to an `Identity` object. The `Identity` object encapsulates all the information about the current user. `Identity` objects also come in three forms:

❑ Windows Identity

❑ Generic Identity

❑ Custom identities

In order to check a user's credentials, the code must be able to get a reference to their identity. The following listing shows an example of how this can be achieved: `ShowIdentity.vb`:

```
Imports System
Imports System.Security.Principal
Imports System.Threading
```

```
Public Class ShowIdentity
  Shared Sub Main()
    AppDomain.CurrentDomain.SetPrincipalPolicy( _
       PrincipalPolicy.WindowsPrincipal)

    Dim UserPrinciple As WindowsPrincipal = Thread.CurrentPrincipal
    Console.WriteLine(UserPrinciple.Identity.Name & " " & _
                      UserPrinciple.Identity.IsAuthenticated)
  End Sub
End Class
```

When this code executes, I see the following information (this will vary depending on what account you are currently logged into your system as):

```
BIGDOG\Administrator True
```

Now that you have your identity and principal objects created, you can use the methods provided by the Framework to interrogate them and determine if the user has enough privileges to access the protected resources. The .NET Framework provides three mechanisms for executing the security check:

❑ Imperative security checks

❑ Declarative security checks

❑ Directly accessing the principal object

Managed code has the ability to perform imperative or declarative security checks in order to determine if a principal object is a member of a known role, has a specific identity, or has an identity acting in a specified role. Imperative security checks involve the creation of an identity object, a principal object, a PrincipalPermission object, and a call to the PrincipalPermission object's Demand() method. Look at the example below:

```
Imports System
Imports System.Threading
Imports System.Security.Principal
Imports System.Security.Permissions

Public Class RoleBased
  Shared Sub Main()

    AppDomain.CurrentDomain.SetPrincipalPolicy( _
      PrincipalPolicy.WindowsPrincipal)
    Dim MyPermission As New PrincipalPermission( _
      Nothing, "BUILTIN\Administrators", True)

    Try
      MyPermission.Demand()
```

```
      Console.WriteLine("Access Granted")
   Catch ex As Security.SecurityException
      Console.WriteLine("Access Denied: " & ex.Message)
   End Try

   End Sub
End Class
```

This constructs the user's identity and the principal in which they are running using a `WindowsPrincipal` object. It specifies that the role for this principal must be `BUILTIN\Administrators`. Before code execution can continue on to the secure aspects of our application, it assigns the principal to the current thread and instantiates a `PrincipalPermission` object. Next, it calls the `Demand()` method of the `PrincipalPermission` object, `MyPermission`. If the authentication fails, a security exception will be thrown and will provide feedback to the user that they are attempting to access a restricted area; otherwise, execution continues.

Declarative security checks work in much the same way but with less code. We are still required to build an identity and principal object and assign the principal to the current thread. However, rather than implicitly calling the `PrincipalPermission` object's `Demand()` method in code, we set a `PrincipalPermissionAttribute` on the method and/or class that we would like to secure. For example, say you have a method called `DropDatabase()`. It's most likely you want to have very tight security on this method. You would declare the method as follows:

```
<PrincipalPermissionAttribute(SecurityAction.Demand, _
                              "BigDog", "AllBeingAllKnowing")> _
Public Sub DropDatabase()
End Sub
```

If the security check fails, a `SecurityException` object will be thrown and access to the method will be denied. In this case, you are limiting access to a user name of `BigDog` who is in the role of `AllBeingAllKnowing`. In the case, where Declarative security is applied at both the class and method level within the same class, the attribute on the method will prevail.

Managing Security Policy

In this section you will see how to manage security policy. You have already looked at this using the command line tools such as `CasPol.exe`. Now we will examine how to accomplish these tasks, as well as some others, using the graphical user interface provided with the .NET Framework as a management console snap-in. We'll start by looking at the various configuration files within .NET. Then we'll look at managing Code Groups and Permission Sets using the .NET Framework Configuration tool. This section is completed by examining Zones.

The Security Config File

Security configuration files provide the detailed information regarding the permissions assigned to the various policy levels (Enterprise, Machine, and User). There is one configuration file per policy, except in the case of the User policy where there will be one security configuration file per user profile on the computer. Each of the files can be found in the following locations (Windows 2000 is assumed):

❑ Enterprise – %runtime install path%\Config\Enterprisesec.config

❑ Machine – %runtime install path%\Config\machine.config

❑ User – %USERPROFILE%\Application Data\Microsoft\CLR Security Config\<version>\security.config.

You can see in the following excerpt from my own user security configuration file, the code group that was created earlier with the CasPol.exe utility.

```
<CodeGroup class="UnionCodeGroup" version="1"
           PermissionSetName="FullTrust" Name="All_Code"
           Description="Code group grants all code full trust and
forms the root of the code group tree.">
    <IMembershipCondition class="AllMembershipCondition" version="1"/>
    <CodeGroup class="UnionCodeGroup" version="1"
           PermissionSetName="LocalIntranet" Name="MyTestGroup"
           Description="Test Adding new code group">
      <IMembershipCondition class="ZoneMembershipCondition"
                            version="1" Zone="Trusted"/>
    </CodeGroup>
</CodeGroup>
```

Having all the security settings in standard XML format makes them very easy to configure and maintain. However, what is even easier is having a graphical user interface to assist with the management of the security policies. This is what will be discussed in the next section.

Managing Code Groups and Permissions

Managing security is an important administrative task required to ensure the safety of your systems and your data. Security is managed by defining code groups, assigning policies to code groups, and then evaluating assemblies against these code groups in order to ensure that the proper rights are granted to them. As you saw earlier, you could manage your security policies using the CasPol.exe utility. Since this tool is a command-line utility, it can get very cumbersome when trying to manage a larger number of code groups and permission sets. Luckily, the .NET Framework ships with the .NET Framework Configuration management console snap-in, which provides a very user friendly interface for managing your security policies. Again, you can see in this UI the code group created earlier with CasPol.exe:

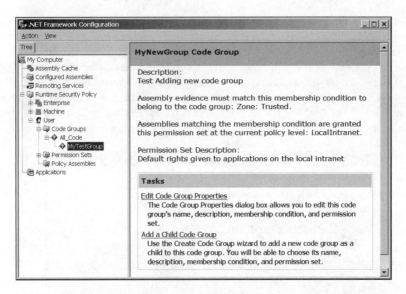

In this section, you will delete the previously created code group and create a new code group with a Machine-level policy. To delete the code group, MyTestGroup, you can simply right-click it and select the Delete menu item, as is common with virtually all Windows applications.

Now, to add a code group to the Machine-level policy, expand the Machine node, and then the Code Groups node. Next, right-click the All_Code node and select New from the menu. The Create Code Group wizard will appear:

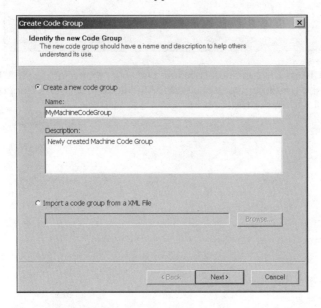

Let's start by specifying the name `MyMachineCodeGroup` and giving the group a description. In addition to specifying the name here, you can also browse to a predefined XML file that contains the information we require for our code group. The XML file will contain all the information that would be entered into the wizard over the next few steps. If you choose to create the code group in this manner, after entering the file path and name into the bottom textbox, you will be presented with the Finish button instead of the Next button. In order to keep in step with the purpose of this exercise, you will simply follow the steps of the wizard. Press the Next button to continue.

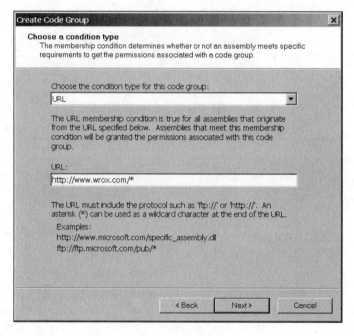

Let's specify a URL as the condition type and http://www.wrox.com/* as the URL. Depending on the condition type specified for the code group, other options would become available. Click the Next button.

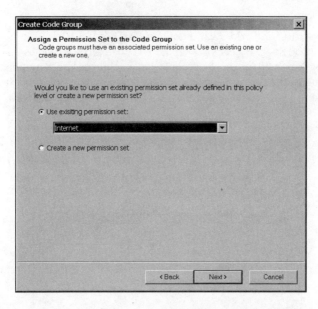

In the next page of the wizard, you can specify an existing permission set or create a new one. For now, choose Internet as your permission set. You can edit this later, should you require this. After clicking Next and then Finish on the wizard, you will see your new code group listed in the treeview under the Machine level policies and All_Code tree nodes. The node code group will look similar to this (depending on what name you gave yours):

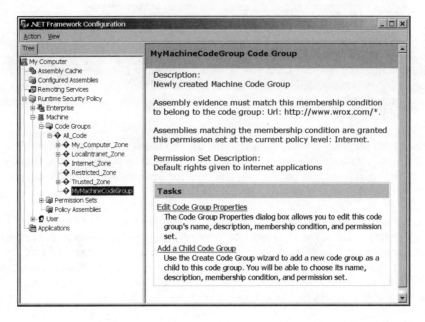

In the right-hand pane, there are some additional links that will permit you to both edit code group properties, and add a child code group. For now, let's just look at editing the code group properties. By clicking on the Edit Code Group Properties link, a standard properties dialog box will appear. You could have achieved the same result by right-clicking the name of the new code group in the treeview pane on the left and selecting the Properties menu item. In the dialog, if you select the Permission Set tab, you will see the following:

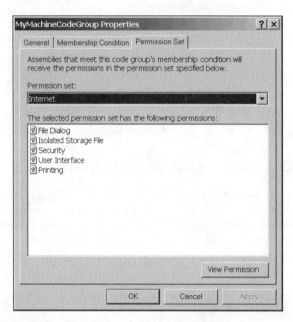

In the drop-down list, you have the ability to view all the pre-defined permission sets and apply a new one to your code group. Select a different permission set, and then click Apply or OK. After you apply your changes, you will be back in the detail view for the code group. On the right side in the details view, you will see the new permission set that you have applied to your code group.

In some cases, you may not want to settle for the pre-defined permission sets. Your assembly may only require a fraction of the rights granted by the Internet permission set. In this case, it is safer to create a new permission set containing just those rights that are specifically needed.

To create a new permission set you can select the Permission Sets node in the treeview, and then from the Action menu, select New. This will display the Create Permission Set wizard. Create a new permission set called MyCustomPermissionSet and give it a description. After selecting the Next button, you are presented with a list of resources on the left-hand side that are available to assign to this permission set, or the option to import a pre-defined XML file containing a list of permissions.

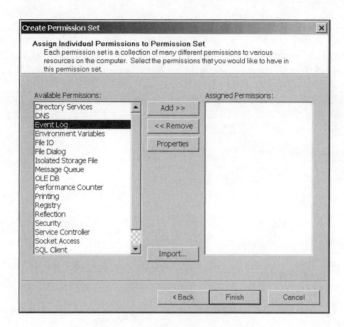

For this example, select the Event Log permission and add it to the permission set. You are immediately presented with another dialog to select individual event logs or unrestricted access to all event logs. Select the latter and press OK.

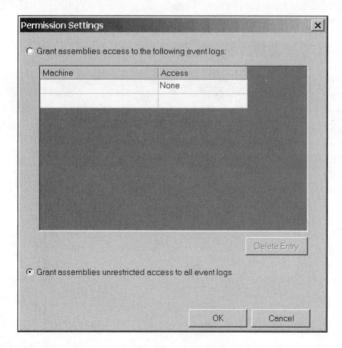

Select the Finish button after assigning the permissions for the event log. You will now be able to see your newly created permission set in the list of available permission sets. If you select your new permission set, then select View Permissions on the right-hand side you will be able to see all the permissions that have been assigned to it:

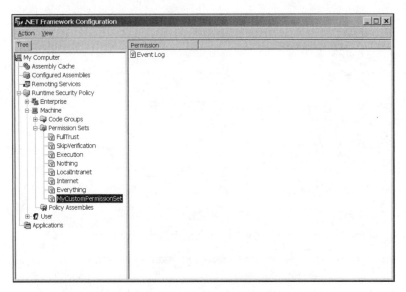

Now, if you go back to the properties of the code group you created, you can assign your new permission set to it (as seen in following screenshot):

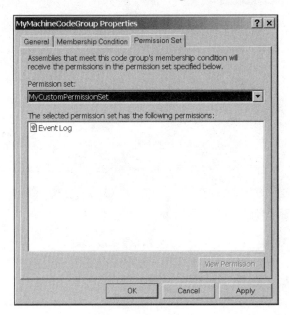

Once you have created your own permission sets, it is quite conceivable that you may want to edit their properties at some later time. You may decide that you can, or perhaps that you need to, allow the code group to grant a few more permissions. If you navigate to your custom permission set and select it on the left-hand side, then from the context menu you can select the Change Permissions option and be presented with the same dialog seen earlier. You can now add new permissions to or remove permissions from the permission set. The changes will be applied to any and all code groups that the permission set is associated with.

Managing Zones

When managing code groups and permissions, it is very important to keep in mind the zones you are trying to grant access to and protect yourself from. For example, you may want to grant full access to assemblies coming from your intranet, but you would not want to do the same for assemblies coming from the Internet. There are five basic zones to consider:

❑　Internet

❑　Local Intranet

❑　Trusted Sites

❑　Restricted Sites

❑　Implicit zone (local machine, MyComputer)

The Internet zone comprises all Internet sites that are not included in the Trusted Sites zone or the Restricted Sites zone. The Trusted Site zone consists of all sites from which code is declared as being safe to execute once downloaded as opposed to Restricted sites which are all of the sites from which code is considered dangerous. The Implicit zone is made up of any code originating from the local computer. Finally, the Local Intranet consists of all code originating within a company's intranet that would typically be behind firewalls, blocking it from the outside world.

The zones can be viewed and amended through the Control Panel using the Internet Options menu:

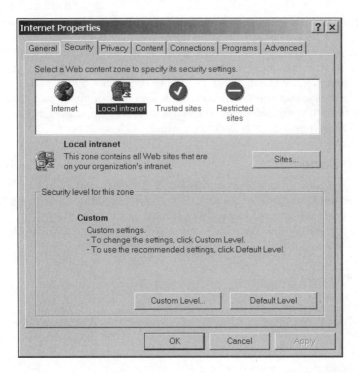

When configuring code groups, it is important to consider each zone. Again, the rule of thumb is not to grant any more access than what is absolutely necessary for the code to run correctly. For example, when specifying that an assembly on the Internet is safe to run, you would not grant full access to the entire Internet zone. You would more likely specify the fully qualified URL of the assembly and only grant it the access it needs.

Summary

In this chapter we started by taking a look at assemblies. We saw how they are the building blocks of .NET applications and examined their structure and how to use them. Then we examined the role of configuration files within .NET and saw an example of how a user's preferences can be persisted using these configuration files.

We looked at security in .NET. The space available in this chapter did not allow us to examine the topic fully (for that we would need an entire book), so we concentrated on introducing topics such as code access security and managing a security policy. We used the `CasPol.exe` command-line utility, and the .NET Framework Configuration tool.

In the next chapter we will look at the important topic of sharing assemblies.

VB.NET

Deployment

Handbook

5

Maintaining and Updating Applications

In this chapter we will look at some of the issues concerning how to maintain and update our applications. These issues could arise if you have discovered a bug in one of your applications that needs to be fixed, or because the users of your applications have new or different requirements.

The topics covered in the chapter are:

❑ **Assembly Resource Files** – These can be used to store strings, images, etc. in a separate location to the application code. For example, a user message can be stored in a file, rather than hard-coded into the application, so that it doesn't need to be recompiled if the message needs to be updated.

❑ **Shared Assemblies** – You will see how to share assemblies between multiple applications, what the advantages are of sharing assemblies, and what some of the issues to be aware of are. This chapter will also examine the role of the Global Assembly Cache.

❑ **Versioning** – You will see how to run more that one version of the same assembly side-by-side on the same machine, and how you can direct the client application to use the correct version.

Assembly Resource Files

Resource files can be used to store such things as strings and images that can be used by our applications. The advantage of using resource files instead of storing strings and images directly in an application's code is that they can be easily updated without the need to search through your code, recompile your code, and then re-deploy your applications. Resources can be easily updated and then compiled into new resource files simply by using a few batch files. It also enables you to change strings or images for different locales.

In this section we'll look at:

❑ The Resource File Generator utility `resgen.exe`

❑ The `ResourceWriter` and `ResXResourceWriter` classes from the `System.Resources` namespace

❑ Using resource files in a Windows application

Creating Resource Files

As previously stated, resource files can contain such things as tables of strings and images. The .NET Framework supports two types of resource files:

❑ Plain text format files, which have a file extension of `.resources`

❑ .NET XML Resources Template files, which have a file extension of `.resX`

Let's examine each of these now.

Plain Text Resource Files

The most important issue is that only resource files with a `.resources` extension can be added to an assembly. They can either be linked to as external files, or they can be embedded directly into an `.exe` or `.dll` file.

As a demonstration, we will use the following text file, `Book.txt`, which contains a key-value pair table, where string values are matched to keys, in a similar fashion to `.ini` files:

```
Book Series = VB.Net Handbook
Title = VB.Net Deployment Handbook
ISBN = 186100771X
Chapter = Maintaining and Updating Applications
Author = Nick Manning
Publisher = Wrox Press
```

The Resource File Generator Utility

Firstly, you need to create a .resources file from book.txt using the resource file generator utility, resgen.exe, at the command prompt:

```
> resgen Book.txt
```

The resulting Book.resources file can be embedded into an assembly, as you will see later. The most important limitation to resgen.exe is that it does not support images.

The ResourceWriter Class

An alternative to the resgen.exe utility is to write a custom program that uses the ResourceWriter class, which can be found in the System.Resources namespace. A major advantage of using this method is that images can be added.

Let's demonstrate this with a simple console application that will add the same resources as are found in Book.txt, as well as an image file (in a real-world scenario you may take the values from a database or other resource):

```vbnet
Imports System
Imports System.Drawing
Imports System.Resources

Public Class Book2
   Shared Sub Main()
      Dim rw as New ResourceWriter("Book2.resources")
      Dim Logo as Image
      Logo = Image.FromFile("wrox_logo.gif")
      rw.AddResource("Wrox Logo", Logo)
      rw.AddResource("Book Series", "VB.Net Handbook")
      rw.AddResource("Title", "VB.Net Deployment Handbook")
      rw.AddResource("ISBN", "186100771X")
      rw.AddResource("Chapter", "Maintaining and Updating Applications")
      rw.AddResource("Author", "Nick Manning")
      rw.AddResource("Publisher", "Wrox Press")
      rw.Close()
   End Sub
End Class
```

This program starts by creating an instance of the ResourceWriter class that will write to a file called Book2.resources. The code creates an Image object to hold the image, in this case the Wrox logo (wrox_logo.gif must exist in the current directory), and then uses the AddResource() method of the ResourceWriter object to add the resources to the file.

.NET XML Resources Template Files

You can also create resource files that are in XML format. They have the `.resx` extension, and you can view and amend the resources using a text editor like Notepad. One limitation of `.resx` files is that they cannot be embedded within an assembly. Let's see how they can be created.

The Resource File Generator Utility

You can use the `resgen.exe` utility to create `.resx` files from `.resources` files at the command prompt:

```
C:\Deployment\Chapter05> resgen Book2.resources Book2.resx
Read in 7 resources from 'Book2.resources'
Writing resource file...  Done.
```

The ResXResourceWriter Class

The `ResXResourceWriter` class is similar to the `ResourceWriter` class, except it produces `.resx` files (in XML format). The class is part of the `System.Resources` namespace, but it is contained in the `System.Windows.Forms.dll` assembly.

Let's change the previous example to use the `ResXResourceWriter()` class:

```
Imports System
Imports System.Drawing
Imports System.Resources

Public Class Book3
   Shared Sub Main()
      Dim rxw as New ResXResourceWriter("Book3.resx")
      Dim Logo as Image
      Logo = Image.FromFile("wrox_logo.gif")
      rxw.AddResource("Wrox Logo", Logo)
      rxw.AddResource("Book Series", "VB.Net Handbook")
      rxw.AddResource("Title", "VB.Net Deployment Handbook")
      rxw.AddResource("ISBN", "186100771X")
      rxw.AddResource("Chapter", _
                      "Maintaining and Updating Applications")
      rxw.AddResource("Author", "Nick Manning")
      rxw.AddResource("Publisher", "Wrox Press")
      rxw.Close()
   End Sub
End Class
```

As the resulting `Book3.resx` file is in XML format, it can be viewed in Internet Explorer.

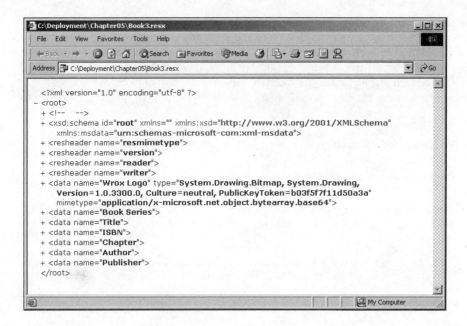

Using Resource Files

You can embed resource files into assemblies using Visual Studio .NET (or the `Al.exe` Assembly Linker tool using the `/embed` option – see .NET documentation for more details). Here, we'll demonstrate how to use the resources from a `.resources` file in a Windows Application at run time.

Create a new Visual Basic .NET Windows Application called `ResourceConsumer` and add a picturebox and six textboxes to the main form. In order to use a `.resources` file, you must add it to the project by right-clicking on the project in the Solution Explorer and selecting Add | Add Existing Item... from the menu. When you have added `Book2.resources` to the project, you can view its properties:

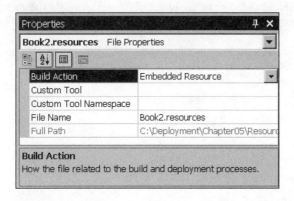

By default, the `Build Action` property of an added resource is set to `Embedded Resource` so that it gets embedded into the assembly output. In order to consume the resources in a `.resources` file, you need to import the `System.Resources` and the `System.Reflection` namespaces (although it is beyond the scope of this book to explain reflection fully, it can be briefly defined as the ability to discover type information at run time by examining an assembly's metadata):

```
Imports System.Reflection
Imports System.Resources
```

Next add the following code to the main form's `Load()` event:

```
Private Sub Form1_Load(ByVal sender As System.Object, _
                       ByVal e As System.EventArgs) _
                       Handles MyBase.Load

    Dim resMan As System.Resources.ResourceManager
    Dim myAssembly As [Assembly] = [Assembly].GetExecutingAssembly

    resMan = New ResourceManager("ResourceConsumer.Book2", myAssembly)

    PictureBox1.Image = resMan.GetObject("Wrox Logo")
    TextBox1.Text = resMan.GetString("Book Series")
    TextBox2.Text = resMan.GetString("Title")
    TextBox3.Text = resMan.GetString("Chapter")
    TextBox4.Text = resMan.GetString("Author")
    TextBox5.Text = resMan.GetString("ISBN")
    TextBox6.Text = resMan.GetString("Publisher")
End Sub
```

The first thing the code does is to create an instance of the `ResourceManager` class. You need to pass two arguments to the constructor of this class. The first argument is the root name of the resources, which is made up of the namespace of the application followed by the name of the resource file without its extension. The second argument is the executing assembly into which you wish to embed the resources, which is acquired using reflection. You can retrieve the resources using the `GetObject()` and `GetString()` methods of the `ResourceManager` object.

When you run the application, you should see the following form, complete with the text and image retrieved from the embedded resource file:

Shared Assemblies

Assemblies can either be private or shared. Private assemblies are the more common and can be found in the same directory as the application (or one of its sub-directories). As such, you don't need to worry about naming conflicts with other assemblies, or with versioning issues.

You may wish to share assemblies between applications, as might be the case if you're a third-party vendor. However, if you decide to share assemblies, then you need to be aware of some issues. For instance, you may need to update a shared assembly for one application and this may cause a problem with another. In order to overcome such a situation, it is important that you maintain the rules for shared assemblies, such as strong naming (which is discussed in this section), and versioning (which is discussed later in the chapter).

In this section, you'll see what needs to be done in order to share assemblies. We'll start by examining where shared assemblies are stored: the Global Assembly Cache.

The Global Assembly Cache

The Global Assembly Cache (GAC) is a machine-wide cache of globally available assemblies that exists on each computer that has the Common Language Runtime (CLR) installed. The GAC is specifically designed for assemblies that are to be shared by more than one application, although it is also possible to store private assemblies there.

There are several good reasons for installing assemblies in the GAC, including:

❑ **Shared location** – Shared assemblies are kept in one place.

❑ **File security** – The GAC is installed in the %System% directory (C:\Winnt by default on Windows NT & 2000). On an NT-based machine, this directory is protected from write access, which will be automatically inherited by the GAC. Microsoft recommends that only those with Administrative privileges be allowed to delete assemblies from the GAC.

❑ **Side-by-side versioning** – The GAC is a convenient location for multiple assemblies with the same assembly name that have different version information.

❑ **Additional search location** – The CLR will check the GAC for a requested assembly before probing or using the codebase information in a configuration file (see the *Configuration* section later).

In order for an assembly to be deployed to the GAC, it must have a unique identifier. This is achieved using a unique name called a **Strong Name**, part of which is a mandatory version number, as shown later. Additionally, the assembly and file name (excluding extension) should be the same. For example, an assembly called mySharedAssembly should have a file name of mySharedAssembly.dll or mySharedAssembly.exe.

However, these factors alone would not create a unique or strong name, as another developer could create an assembly with the same name and version number. To ensure uniqueness, you must sign the assembly with a public-private key, as you will see in *Creating Shared Assemblies*.

Microsoft recommends that only assemblies that require to be deployed to the GAC should be. Assemblies should be kept private and located in the application directories whenever possible.

Assemblies can be deployed to the GAC in various ways:

❑ The preferred option is to use an Installer tool designed to work with the GAC to produce .msi files

❑ The .NET Framework SDK provides the Global Assembly Cache Tool (gacutil.exe)

❑ The assembly can be dragged and dropped into the GAC using Windows Explorer

❑ We can use the Microsoft .NET Framework Configuration Tool

The advantage with the installer option above is that the developer does not need to be on site; they can ship the setup disks to their clients to install.

Global Assembly Cache Viewer

The GAC on any machine can be viewed and manipulated with the help of the **Assembly Viewer** (shfusion.dll), which is a Windows shell extension. Simply navigate to the \assembly subdirectory of the Windows directory (usually c:\winnt\assembly) in Windows Explorer. The Assembly viewer displays the Global Assembly Name, Type, Version, Culture, and Public Key Token (an 8 byte hash of the public key used to save space) for each assembly, as can be seen in the following screenshot:

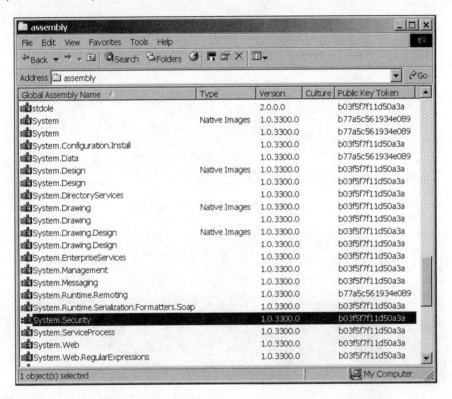

The Type denotes whether the assembly was installed using the native image generator, ngen.exe (see .NET documentation for further details). By right clicking on an assembly you can either delete the assembly or view its properties, as shown in the following screenshot:

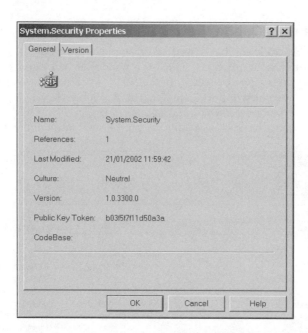

To see the actual files and directory structure, we must use the command prompt.

Global Assembly Cache Tool

The Global Assembly Cache Tool, gacutil.exe, provides the same functionality as the GAC viewer, shfusion.dll, with the added benefit that it can be used in scripts, batch files, etc. The tool can be used to install, uninstall, and list the assemblies in the GAC. Some of the available options are shown below:

❑   gacutil /l – Lists all the assemblies in the GAC

❑   gacutil /i mySharedAssembly – This installs the shared assembly called mySharedAssembly into the GAC

❑   gacutil /u mySharedAssembly – This uninstalls the shared assembly called mySharedAssembly from the GAC

You may need to add the location of gacutil.exe, which is:
C:\Program Files\Microsoft Visual Studio .NET\FrameworkSDK\Bin (if Visual
Studio .NET is installed) or: C:\Program Files\Microsoft.NET FrameworkSDK\bin
(for the .NET Framework SDK), to you PATH environmental variable in order to be able
to use it from the command prompt.

It needs to be noted that access to a client machine is required to use gacutil.exe,
and that it is not installed with the .NET Redistributable files on Windows 98 machines.

Creating Shared Assemblies

The default is to *not* share an assembly and to install it in the application's directory or
one of its subdirectories. In this section you will see how to create and use shared
assemblies. In particular, you will learn about:

❏ Public Key Cryptography

❏ Strong Names

❏ Creating shared assemblies

❏ Installing shared assemblies into the GAC

❏ Using shared assemblies

❏ Delayed Signing of shared assemblies

Public Key Cryptography

Cryptography is a set of mathematical techniques used for encrypting and decrypting
data. A simple form is *symmetric* key cryptography, in which the same key is used to
both encrypt and decrypt the data. However, a more advanced technique is public key
cryptography, which is also known as *asymmetric* key cryptography.

Public key cryptography is known as asymmetric because it uses a pair of
mathematically related keys: the public key and the private key. If data is encrypted
with one of the keys, then it can only be decrypted with the other. To make the system
secure, the private key must be kept safe from non-authorized persons, so that the real
owner is the only one who can use it.

For example, if you have a business associate who wishes to send you confidential
data across the Internet that is not to be seen by anyone but you, they can encrypt the
data with your public key (which is freely available), send the data to you, and you
can then decrypt it with your private key. If the data is intercepted en-route by a
hacker, then they will not have the private key and will not be able to decrypt the data.

155

Similarly, if you need to send the same business associate some data that they need to know came from you, then you can encrypt the data with your private key and it will only be your public key (which the receiver has a copy of) that can decrypt the data. This does not mean that the data cannot be intercepted and decrypted, for that you must use the associate's public key for them to decrypt with their private key (which only they have). What it does do is ensure that the data came from you.

How does your associate know that your public key is really your public key and not one substituted for it en-route by a hacker? Well, this is where third-party certificate authorities, such as VeriSign, join the party. For a fee, you can obtain a certificate from one of these third-party authorities, so your associate can verify the public key they think is yours with the relevant authority.

Strong Names

The aim of a shared assembly name, or **Strong Name**, is twofold:

- ❑ It must be globally unique to ensure that the assembly is at no time confused with another assembly

- ❑ It must be possible to protect the assembly from tampering by any one else

Both these aims are achieved with strong names, which comprise of the following four parts:

- ❑ The assembly's name.

- ❑ A version number so that different versions of the assembly are possible in the same location. Different versions of an assembly can even be loaded together in the same process.

- ❑ A public key, which guarantees that the name is unique and that the assembly cannot be amended or replaced, by verifying the hash code encrypted using the private key.

- ❑ A culture or set of preferences based on the user's language and culture.

Now let's look at creating a shared assembly.

Creating a Shared Assembly

We'll demonstrate what has been discussed so far with a simple example, where you will:

- ❑ Create a simple assembly containing just one class that does some simple math calculations

- ❑ Create a strong name for the assembly, including public-private key pair used to sign the assembly

- ❑ Install the assembly in the GAC

❑ Create a simple console application to demonstrate how to use a shared assembly

> **For the following exercises to be more realistic, it is preferable to have two machines. The first is used to develop the assemblies and setup projects, and the second to install the application on. However, the exercises can be carried out equally well on a single machine.**

Creating an Assembly

Create a Visual Basic .NET class library project called `SharedMathAssembly`, and add a class named `SharedMath`. This will contain the public methods. The code is as follows:

```vbnet
Imports System
Imports System.Reflection

Public Class SharedMath
  Private Sub New()
    ' No constructor
  End Sub

  Public Shared ReadOnly Property AboutMe() As String
    Get
      Dim A As [Assembly] = [Assembly].GetExecutingAssembly()
      Return (A.FullName)
    End Get
  End Property

  Public Shared Function SquareArea(ByVal length As Single) _
               As Single
    Return (length * length)
  End Function

  Public Shared Function CircleArea(ByVal radius As Single) _
               As Single
    Return (3.14 * radius * radius)
  End Function
End Class
```

The `AboutMe()` property requires a little explanation. The method uses reflection to get the `FullName` property of the currently executing assembly and returns this to the calling client. The information provided would be the same as shown by the GAC Viewer, as we shall see shortly when we develop a client application. The other two methods are very straightforward so they really don't require any explanation, so let's move on to creating a strong name.

Creating a Strong Name

To create the strong name you need to make this assembly shared, use the strong name utility, `sn.exe`, to create a public-private key pair from the command prompt as follows:

```
> sn -k myKey.snk
```

This creates a file containing the key pair that we can reference from the `AssemblyInfo.vb` file in our `SharedMathAssembly` project. Add the following entries:

```
<Assembly: AssemblyDelaySign(False)>
<Assembly: AssemblyKeyFile("../../myKey.snk")>
<Assembly: AssemblyKeyName("")>
```

The path to the key file must be either absolute or relative to the `.dll` file created when building the project (in this case the file is in the root folder of the project).

After the project has been rebuilt, you can see the public key present in the assembly's manifest by using the `ildasm.exe` utility that was introduced in Chapter 4 (you can also see the version number that will be discussing in *Versioning*).

```
MANIFEST                                                        _ □ ×
.publickey = (00 24 00 00 04 80 00 00 94 00 00 00 06 02 00 00   //
             00 24 00 00 52 53 41 31 00 04 00 00 01 00 01 00   //
             B7 57 43 96 36 91 F6 5A DB 7B 79 D7 91 CE D6 CA   //
             6D F5 DB 7C 02 04 CA 92 6E C0 0F 33 63 B7 37 8A   //
             D9 6F B1 45 50 65 33 6A DB D4 20 C1 0E FF 27 CF   //
             C9 06 D8 30 3C 6B 3A 6E F3 7C ED 33 05 CF 99 D7   //
             98 BF 6C CC 51 B3 F6 EC 77 05 BF 99 C6 E8 8A A7   //
             AF 7A DA 33 26 7D 56 87 37 F1 3C 49 DE B5 60 A5   //
             2E 08 F5 7B 06 0B 1D E2 DD F5 5A C7 74 8C FD FF   //
             8E 8C 4D 55 1D 66 4A 40 32 DC E7 FB D5 3D 30 C4 ) //
.hash algorithm 0x00008004
.ver 1:0:932:20434
}
.module SharedMathAssembly.dll
```

Installing an Assembly in the GAC

As we mentioned earlier, we have various ways in which to install a shared assembly in the GAC:

❑   Creating an Installer Package

❑   Using the GAC utility, `gacutil.exe`

❑   Using the Microsoft .NET Framework Configuration Tool

Let's examine each of these now, including when they are most appropriate.

Using an Installer Package

Using the Windows Installer is Microsoft's recommended way of installing shared components. The main benefit is that the developer does not need access to the client's machine, as the installation will be taken care of by the installer package. It also provides reference counting of assemblies in the GAC and ease of use for the user.

Let's start by adding a new setup project to our solution and calling it `SharedMathSetup`. After the new setup project has been added you should see the File System Editor in Visual Studio .NET's main window. The default installation for an assembly is the application's folder, so you must add a folder for the GAC. You can do this by right-clicking on the File System on Target Machine node and selecting Add Special Folder | Global Assembly Cache Folder. This will add a new child node for the GAC. Now you must add the `SharedMathAssembly` to the setup project by right-clicking on the Global Assembly Cache Folder node and selecting Add | Project Output. The Add Project Output Group dialog box will appear and you now select `SharedMathAssembly` from the Project: combobox, and Primary output from the listbox.

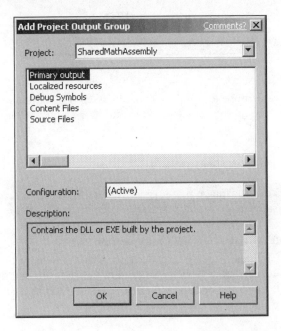

You are now ready to build the setup project by right-clicking on SharedMathSetup in the solution explorer and selecting Build. If you examine the contents of the `SharedMathSetup\Debug` folder, you will see the `.msi` and other files discussed in Chapter 2. If you run the installer then you'll be able to verify that the assembly has been installed successfully in the GAC by using the GAC viewer described earlier.

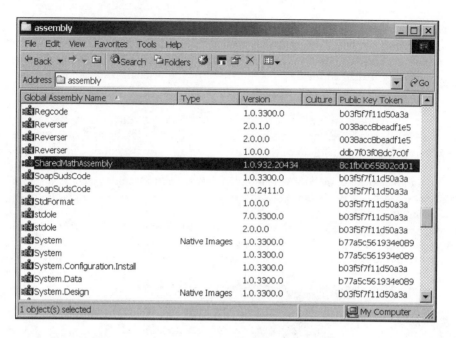

Using the GAC Utility

The next method we can use to install our shared assembly in the GAC of a client machine is by using the gacutil.exe utility with the /i option from the command prompt:

```
> gacutil /i SharedMathAssembly.dll
```

The GAC utility has the advantage that it is convenient for using in scripts, batch files, makefiles, etc. A disadvantage is that you need access to the client's machine.

Using the Microsoft .NET Framework Configuration Tool

The third method examined is using the Microsoft .NET Framework Configuration Tool, which is located in Administrative Tools in the Control Panel. Select the Assembly Cache node and right-click to get the Add... option that opens the Add an Assembly dialog, which allows you to navigate to the desired assembly.

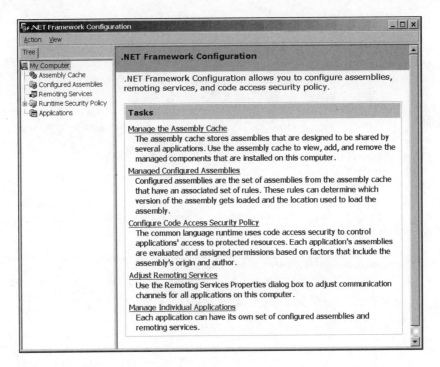

We will be discussing the Microsoft .NET Framework Configuration Tool in more detail later in the chapter.

Using a Shared Assembly

In this section we will demonstrate how to use our shared assembly by building a simple console application that will use its math methods and then build an installer for that simple console application.

Building a Shared Assembly Consumer Application

Start by building a simple console application called `UsingShared` that contains the following code:

```
Imports System
Imports SharedMathAssembly

Module Module1
  Sub Main()
    Dim myMath As SharedMathAssembly.SharedMath
    Dim i As Integer
    i = 3
    Console.WriteLine("We are using: " & myMath.AboutMe())
    Console.WriteLine("The area of a circle with a radius of " & _
                i & " is " & myMath.CircleArea(i))
```

```
        Console.WriteLine("The area of a square with sides of " & _
                            i & " is " & myMath.SquareArea(i))
        Console.ReadLine()
    End Sub
End Module
```

In order to use the shared assembly, the first thing you must do is set a reference to the assembly. Do this by right-clicking on References in the Solution Explorer and selecting Add Reference... from the context menu. Then click the Browse... button and navigate to the path of `SharedMathAssembly.dll` (the `\bin` directory of the `SharedMathAssembly` project).

The next task is the most important when using components from the GAC. Right-click on the newly created reference in the Solution Explorer and set its `Copy Local` property to `False` as shown in the following screenshot.

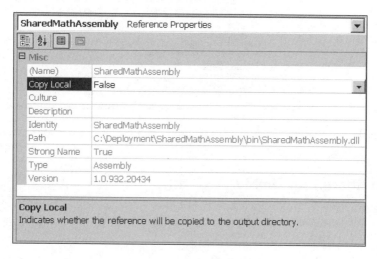

This ensures that the assembly is not compiled into the project, which is what you want. If you had left the `Copy Local` property to `True`, then a copy of `SharedMathAssembly.dll` would have copied to your `\bin` directory and that assembly, not the one in the GAC, would have been used by the application.

If you run the application from within Visual Studio .NET, you will get the following results.

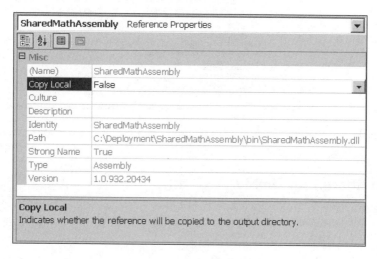

Installing a Shared Assembly Consumer Application

Now let's create the Installer package. Add a new Project to this project, and create a Setup project called `UsingSharedSetup`. You must add the `UsingShared` project by right-clicking on the Application Folder node in the File System editor and selecting Add | Project Output... from the context menu. In the Add Project Output Group dialog box select `UsingShared` and Primary Output.

The next thing we must do is very important. As can be seen from the following screenshot, Visual Studio .NET has included `SharesMathAssembly.dll` in output to the Application Folder, whereas we wish it to be in the GAC. Our application would still work; however, it would use the assembly in its installation folder and not one in the GAC. Additionally, other applications would not be able to use our assembly, as it would not be available in the GAC.

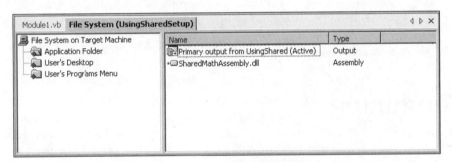

We can rectify this by right-clicking on the File System on Target Machine node and selecting Add Special Folder | Global Assembly Cache Folder, and then dragging and dropping `SharesMathAssembly.dll` into the new folder.

The package is now ready to be built and installed on a target machine. Note that if the target machine does not already have the `SharedMathAssembly` installed, then it will be installed into the GAC by this package.

Delayed Signing of Shared Assemblies

The most important issue when using a public-private key pair is that the private key **must** be kept safe. For this reason, it is often not desirable for all the developers in a company to have access to it. To allow for this, .NET uses the concept of delayed signing in which only the public key portion is used during the development stage, and an authorized individual uses the private key immediately prior to deployment.

The delayed signing of assemblies is a four-stage process. Firstly, create a public-private key pair using the strong name utility in exactly the same way as we did before at the command prompt:

```
> sn -k myKey.snk
```

Secondly, extract the public key portion of the key pair and make it available to relevant developers. This is also done at the command prompt with the strong name utility using the –p option as follows:

```
> sn -p myKey.snk myPublicKey.snk
```

Thirdly, the relevant developers then use the public key, in our case myPublicKey.snk, to sign their assemblies. However, for this to work, they must set the following attributes in the AssemblyInfo.vb file:

```
<Assembly: AssemblyDelaySign(True)>
<Assembly: AssemblyKeyFile("../../myPublicKey.snk")>
```

Finally, the assembly must be resigned immediately prior to distribution with the original key pair. This is done using the –R option of the strong name utility:

```
> sn -R MySharedAssembly.dll myKey.snk
```

Versioning

No matter how well you develop your assemblies; at some point in the future they are likely to need updating. It may be that you'll encounter a bug that needs to be fixed, or that the users of the assembly will have new or changed needs. For legacy COM components this can lead to the scenario commonly known as DLL Hell. When you update or fix a bug in a shared COM component to fix a problem for one application, it may cause a new problem for another. The .NET Framework solves this problem by allowing you to install different versions of the same assembly on the same machine – you can even use more than one version at the same time within the same application.

For private assemblies versioning is not really an issue as the referenced assemblies are copied with the client into its application directory or sub directories. For shared assemblies, however, you need a way to ensure that the client applications will use the correct version, and this is solved in .NET by the use of version numbers.

Version Numbers in .NET

All .NET assemblies have a four-part version number in the following format:

```
<Major>.<Minor>.<Build>.<Revision>
```

The version number is located inside the AssemblyInfo.vb file and for a newly created assembly the version will be:

```
<Assembly: AssemblyVersion("1.0.*")>
```

The first two numbers represent the major and minor numbers, while the "*" character means that the build and revision numbers will be auto-generated. The default for the build number is the number of days since January 1st 2000 and the default for the revision is the number of seconds from midnight (local time). You can see the version number when examining the assembly using the ildasm.exe utility seen earlier.

> *The values that you see for the build and revision numbers will not be the same as in this chapter.*

While useful in some ways, auto incremented versioning has its disadvantages: especially when developing strong-named assemblies. For example, every time you rebuild a strong-named assembly the version number will alter regardless of whether there have been any changes to the assembly – this means that all the components referencing the assembly will need to be rebuilt. In addition, there is no easy way of determining which assembly relates to what version number, which may prove problematic of you are supporting multiple versions in a live environment. The major advantage is that you are guaranteed a unique version number.

If you choose to, you can specify all four numbers. One good policy would be to change the major and minor values when the changes made are incompatible with previous versions, and the build and revision numbers when the change will be compatible. This ensures that you can safely redirect a client to a new version of the assembly when only the build and revision numbers have changed.

When you reference an assembly in a client application, the version number will be stored in the manifest of the client application. For instance, the following shows the manifest for the UsingShared application.

```
MANIFEST                                               _ □ x
.assembly extern System.Xml
{
    .publickeytoken = (B7 7A 5C 56 19 34 E0 89 )
    .ver 1:0:3300:0
}
.assembly extern SharedMathAssembly
{
    .publickeytoken = (8C 1F B0 B6 58 02 CD 01 )
    .ver 1:0:932:20434
}
```

Building New Versions of Assemblies

The observant among you may have noticed that the demonstration assembly, SharedMathAssembly, did not calculate the area of a circle in the best way possible in .NET. Rather than hard-coding in a value of 3.14, you could have used the .NET constant System.Math.PI. Let's change the code so that the updated version of SharedMathAssembly is going to do precisely that.

Start by reopening the solution that contained both the `SharedMathAssembly` and `SharedMathSetup` projects. Update the `CircleArea()` method in `SharedMath.vb` as follows:

```
Public Shared Function CircleArea(ByVal radius As Single) _
                       As Single
    Return (Math.PI * radius * radius)
End Function
```

The next thing you must do is to update the `AssemblyInfo.vb` file. You could allow Visual Studio .NET to update the build and revision numbers for you and leave it at that as you will have no compatibility issues with our update. However, let's manually update the minor number for clarity as shown:

```
<Assembly: AssemblyVersion("1.1.*")>
```

Now rebuild the `SharedMathAssembly` project. Don't rebuild the setup project; instead install the new assembly into the GAC using the `gacutil.exe` tool (alternatively create a second setup project). At the command prompt, navigate to the `bin` directory of the `SharedMathAssembly` project and execute the following command:

```
> gacutil /i SharedMathAssembly.dll
```

Now, if you view the contents of the GAC you will see two versions of the assembly side-by-side:

Redirecting Clients

After you have created an updated assembly and distributed it to the relevant target machine, you need to ensure that client applications on those machines use this updated assembly. You could recompile and redistribute the client applications but that might be resource intensive and not very practical. Fortunately, the .NET Framework provides you with some straightforward, quick, and easy ways to redirect clients to updated assemblies. Let's start with application configuration files.

Application Configuration Files

We can use an application's configuration file to redirect its binding from one version of an assembly to another. Let's try this out using the client we created earlier. Navigate to the `Program Files\CompanyName\UsingSharedSetup` directory and execute `UsingShared.exe`. You should get the following output:

```
C:\Program Files\Deployment\UsingSharedSetup\UsingShared.exe
We are using: SharedMathAssembly. Version=1.0.932.20434. Culture=neutral, Public
KeyToken=8c1fb0b65802cd01
The area of a circle with a radius of 3 is 28.26
The area of a square with sides of 3 is 9
```

As you can see, the executable is still using the original version of the shared assembly. Let's see how you can go about redirecting it so that it uses the new version. You could do this manually by creating an application configuration file called `UsingShared.exe.config` manually in Notepad. However, in this case we will use the Microsoft's .NET Framework Configuration Tool that was introduced earlier.

The first task is to tell the tool on the client machine that you wish to configure the `UsingShared.exe` application. You do this by right-clicking on the Applications node and selecting Add.... The Configure an Application dialog box is shown, from where you can navigate to the application if it is not already given in the list (make sure you choose the one in the `Program Files` directory, and not the one in the `bin` directory of the Visual Studio .NET project if you installed the application on the same machine that you developed it).

Once you've added an application, you can view the assemblies upon which it depends by selecting the Assembly Dependencies node.

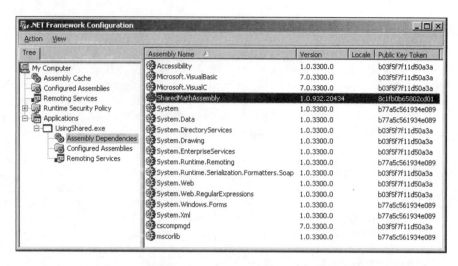

If you select the Configured Assemblies node you can choose the Configure an Assembly option to configure the application to use the new version of our assembly.

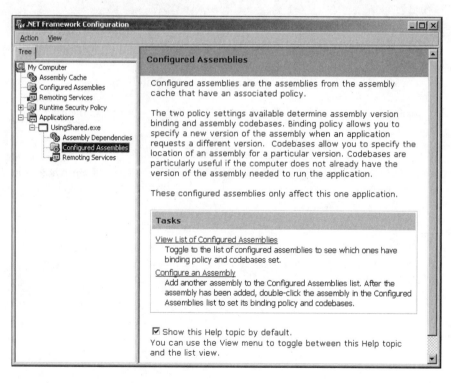

By using the Configure an Assembly dialog box you can select the first option and press the Choose Assembly... button.

You can now select the appropriate assembly from the
Choose Assembly From Dependent Assemblies dialog box, press Select, and then Finish.

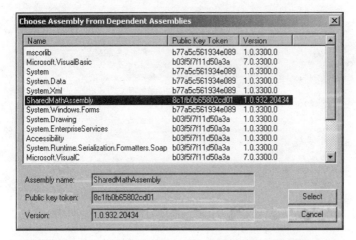

This will open the properties dialog box for the assembly. Navigate to the Binding Policy tab, which is used to redirect from a requested version to a new version. Enter a value for the Requested Version, which is the old version number that is referenced in the client application's manifest, and enter a New Version number. Take note of the rules stated on the tab.

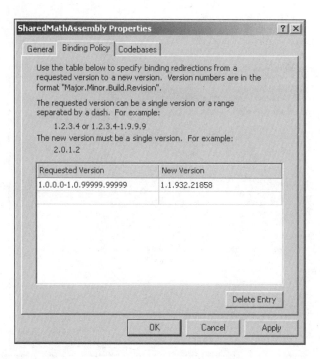

When you press OK, the tool will create or amend the application's configuration file. In our case, the UsingShared.exe.config file will look as follows:

```xml
<?xml version="1.0"?>
<configuration>
  <runtime>
    <assemblyBinding xmlns="urn:schemas-microsoft-com:asm.v1">
      <dependentAssembly>
        <assemblyIdentity name="SharedMathAssembly"
                          publicKeyToken="8c1fb0b65802cd01" />
        <bindingRedirect oldVersion="1.0.0.0-1.0.99999.99999"
                         newVersion="1.1.932.21858" />
      </dependentAssembly>
    </assemblyBinding>
  </runtime>
</configuration>
```

If you now run UsingShared.exe, it will reference the new assembly and the output will show the following.

```
C:\Program Files\Deployment\UsingSharedSetup\UsingShared.exe
We are using: SharedMathAssembly. Version=1.1.932.21858. Culture=neutral. Public
KeyToken=8c1fb0b65802cd01
The area of a circle with a radius of 3 is 28.27433
The area of a square with sides of 3 is 9
```

Publisher Policy Files

Publisher policy files are a method by which a vendor of a shared assembly can redirect all the clients of that assembly to a new version. For instance, if the vendor discovers a bug in a version of an assembly, they can deploy an update to the GAC, create a redirection policy file, and deploy that policy to the GAC (along with the new assembly) and have all clients use the update without the need to create or amend application configuration files for all the clients.

In this section will see how to:

❑   Create a publisher policy file

❑   Create a publisher policy assembly

❑   Add a publisher policy assembly to the GAC

❑   Override a publisher policy

❑   Fix an application broken by a publisher policy

Creating Publisher Policy Files

A publisher policy file is an XML file that redirects all client applications that are using an existing version (or version range) of a shared assembly in the GAC to use a newer version instead. The file is placed in the GAC on the client machine.

The syntax is actually the same as for application configuration files. As such, you can use a file with exactly the same contents as the `UsingShared.exe.config` file that was created in the previous section. However, rename it `SharedPolicy.config` and move it to the folder containing the `SharedMathAssembly` project:

```xml
<?xml version="1.0"?>
<configuration>
  <runtime>
    <assemblyBinding xmlns="urn:schemas-microsoft-com:asm.v1">
      <dependentAssembly>
        <assemblyIdentity name="SharedMathAssembly"
                          publicKeyToken="8c1fb0b65802cd01" />
        <bindingRedirect oldVersion="1.0.0.0-1.0.99999.99999"
                         newVersion="1.1.932.21858" />
      </dependentAssembly>
    </assemblyBinding>
  </runtime>
</configuration>
```

In order to demonstrate that the publisher policy is actually going to work, return to the directory containing the `UsingShared.exe` client application and remove the `UsingShared.exe.config` file. If you run `UsingShared.exe` now, you will see that it uses the original assembly, as it is no longer redirected to our updated assembly by its configuration file.

Creating Publisher Policy Assemblies

The next step is to associate the `SharedPolicy.config` publisher policy file with the shared assembly in order to create a publisher policy assembly that you can deploy to the GAC of the client machines. To do this you use the Assembly Linker utility, `al.exe`. There are two specific rules you must follow when creating the publisher policy assembly:

❑   The name must start with `policy.`, followed by the major and minor version numbers, and the filename of the shared assembly that you wish to redirect. In our case, the name will be `policy.1.0.SharedMathAssembly.dll`.

❑   You must sign the publisher policy assembly with the same public-private key pair that you used to sign the original shared assembly. In this case: `myKey.snk`.

You now need to execute the following line at the command prompt:

```
> al /link:SharedPolicy.config /out:policy.1.0.SharedMathAssembly.dll
/keyfile:myKey.snk
```

Add a Publisher Policy Assembly to the GAC

To publish the publisher policy assembly to the GAC, use the following command-line expression:

```
> gacutil -i policy.1.0.SharedMathAssembly.dll
```

Now you can run the `UsingShared.exe` client application again and this time it will be redirected by the new publisher policy to use the updated assembly.

Overriding Publisher Policies

It may be after a publisher policy has been applied, that you want a specific application to continue using the older version. You can do this by overriding the publisher policy in the application's configuration file. You can do this by either manually amending the configuration file, or by using the .NET Framework Configuration tool used earlier. The first tab of the shared assembly's property pages has an Enable publisher policy checkbox.

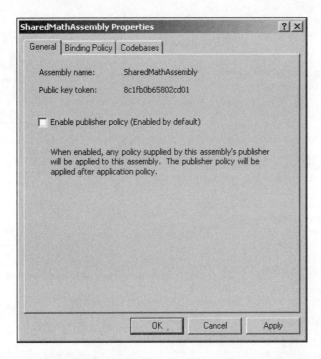

Alternatively, you can right-click on the client application's child node and select Properties.

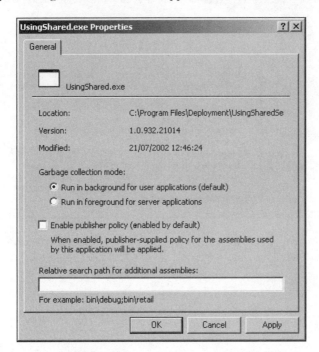

After you override the publisher policy, the tool will add a `<publisherPolicy>` element to the application's configuration file:

```xml
<?xml version="1.0"?>
<configuration>
  <runtime>
    <assemblyBinding xmlns="urn:schemas-microsoft-com:asm.v1">
      <dependentAssembly>
        <assemblyIdentity name="SharedMathAssembly"
                          publicKeyToken="8c1fb0b65802cd01" />
      </dependentAssembly>
      <publisherPolicy apply="no" />
      <probing privatePath="" />
    </assemblyBinding>
    <gcConcurrent enabled="true" />
  </runtime>
</configuration>
```

After disabling the publisher policy, you can configure a different version redirection within the configuration file if you wish.

Fixing Applications

If you find that an application is not working correctly due to a version change that you have just made, you can use the .NET Framework Configuration tool to help rectify the situation. You can do this by selecting the Fix this Application hyperlink.

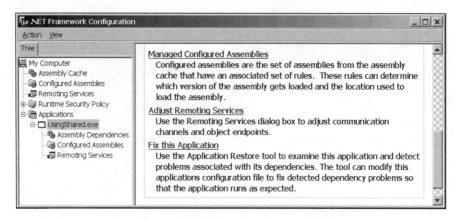

Firstly, the .NET Application Restore dialog box will ask you if you wish to restore the application to the previous configuration.

If you click the Advanced button, you will be presented with a list of previous configurations to choose from. If you select Application SafeMode, you will disable publisher policies.

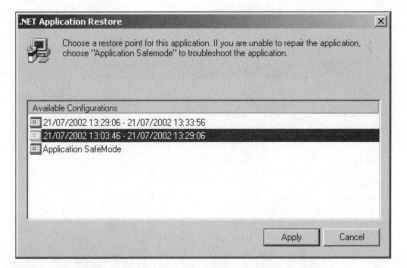

Configuring Directories

You've seen two methods of redirecting clients to new assembly version. Now you'll see two more:

- ❑ codeBase configuration, which is only available for shared assemblies
- ❑ probing, which is available for private assemblies

<codeBase>

It may be the case that you want to share assemblies but not put them in the GAC. For instance, you may want an assembly to be made available to some applications but not generally available to others, or you may wish to place assemblies on network shares.

As with other configuration methods, you can use the .NET Framework Configuration tool.

175

In the above screenshot, the client application has been configured to load version `1.0.932.20434` of the assembly from the web server http://localhost/SharedUtilities. This would produce the following configuration file:

```
<?xml version="1.0"?>
<configuration>
  <runtime>
    <assemblyBinding xmlns="urn:schemas-microsoft-com:asm.v1">
      <dependentAssembly>
        <assemblyIdentity name="SharedMathAssembly"
                          publicKeyToken="8c1fb0b65802cd01" />
        <codeBase version="1.0.932.20434"
                  href="http://localhost/SharedUtilities" />
      </dependentAssembly>
    </assemblyBinding>
  </runtime>
</configuration>
```

> **When you wish to use assemblies from network shares, you must ensure that the appropriate permissions are granted. Otherwise a `System.Security.SecurityException` occurs.**

\<probing\>

When an assembly is not stored in the GAC and no `codeBase` configurations have been set, the runtime tries to find the assembly using **probing**. The runtime will try to find an assembly with either an `.exe` or `.dll` extension with the same name as the assembly in the application's directory and subdirectories. You can configure the runtime to search additional locations using the .NET Framework Configuration tool.

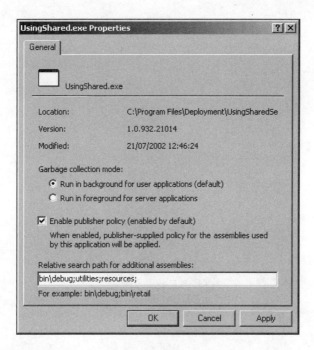

The configuration produced from the entries in the above screenshot will look like this:

```
<?xml version="1.0"?>
<configuration>
  <runtime>
    <assemblyBinding xmlns="urn:schemas-microsoft-com:asm.v1">
      <probing privatePath="bin\debug;utilities;resources;" />
    </assemblyBinding>
  </runtime>
</configuration>
```

> **It is not possible to use this method for assemblies located outside the application's path.**

Summary

In this chapter you saw some of the ways in which you can maintain and update your applications. You saw how you could maintain applications using resource files, obviating the need for recompilation. You saw how to share assemblies using the Global Assembly Cache, and you also saw how you could use versioning to have more than one version of the same assembly running side-by-side at the same time on the same machine.

VB.NET

Deployment

Handbook

6

6

Licensing

Many developers enjoy learning how to accomplish new and interesting things using their favorite languages and tools. Learning new things keeps a programmer's skills fresh and marketable. However, as much as we might like to think that the entire business of producing software revolves around producing "cool" and innovative code, it doesn't. The bottom line is that everything revolves around money.

Your product might be the best piece of software engineering the world has ever seen, and it might be worth millions of dollars. But there is a catch: If you can't license your software, you won't make money from it. If you don't have a really solid method of charging for your software and limiting your software to only those with valid licenses, then the sad truth is that you will make little or no money from your application or component.

This chapter will give you an overview of some of the most commonly used methods of licensing software, the programming challenges they present, and the code that will solve those challenges and make licensing a reality for the .NET developer. In overview, you will see:

❑   The importance of software licensing and some of the issues involved with your choice of license

❑   Code that can be implemented to take advantage of these different models

❑   Developer-to-developer licensing and how the .NET Framework licensing scheme assists you with this

❑   How to use the licensing framework with the encryption classes to create secure licenses for your components

First, you'll see an overview of the more commonly used methods of licensing software and some examples of application types that might take advantage of those licensing methods. Then, you'll see some of the common programming tasks involved in supporting the various licensing models with an eye for reusing various programming tasks for different models.

Licensing Models

A *Licensing Model* is really just a way in which a particular application deals with the legalities of providing functionality to valid customers, denying functionality to others, and possibly demonstrating functionality (maybe restricted) to potential customers. This section of the chapter will give you an overview of some of the most commonly used licensing models, and give you some practical examples of when these licensing models would be used. The models we'll be discussing here are:

- ❏ Free (Freeware, Open Source, Shared Source, etc.)
- ❏ For Purchase (Shrink-wrapped)
- ❏ Trial or Time-Limited Evaluation
- ❏ Per Seat/Processor/Server
- ❏ Install-On-Demand
- ❏ Third-party
- ❏ Pay-Per-Use

Free

It may seem trivial to cover free software in its own section, but there is more to distributing free software than might first appear. For example, you could be distributing it free of charge *and* requiring that no one else distribute it on your behalf. If you want other people to be able to distribute your free software, do you wish to allow them to make changes to your software and still distribute the software as if it was your original product? Just because you plan on distributing your software without charging for it doesn't mean that you're distributing it without restrictions. Free software licenses can range from complete Freeware, such as much of the software you can download, to Open-Source licensing, to licensing providing for free software for research purposes only.

There are actually quite a few decisions that need to be made about deploying free software. One increasingly common method of licensing free software is to deploy the software under the GNU Public License (GPL). Essentially, the GPL allows you to copyright the source code of the software, and then provides license to distribute, modify, and copy the software as long as the modified source code is distributed with it. The GPL is intended to protect the author's rights at the same time as providing quality free software to the general public. For more information on the GPL, see http://www.gnu.org/copyleft/gpl.html.

Another kind of free software licensing is that which Microsoft has done with its public implementation of the .NET Framework's ECMA standard elements for Windows and FreeBSD (codenamed 'Rotor'). This "Shared Source" licensing method allows for people to use the software and its accompanying source code for non-commercial use, such as for teaching, education, and personal experimentation. Any re-distribution of the software and its source code must be intact, original, and contain a copy of the license.

You can also find a large amount of public, free, and open-source software projects available at http://www.sourceforge.net, which is an online source-control repository for open-source projects.

For Purchase

This licensing model can be thought of as the "shrink-wrap" model. Essentially, software is produced, packaged, and purchased outright. There is no trial period, no expiration, and no renewal required. A single purchase of the application grants the customer usually unlimited use of the compiled software on one machine, although further freedoms or restrictions can be provided.

This particular form of licensing does present a few problems. As with almost all forms of selling software, piracy is a big issue. A problem occurs when determining if the person using the application is licensed to use it. An extension of that problem is that often someone will purchase a single copy of an application, duplicate it, and distribute it to dozens of other people; a practice extremely common with games on the PC and even for some gaming consoles. In general, it is impossible to completely prevent this kind of piracy, but there are some ways to restrict its possibility. The most common is by identifying a CD as a valid publisher-produced CD (as opposed to a duplicate burned at some other location). The second approach taken by Windows XP requires you to authenticate your installation of the software by connecting to an online verification service. This service remembers each time a license key is used to validate software to prevent illegal duplicate installations. This kind of approach is extremely costly and difficult to implement for all but the largest software development firms. The downside of this model is that it is so restrictive that it might prevent a valid licensed user from installing and running their application simply because they change or re-configure their computer more often than Microsoft expects. You have to be relatively certain that your customers won't go elsewhere to a software product that does not have such a restrictive licensing scheme.

Applications that typically utilize the for-purchase license model are ones that you would find on the shelf in a computer store, such as games, productivity applications, and some utilities.

Trial or Time-Limited Evaluation

Trial software is just that, a trial. You are allowed to download (or order on CD, possibly for a shipping fee) a functioning (or functionally-limited) copy of the software, and use it for a pre-determined period in order for the clients to determine if they want to buy the full version of the software.

Licensing models like this are often employed for software that requires a large amount of up-front cost. Enterprise style software, such as RDBMS servers like SQL Server and Oracle, typically require a large investment to purchase and implement. Before considering such an investment, many companies and programmers want to be able to use, test, and analyze the software before buying it.

On the other hand, many people like to take advantage of trial software as a way of getting the functionality of the software without paying for it. The key to trial software is making sure that it *actually* expires at the appropriate time. It should be immune to tampering, such as by modifying the system clock on the installed system, or even re-installation. For example, many people will re-install trial software every 90 days or so to keep using it without paying. Such an action should prevent the customer from accessing any of their data in the demo/trial version until such time as they convert their trial into a fully functioning copy of the software.

Another variation on the trial period licensing model is the time-limited application or the subscription model. Some applications will allow you to purchase, say, six months use or *subscribe* to use the application and its services for regular periods. Once that time period is up, the customer must renew the subscription or stop using the application. Again, the key to enforcing this licensing model is ensuring that you do not allow your customers to use more of your application than they have paid for.

Per Seat/Processor/Server

In many large enterprise applications or application suites, the per-processor/server licensing model is prevalent. It is especially prevalent in applications that serve large numbers of clients where it would be inappropriate to bill on a per-client basis.

In other applications, such as a "fat client" intranet application, it is more appropriate to license on a "per seat" basis. This means that the customer will be paying for each installation of the application.

These types of licensing models are often the hardest to enforce programmatically. For example, how can your application not only determine the number of processors on the installed machine, but also determine the number of processor licenses purchased in order to compare and validate these licenses? It is possible, but still difficult and requires complex programming to prevent the customer from tampering with the license information. One method you will see at the end of this chapter in the *Creating a New LicenseProvider* section is to digitally sign the license and hardcode the public key necessary for confirming the signature into the assembly.

SQL Server and Oracle both follow licensing models similar to the one just described. Enterprise management software like CA's Unicenter and other similar products also take advantage of this licensing model.

Install-On-Demand

Install-on-Demand is a fairly new type of licensing and deployment approach. The customer obtains an application that supports the core functionality only, by downloading it or by installing it from a CD. As the customer uses the application and attempts to utilize features not available in the application, the application will automatically install the feature requested. It is also possible to implement billing operations into this procedure so that the features being automatically installed can be purchased and licensed at the time they're downloaded.

The possibilities for various different deployment strategies in this licensing model are fairly diverse. The main concern for programmers with this licensing model is that not only should you prevent customers from downloading functionality they haven't paid for, but you should also not charge the customer for functionality that never made it to their desktop due to connection problems, etc. – charging for services not rendered.

Third Party

This type of licensing is possibly one of the most complex types currently available. When your application provides a feature that is actually supported by *another* company's product that requires licensing fees, you would apply third-party licensing. For example, suppose your application provides reports against the data it manages. An API for another company's software might also provide this reporting functionality and some so third-party licensing is needed.

Another example that might become far more common in the near future is the use of XML Web Services. It is very likely that when customers are paying for services your application provides then other companies, through these web services, will also provide portions of those services. This kind of licensing model will have to be structured so that appropriate license fees are paid for the use of the service, and the appropriate costs are forwarded on to the customer.

There aren't any new difficulties in enforcing this licensing method, as you still have to enforce your own licensing policy. The only difficulty here is in making sure that the third party supplying your support product gets paid and you avoid invalidating all of your own application installations due to third-party licensing problems.

Medium-sized companies typically employ licensing models like this. Larger companies usually have enough resources to provide their own services and application features, whereas smaller companies that specialize in providing a specific service might gain more customers by consuming third-party services as value-added functionality for their customers.

Pay-Per-Use

Pay-per-use licensing essentially involves billing the customer each and every time they use the application. There are variations to this theme, such as monthly billing, or licensing a certain number of uses or certain periods of time. The bottom line is that when it comes down to enforcing this particular type of licensing, there is one task that must be accomplished: monitor the customer's usage of your application.

You see this kind of model quite often with Internet entertainment. Internet gambling sites often require you to purchase virtual "chips" with which you can use to gamble with the gambling site. Online games, virtual worlds, realities and chat environments often bill usage in terms of hours spent using the application or monthly fees. Some games considered simple by today's standards that initially showed up in the early days of the Internet on Compuserve and Genie were known to charge as much as $30 per *hour!*

Once an application is monitoring the customer's usage, there is another problem that arises: communicating that usage to the billing company. Applications that follow this licensing model must track customer usage, and communicate that usage to the publisher as well as attempt to prevent customers from tampering with the usage information.

A licensing model like this is not usually appropriate for a small company or application. Generally companies opt for a pay-per-use model because the cost of resources to maintain the application or the application's services is considerable. For example, to maintain a stock purchase and financial application that charges per transaction requires the maintenance of numerous powerful computers, and a complex backbone network. The maintenance of Internet games such as online role-playing games and gambling sites often requires hundreds of servers.

Common Scenarios

In the first section of this chapter, you saw some of the more common ways in which applications are licensed and deployed. In this section, you'll look at some of the more common programming tasks involved in enforcing those kinds of licensing models, and some examples of how to implement those using Visual Basic .NET. As said before, the usefulness of an application alone cannot support a company. The company needs to be able to receive revenue for the application and to prevent piracy.

Acknowledgement of Policy

Any time a company wishes to enforce that its application can only be used in specific circumstances, something typically called an End-User License Agreement (EULA) is displayed. Before the application can be used, the user must agree to that license. Also, included in the wording of that license is clicking an acceptance button after reading the agreement, the reader accepting that they considered party to a legally binding contact.

This *sometimes* allows software publishers to have court-enforceable policies against piracy, duplicate installations, or even application misuse. You should definitely consult legal counsel before attempting to publish and enforce your EULA. The bottom line is that, in order for such an EULA or policy against piracy to be considered legally binding, the user has to accept it. The user should not be allowed to install and so use the application until they have accepted that agreement.

To illustrate the principal of working with an EULA and forcing the user of your application to accept the EULA, we'll use an example of a new VB.NET Windows Application called `EulaDemo`.

To allow the user to accept the EULA, you need a form to display it and provide the appropriate accept button. Add a new Windows Form to your application and call it `DisplayEulaForm`. Add a textbox control to contain the EULA, and two radio buttons (one for "Accept" and one for "Reject"). Also, add an OK button and a Cancel button. Set the `DialogResult` property of `OKButton` to `OK`, and the `DialogResult` property of the `CancelButton` to `Cancel`.

You'll need to rename `Form1.vb` to `MainForm.vb` (and change the class name to `MainForm` also). What we want to do is code it so that our main form will refuse to load if the EULA has not been accepted. To accomplish this, we'll set up the following event handler for `MainForm`'s load event:

```
Private Sub MainForm_Load(ByVal sender As System.Object, _
                    ByVal e As System.EventArgs) _
                    Handles MyBase.Load
    Dim eulaForm As DisplayEulaForm
    Dim LoadOk As Boolean
```

```
eulaForm = New DisplayEulaForm()
LoadOk = False
If (eulaForm.ShowDialog(Me) = DialogResult.OK) Then
  LoadOk = eulaForm.AcceptedAgreement
End If

If Not LoadOk Then
  MessageBox.Show(Me, "You did not accept the License")
  Me.Close()
  End
End If
End Sub
```

This is straightforward Windows Forms programming. The application will first display the EULA, as follows:

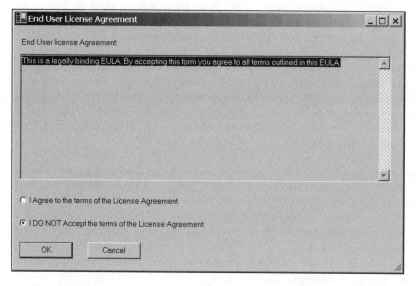

If the user chooses to accept the terms of the EULA (this is NOT the default behavior, the user must actively *choose* to accept the agreement rather than accept the default) then the application will simply display the main form:

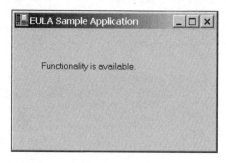

On the other hand, if the user does not accept the license agreement, the application will not load at all and they will be informed that the license was not accepted:

The issue with this sample application is that it presents the EULA each and every time the application loads. There are types of applications where this is required (such as online multiplayer games), but it is possible to allow the user to accept the EULA once, store that fact, and then allow them to use the application without further dialogs. You should definitely consult an attorney who deals with EULAs to determine which approach is the best legal option for your particular application.

Submit License Number

In this scenario, the user is prompted for a license number or key that identifies the installation as a valid one. Typically these numbers are validated through an algorithm that determines that the number is one of the many possible valid license numbers. These algorithms on their own are incapable of determining whether that number has been submitted dozens of times already by different people in the case of software piracy. To detect multiple installations, a central repository of installation records must be used, which you'll see in the next section, *Register Online*.

Our next example will illustrate an application that will not allow you to access the main form (and all subsequent forms) unless you enter a valid license code. For our purposes, we'll use a fairly simple code. The code must be 14 digits long, and it must start with the number 7. Therefore, the following code is valid for our sample application:

```
720486038492945
```

The purpose of our example is to show you in general how something like this is accomplished. It will be left as an exercise to come up with an algorithm that is worthwhile for use in a production environment. Our format is far too simple for a production application.

To create this example, you'll follow a routine similar to the last one. Create a new Windows Forms application and call it `SubmitLicense`. Rename the main form file and class to `MainForm`. As with the last example, to prompt the user for the information needed to license the application, you need a form to display the prompt. To do this add a new Windows Form to the application and call it `LicenseInputForm`. Add a textbox to the form for license code entry and call it `LicenseTextBox`. Then, add a property to the form that exposes that textbox's string by adding the following code to the form:

187

```
Public Property LicenseCode() As String
  Get
    Return LicenseTextBox.Text
  End Get

  Set(ByVal Value As String)
    LicenseTextBox.Text = Value
  End Set
End Property
```

Now you need to modify the main form's Load event handler to trigger the license input form and validate the code itself:

```
Private Sub MainForm_Load(ByVal sender As System.Object, _
                          ByVal e As System.EventArgs) _
                          Handles MyBase.Load
  Dim LoadOk As Boolean = False

  Dim licenseForm As LicenseInputForm
  licenseForm = New LicenseInputForm()

  If (licenseForm.ShowDialog = DialogResult.OK) Then
    Dim code As String = licenseForm.LicenseCode
    If code.Length = 14 And code.Chars(0) = "7" Then
      LoadOk = True
    End If
  End If

  If Not LoadOk Then
    MessageBox.Show(Me, "Invalid license code entered")
    Me.Close()
    Throw New ApplicationException("Invalid Key")
  End If
End Sub
```

You can catch and examine the thrown exception in the main loop and exit the application. When you compile and run the program, we're presented with our license code dialog:

If you enter a valid license code, then you are presented with the application's main form. Also, as you might expect, if you enter an invalid license code you are given a warning message and the application will shut down, not allowing you to access any of the application's functionality.

One thing to keep in mind with algorithms like this is that it is possible for a developer to use MSIL Disassembler utility, `ildasm.exe`, or any other disassembly tool to inspect the IL code that your application generated. This might allow that customer to decipher your license code validation algorithm and circumvent it. You'll see more about methods of protecting your code and intellectual property in the next chapter.

Register Online

The Register Online licensing scenario requires that the end user have some form of Internet connectivity when they install the application or run it for the first time. The Internet connection is used to connect to the publisher and perform one of two tasks:

❑ Verify an existing registration or license number

❑ Register a new installation by supplying registrant information (name, etc.) and the license number (probably a CD Key) provided with the installation itself.

Before you see the source code that accomplishes all this, let's discuss the sample application that you will write to illustrate this principal. This application is called `RegisterOnlineClient` and is a Windows Forms application.

When you first start the application up, you are prompted for the license number. This is typically where an application would prompt you for the CD Key or some unique number that you and *only* you should have. This licensing method only works if customers have their own unique identifier. Because this method has an online backend that should be fairly tamper-proof, you could actually just use GUIDs (Globally Unique IDentifiers) and have the customers enter those values. The license number prompt looks like this:

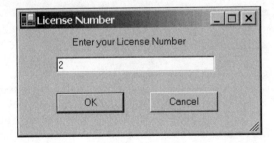

What you don't see happening after you click OK is the client application making a call to a web service. This web service would accept the license number as an argument and return `True` or `False` depending on whether that license number has already been registered. Because of this, you should definitely use complex license numbers, as you wouldn't want people to be able to run the application after randomly picking a valid license number. This is another argument for GUIDs or some variation on the concept of an always-unique identifier. Assuming the license number you supplied is valid, the application will "unlock" its secured functionality, and you'll see something like this:

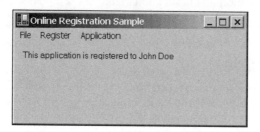

If you enter some value for the license number that you know isn't going to be valid (such as blank) or you cancel the input dialog for the license number, the application will open in "Unregistered" mode. All functionality that requires a registered customer (essentially everything you want to charge for) will be disabled, grayed out, or otherwise unavailable. One option that *will* be available to you after skipping the license number prompt will be the option to register online. When you decide to register online, you'll see a prompt that looks like this:

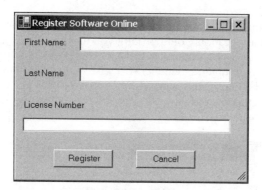

When you hit the *Register* button, another call is made to the web service that will perform a registration, which is essentially nothing more than an association of a license number with a particular customer. After that point, *no one* else can register that license number. Because you have a central database in place containing licenses and registered persons, you can monitor the use of licenses, keep track of who has paid you and who hasn't, and add in other features such as monitoring (see the pay-per-play licensing method above). The use of a web service as an information-store back-end is the most secure way to lock down your application to prevent piracy, as well as keep track of demographic information on your customer base.

We used a web service to perform the registration but you could actually use a standard web page. The difference is that for that method you would lose the ability to register the application while running it.

First, let's take a look at the code for the web service. Simply create a new VB.NET Web Service solution and called it `RegisterOnline`. Rename the service file and the associated class to `RegisterService`. Here's the source code for `RegisterService.asmx.vb`:

```vbnet
Imports System
Imports System.Web.Services
Imports System.Xml

<WebService(Namespace:="http://tempuri.org/")> _
Public Class RegisterService
  Inherits System.Web.Services.WebService

  <WebMethod()> _
  Public Function RegisterOnline(ByVal licenseNumber As String, _
                                 ByVal firstName As String, _
                                 ByVal lastName As String) As Boolean
    Dim licenseesDoc As XmlDocument
    licenseesDoc = New XmlDocument()

    licenseesDoc.Load(Server.MapPath("licensees.xml"))

    Dim selectString As String = _
      "//licensee[@licensenumber=" & Chr(34) & licenseNumber & _
      Chr(34) & "]"
    Dim licenseeNode As XmlNode
    licenseeNode = licenseesDoc.SelectSingleNode(selectString)
    If (licenseeNode Is Nothing) Then
      Dim licenseeElem As XmlElement
      licenseeElem = licenseesDoc.CreateElement("licensee")
      licenseeElem.SetAttribute("licensenumber", licenseNumber)
      licenseeElem.SetAttribute("firstname", firstName)
      licenseeElem.SetAttribute("lastname", lastName)
      licenseesDoc.DocumentElement.AppendChild(licenseeElem)
      licenseesDoc.Save(Server.MapPath("licensees.xml"))
      Return True
    Else
      Return False
    End If
  End Function

  <WebMethod()> _
  Public Function IsRegistered(ByVal licenseNumber As String, _
                               ByRef firstName As String, _
                               ByRef lastName As String) As Boolean
    Dim licenseesDoc As XmlDocument
    licenseesDoc = New XmlDocument()
```

```
      licenseesDoc.Load(Server.MapPath("licensees.xml"))

      Dim selectString As String = _
        "//licensee[@licensenumber=" & Chr(34) & licenseNumber & _
        Chr(34) & "]"

      Dim licenseeNode As XmlNode
      licenseeNode = licenseesDoc.SelectSingleNode(selectString)

      If (licenseeNode Is Nothing) Then
        firstName = "UNREGISTERED"
        lastName = "USER"
        Return False
      Else
        firstName = _
          licenseeNode.Attributes.GetNamedItem("firstname").Value
        lastName = _
          LicenseeNode.Attributes.GetNamedItem("lastname").Value
        Return True
      End If
    End Function
  End Class
```

The web service uses an underlying XML file that essentially makes up the database of users. In order to actually get this to work you need to modify the permissions on the licensees.xml file to allow write access. Using an XML file allows you to get a sample running without a SQL Server or an Oracle data source. You should be able to easily modify the example created to replace the XML backend with whatever data source is required.

As you can see the web service has two methods:

❑   IsRegistered() – A method that takes a license number as an argument and returns True or False depending on whether the license number is registered or not.

❑   RegisterOnline() – A method that takes a license number, first name, and last name as arguments and will store that information if that license number has not already been registered. Returns True if the registration is successful, or False if the license number has already been registered.

Now let's look at the code for the Windows Forms client. It has three forms, a class for maintaining global information, and a web reference to the web service shown above:

❑   Form1 – This is the main form that houses the main UI

❑   frmLicensePrompt – This is the form that prompts the user for a license number when the application first starts up

❑   frmNewRegistrant – This is the form that prompts the user for their first and last name as well as their valid license number

❑   GlobalData – This is a class that contains shared members that allow us to store information globally

Here's the code for Form1:

```
Public Class Form1
    Inherits System.Windows.Forms.Form

    Private Sub Form1_Load(ByVal sender As System.Object, _
                            ByVal e As System.EventArgs) _
                            Handles MyBase.Load
        GlobalData.LicenseNumber = "-1"

        Dim licensePrompt As frmLicensePrompt
        licensePrompt = New frmLicensePrompt()

        If (licensePrompt.ShowDialog = DialogResult.OK) Then
            GlobalData.LicenseNumber = licensePrompt.LicenseNumber
        End If

        licensePrompt.Dispose()

        Dim regProxy As RegisterOnline.RegisterService
        regProxy = New RegisterOnline.RegisterService()

        GlobalData.IsRegistered = _
            regProxy.IsRegistered(GlobalData.LicenseNumber, _
                            GlobalData.FirstName, _
                            GlobalData.LastName)
        regProxy.Dispose()

        If (GlobalData.IsRegistered) Then
            lblRegStatus.Text = "This application is registered to " & _
                GlobalData.FirstName & " " & GlobalData.LastName
        Else
            lblRegStatus.Text = "This application is NOT registered"
        End If
    End Sub

    Private Sub MenuItem6_Click(ByVal sender As System.Object, _
                            ByVal e As System.EventArgs) _
                            Handles MenuItem6.Click
        If (GlobalData.IsRegistered) Then
            MessageBox.Show(Me, _
                "You can do this because this app is registered")
        Else
            MessageBox.Show(Me, _
                "You cannot do this because this app is NOT registered")
        End If
    End Sub
```

```
      Private Sub MenuItem4_Click(ByVal sender As System.Object, _
                                  ByVal e As System.EventArgs) _
                                  Handles MenuItem4.Click

        If GlobalData.IsRegistered Then
          MessageBox.Show(Me, "You do not need to register, " & _
                          "this application is already registered.")
        Else
          Dim regProxy As RegisterOnline.RegisterService
          regProxy = New RegisterOnline.RegisterService()

          Dim newRegForm As frmNewRegistrant
          newRegForm = New frmNewRegistrant()

          If (newRegForm.ShowDialog = DialogResult.OK) Then
            GlobalData.IsRegistered = _
              regProxy.RegisterOnline(newRegForm.LicenseNumber, _
                                      newRegForm.FirstName, _
                                      newRegForm.LastName)
            If GlobalData.IsRegistered Then
              GlobalData.FirstName = newRegForm.FirstName
              GlobalData.LastName = newRegForm.LastName
              lblRegStatus.Text = _
                "This application was just registered to " & _
                newRegForm.FirstName + " " + newRegForm.LastName
            End If
          End If
          regProxy.Dispose()
        End If
      End Sub
    End Class
```

The only change made to frmLicensePrompt was to abstract the license number
textbox control under a standard string property as follows:

```
Public Property LicenseNumber As String
  Get
    Return txtLicense.Text
  End Get

  Set(ByVal Value As String)
    txtLicense.Text = Value
  End Set
End Property
```

Add the following property definitions to the frmNewRegistrant class:

```
Public Property LicenseNumber As String
  Get
    Return txtLicense.Text
  End Get
```

```
    Set(ByVal Value As String)
      txtLicense.Text = Value
    End Set
  End Property

  Public Property FirstName As String
    Get
       Return txtFirst.Text
    End Get

    Set(ByVal Value As String)
      txtFirst.Text = Value
    End Set
  End Property

  Public Property LastName As String
    Get
       Return txtLast.Text
    End Get

    Set(ByVal Value As String)
      txtLast.Text = Value
    End Set
  End Property
```

Here's the simple definition for the `GlobalData` class:

```
Public Class GlobalData
  Private Sub New()
  End Sub

  Public Shared LicenseNumber As String
  Public Shared IsRegistered As Boolean
  Public Shared FirstName As String
  Public Shared LastName As String
End Class
```

This particular example can be adapted to any number of licensing problems. It demonstrates one of the most secure ways to license your application. Store all vital information that you don't want customers to be able to tamper with at *your* facility and allow the applications to communicate with your facility via the Internet.

The only downside to this method is a large one: The user cannot register or even validate their own copy if they do not have an Internet connection. For applications that require the Internet to function (search engines, online games, stock tickers, news delivery services, weather delivery services, etc.) this downside is a non-issue. However, for other applications that do not require the Internet to perform their main function, a hybrid of this solution might be required. In other words, require that they use the Internet to register their installation *once* and then store that they registered the application somewhere discrete and tamper-proof (perhaps in Isolated Storage) to avoid the need to access the Internet each and every time the application runs.

Time-Limited Trial

In this licensing model (and those similar to it) the key to enforcing the proper licensing is in storing the date of the first run of the application (not necessarily the installation date). It is frustrating when an application starts ticking down five days before it is actually tried.

The problem with storing the date of the first run of the application is that you're storing it on the customer's hard drive (you could store it on yours using a web service, but see the previous example for the drawbacks to that alternative). There are a couple of problems with this model that need to be worked out before it can be used:

❑   If the Registry is used, then undoubtedly any clever customer is going to find it and manually set it back.

❑   If you use some binary file in the application directory, it can be encrypted, but eventually a clever cracker will figure out which parts to tweak and the application will simply never expire.

❑   If you use some file with a proprietary format and decide to put it somewhere on the user's hard drive where they're likely to never look for it, then we are at the mercy of the user's security permissions on the hard drive. It is extremely likely that our application will not have sufficient permission to create the file needed to log the application creation date.

There is one solution that looks like a fairly ideal workaround to the above problems: **Isolated Storage**. This facility allows you to create files that the user is not immediately aware of, and these files are *not* subject to the same permission restrictions as the user's hard drive. If the user restricts the Assembly from writing to Isolated Storage, you can catch that exception and simply quit the application – if the application can't create the file, then it doesn't run.

Essentially, what we're going to do is create a file within the Isolated Storage *Store*, which is a partitioned piece of the hard drive. This file will contain a single line that is just a simple string representation of the current date and time at the time of the first running of the application. On all subsequent executions, the application will read this date/time from the Isolated Storage file and use that data to determine how many days are remaining in the trial period.

Let's look at the application running before diving into the code. When you run the application (called `TimeTrial.exe`) from its `bin` directory, you should see the following output:

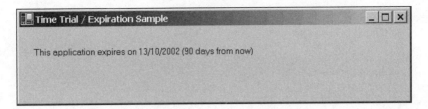

What the end user doesn't see is that this application has created a file that is difficult to find in the Isolated Storage partition for this particular Assembly. Normal file restrictions won't apply and it will be a fairly difficult process for the average user to prevent this application from creating this file.

If you go into the Visual Studio .NET Command Prompt, you can use the Isolated Storage Tool, `storeadm.exe`, and execute the following command:

```
> storeadm /LIST
```

You should see some output that contains a listing of records and some XML data about the various files contained the Isolated Storage store. Here's the output received after running the example:

```
Visual Studio .NET Command Prompt                           _ □ x

C:\>storeadm /LIST
Microsoft (R) .NET Framework Store Admin 1.0.3705.0
Copyright (C) Microsoft Corporation 1998-2001. All rights reserved.

Record #1
[Assembly]
<System.Security.Policy.Url version="1">
    <Url>file://C:/771X/rich/rich/Sources/PuzzlePix.exe</Url>
</System.Security.Policy.Url>

        Size : 0
Record #2
[Assembly]
<System.Security.Policy.Url version="1">
    <Url>File://C:/771X/Chapter06/TimeTrial/bin/TimeTrial.exe</Url>
</System.Security.Policy.Url>

        Size : 1024

C:\>_
```

In the above output you can see that you have indeed created something in the Isolated Storage for this particular Assembly. This something is a text file that contains the installation date. To be even more secure you could actually encrypt the contents of this text file and store more information than just the installation date.

Let's look at the code for the main form of the application (`frmMain.vb`). You can find all of this code in the download for this chapter in the `TimeTrial` solution folder:

```
Imports System.IO
Imports System.IO.IsolatedStorage

Public Class frmMain
  Inherits System.Windows.Forms.Form

  Private installDate As DateTime

  Private Sub frmMain_Load(ByVal sender As System.Object, _
                            ByVal e As System.EventArgs) _
                            Handles MyBase.Load
    Dim isoStore As IsolatedStorageFile
    isoStore = _
      IsolatedStorageFile.GetStore(IsolatedStorageScope.Assembly Or _
      IsolatedStorageScope.User, Nothing, Nothing)

    Dim fileNames As String()
    fileNames = isoStore.GetFileNames("secret_stuff.secret")

    If (fileNames.Length = 0) Then
      ' create a new store file
      Dim writer As New StreamWriter(New _
          IsolatedStorageFileStream("secret_stuff.secret", _
                                    FileMode.CreateNew, isoStore))
      writer.WriteLine(DateTime.Now)
      installDate = DateTime.Now
      writer.Close()
    Else
      Dim reader As New StreamReader(New _
          IsolatedStorageFileStream("secret_stuff.secret", _
                                    FileMode.Open, isoStore))
      Dim tempString As String
      tempString = reader.ReadLine()
      installDate = DateTime.Parse(tempString)
    End If

    Dim dateExpires As DateTime
    dateExpires = installDate.AddDays(90)

    lblStatus.Text = "This application expires on " & _
      dateExpires.ToShortDateString()

    Dim daysLeft As Integer
    daysLeft = DateDiff(DateInterval.Day, installDate, dateExpires)

    lblStatus.Text = lblStatus.Text & " (" & daysLeft & _
      " days from now)"
  End Sub
End Class
```

As you can see in the above code, we are reading and writing from a file in our Isolated Storage store called secret_stuff.secret. If you do a search on your hard drive and include hidden files, you will not find a file that matches this name.

It wouldn't take much work to extend this example to shut down all the features if the current date is equal to or greater than the date the application should expire. Also, for a commercial version of this, the application should shut itself down if it is unable to create the file in the Isolated Storage store in case someone has tightened the security against it, or limited the Assembly's quota for Isolated Storage.

If you look at other code in the previous examples, you probably realized that you could easily adapt the other examples to plug into this example and give the user the ability to extend their trial time by purchasing more time on the application through the use of a web service. This would facilitate a vendor's ability to charge customers over long periods, such as on a per-month or twice monthly basis. When the user's time period is up, they simply order more time through a dialog box and extend the life of the application by modifying the data in the Isolated Storage file.

Install-on-Demand

There are a variety of ways to deal with Install-on-Demand model licensing. Microsoft has provided a method built directly into the .NET Framework. You have the ability to load any type from any Assembly, including Assemblies sitting in public directories out on the Internet somewhere.

What this means is that the user can download the application, which is really nothing more than a Windows Form that launches other forms, as shown below:

When you click on the Form menu item, you are presented with Load Remote Form as an option. The application will actually *download* a feature that it wants to use. This allows you to deploy an incredibly small application and then users who want (or who pay for) more features can simply download them as and when required.

Unlike other applications where the user has to click something to download, watch the download, and possibly wait for the computer to reboot while their software is uploading, .NET does everything for us. We simply request the Assembly we want to load a remote type from, load the remote type, and then activate it. The following form was actually downloaded from an Internet location:

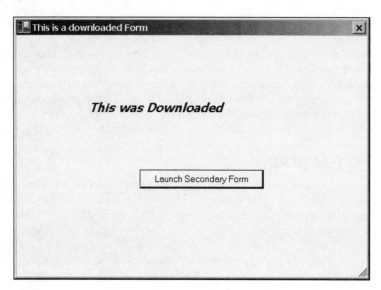

So now you have a form running on your machine that was downloaded from the Internet. This could easily be the main form for an entire application. For example, you could have a "launcher" application that is basically the "Human Resources" department. Some desktops will have downloaded the main form for Payroll, other desktops will have downloaded the main form for Vacation, others will have downloaded the main form for Health Benefits, and yet others will have downloaded the main form for Retirement Plans. All of this looks to the user as if it is the same application, but with some subtle differences. The people who don't have access to the Payroll system can't request the main form for the Payroll system and those without access to Payroll don't even have that module on their hard drive, so they aren't wasting disk space with it and can't try and hack into it.

When you click Launch Secondary Form, the Runtime knows where the first form came from (in our case the local web site) and will automatically get the type of that other form from the same place, seamlessly allowing you to activate even more classes contained in the remote Assembly:

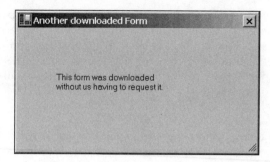

All of the Assemblies that we are downloading from the Internet in order to support this application are stored in the **Download Cache**. This is a central repository of downloaded material. What this means is that if you have five applications on the local desktop that *all* attempt to download the same remote Assembly (for example, a suite of office applications that all attempt to download the same "File Save" dialog form), then only the first application will have to download the Assembly and all other applications can simply service the request from the cache and not have to go over the Internet.

Let's look at the contents of the Download Cache on a machine after running the above example (which downloaded one Assembly and launched one form manually and the other form implicitly). You can obtain the contents of the Download Cache by using the Global Assembly Cache utility, gacutil.exe, and issuing the following command at the command prompt:

> **gacutil /ldl**

```
C:\>gacutil /ldl

Microsoft (R) .NET Global Assembly Cache Utility.  Version 1.0.3705.0
Copyright (C) Microsoft Corporation 1998-2001. All rights reserved.


The cache of downloaded files contains the following entries:
        DownloadedForm, Version=1.0.926.28833, Culture=neutral, PublicKeyToken=n
ull, Custom=null
        DownloadedForm, Version=1.0.0.0, Culture=neutral, PublicKeyToken=null, C
ustom=null

Number of items = 2

C:\>_
```

What we see here is that there are *two* copies of the DownloadedForm form in the Download Cache. The reason for this is that it had been downloaded once before it was assigned a version number while debugging, and then downloaded *again* after it was updated it to launch the secondary form. The cache retains both, so Assemblies that need a *specific* version of the DownloadedForm Assembly can obtain it. The default behavior is to automatically use the newest version of the Assembly in the cache.

To create this example, create a Windows Forms application called `DownloadedForm`. Then, create the two forms seen above (`frmDownloaded` and the secondary form). Once you have the forms looking the way desired, and they've been tested to your satisfaction, change the output type of the project to Class Library. This gives you a DLL that can be put in a public place for distribution to the client application. You will want to strong name it also (as described in the previous chapter) to reduce the security implications of downloading and running code over the Internet.

For the client, create a new Windows Forms application called `InstallOnDemand`. Rename the main form to `frmMain` and point the project to the new location of `Sub Main()`. Then, add the menu items for Form and Load Downloaded Form. The following is the code for the `MenuItem3_Click` event:

```
Private Sub MenuItem3_Click(ByVal sender As System.Object, _
                            ByVal e As System.EventArgs) _
                            Handles MenuItem3.Click
   Dim remoteAssembly As [Assembly]
   remoteAssembly = [Assembly].LoadFrom( _
       "http://localhost/RegisterOnline/DownloadedForm.dll")

   Dim formType As System.Type
   formType = remoteAssembly.GetType("DownloadedForm.frmDownloaded")

   Dim formX As Form
   formX = Activator.CreateInstance(formType)
   formX.ShowDialog()
   formX.Dispose()
End Sub
```

This menu item handler is the perfect location to place code to check and see if the user (or application) is actually authorized to download that particular module. Here is where the application would ideally make a call to a web service and find out what modules the user has purchased, or has been licensed to use. If the module attempting to run isn't in the list of modules the user has access to, then the application should give the user a warning and not download the new feature.

Applications written in this manner have tremendous benefits above and beyond that of having a robust licensing mechanism. They can be updated centrally and have those updates automatically propagated down to all installed clients as those clients are executed. Changes to the backend logic can take place in a Windows Forms application without the end users ever knowing about it, and you can easily keep track of who is downloading what features by simply logging the request-for-access calls that come in for your associated web service with an application like this.

The possibilities are endless, but you should have enough to give you some ideas on how to license your application, and how to enforce the licensing of your application in a way that doesn't hinder the users' ability to get the most out of it while not hindering your ability to actually collect on the licensing fees due to you or your company.

Developer-to-Developer Licensing

In addition to licensing your application to customers, there are times when you might actually want to license your code to other developers. This happens for custom controls in ASP.NET and for Windows Forms. You can license your controls so that only those developers who have purchased the licenses for those controls can actually use those controls in their applications. Typically, the controls should detect whether or not they are licensed and modify their behavior accordingly. For example, a custom Label control might only display the phrase "Unlicensed Control" when no valid license has been detected when the programmer is working with the control.

Fortunately, the .NET Framework provides us with a standard facility for working with licenses for controls. The Framework itself actually makes no distinction between ASP.NET controls and Windows Forms controls in terms of the ability of those controls to make use of the underlying licensing framework. This is accomplished through the use of three specialized classes with special purposes:

❑ LicenseProvider

❑ LicenseManager

❑ License

These classes can be used to check the existence of a valid license for a component at run time or design time.

LicenseProvider

The System.ComponentModel.LicenseProvider class provides the abstract (MustInherit) base class from which all license providers must inherit. The LicenseProvider class has a method called GetLicense() that will retrieve a license based on an instance of a particular component. If the component is not licensed, then the license returned will either be Nothing, or an exception will be thrown.

This class has a protected default constructor that you call into from the first line of your constructor, and as well as those members inherited from System.Object, the GetLicense() method must be overridden in your derived class.

GetLicense()

This method has the following definition:

```
MustOverride Public Function GetLicense( _
        ByVal context As System.ComponentModel.LicenseContext, _
        ByVal type As System.Type, _
        ByVal instance As System.Object, _
        ByVal allowExceptions As System.Boolean) _
        As System.ComponentModel.License
```

The licensing framework will call this method automatically for you, so you need to provide an accurate derived implementation when you create your own license provider. The arguments are described below:

❑   `context`
     This provides the context in which this component is being accessed, whether embedded in another application during compile time, or instantiated during run time. It contains a `UsageMode` property that will contains one of two enumerated values:
     `LicenseUsageMode.DesignTime`, and `LicenseUsageMode.RunTime`.

❑   `type`
     This indicates the `System.Type` of the component that requires a license.

❑   `instance`
     This object contains the actual instance of the object requiring a license.

❑   `allowExceptions`
     When this value is `True`, this means that in most cases you would throw a `LicenseException` whenever there is a problem retrieving or validating a license. If you set this to `False` then this method will just return `Nothing` if a valid license cannot be acquired.

The `License` type is described in the section headed *License*.

LicenseManager

The `LicenseManager` class is a class that implements only shared methods for adding a license to components (ASP.NET and Windows Forms controls) and for managing a specific `LicenseProvider`. The method and properties of this class are used as the entry points into `LicenseManager` and other related classes and types for the licensing framework.

The properties of this class are shown below:

Name	Return Value	Description
CurrentContext	LicenseContext An execution context in which a license is requested.	The context in which a license is being requested. The return value is passed to the `LicenseProvider.GetLicense()` method in the licensing framework. A `LicenseContext` contains the `UsageMode` property, and methods to retrieve the license key for the component.

Name	Return Value	Description
UsageMode	LicenseModeUsage An enumeration that specifies what context a license is valid for: DesignTime or RunTime	**Read Only** When a license has been acquired, it will be valid for only one of two contexts: design time or run time. This indicates where this license is valid.

This class also contains six shared methods. We detail three of those you are likely to use below. The descriptions for the other three can found in the .NET Framework SDK.

IsLicensed()

This method is used to see if the object of specific type has a license. It allows you to check if a license exists elsewhere in your code if you have a number of different components each requiring licenses. Its method stub is shown below:

```
Public Shared Function IsValid(type As System.Type) As Boolean
```

The type of the object requiring a license is given as its argument, and it returns True if a valid license exists.

IsValid()

This checks to see if a valid license can be granted to the specified component or type. Once the license is granted, the class can be used, but this tests to see if a license can be granted for its use. It has two overloads, and the first is shown below:

```
Public Overloads Shared Function IsValid(type As System.Type) _
                  As Boolean
```

Given a specified System.Type, this method checks to see if a valid license can be acquired for this type. The conditions for success will depend on the implementation code for the LicenseProvider.GetLicense() method, but they would normally require a file to be present in a specified place, and for that file to contain specific contents.

The second overload is shown below:

```
Public Overloads Shared Function IsValid(type As System.Type, _
                  object As System.Object, _
                  ByRef license As License) _
                  As Boolean
```

This actually performs the same task as the `Validate()` method shown below, calling into the `GetLicense()` method, except that this function will never throw an exception. This method will attempt to retrieve a license for a specific `object` and if successful, it will return `True`, and store the license in the `license` variable passed as an argument. If it fails, it will return `False` and the `license` variable will point to `Nothing`.

Validate()

This method has two overloads with different return values. The first has a null return value (is a `Sub`) and is shown below:

```
Public Overloads Shared Sub Validate(type As System.Type)
```

This determines if a license can be retrieved for a specific type. If not, a `LicenseException` is thrown. If so, it completes and exits successfully. The second overload is more interesting:

```
Public Overloads Shared Function Validate(type As System.Type, _
                                          instance As System.Object) _
                                          As License
```

This works in the same way as the first overload, throwing an exception if a license cannot be given, but if it succeeds, it will grant a license to the specific object `instance` and return it to the calling code.

License

The `License` class is an abstract (`MustInherit`) class that represents the license itself. It contains a property called `LicenseKey` that is a simple string that represents the key for the license. Typically, the key here is either encrypted or significantly complex so the format of the key is not easy to determine just by looking at it. You can choose your own method of determining this key; suggestions include a registration key of 4 or 5 sets of digits, a 128-bit ID that represents a given network card, processor ID, or otherwise, a piece of data signed with an RSA private key that can be confirmed in code using the public key, or any other identification scheme. The key should be unique and difficult to determine, or it should be tied to some other unique code.

This class must also be derived from and it specifies a method and a property that each must be overridden in the derived class. The derived class would have a name that is specific to its purpose – perhaps called `RestrictedUseLicense`, or `DesignTimeLicense`.

LicenseKey

This property contains the unique key for the license. It is a read-only property and its stub is as shown:

```
Public MustOverride ReadOnly Property LicenseKey As String
```

The license key would normally be passed to the license on construction and it can be retrieved through this method.

Dispose()

The base method implements `IDisposable.Dispose` and is required to be overridden (although it needn't have any implementation). It provides cleanup code for any objects that this license may contain.

```
Public MustOverride Sub Dispose() Implements IDisposable.Dispose
```

When you override this method, you can give it no implementation, if the class only contains primitive types, but if new objects are created during construction, then ensure they are cleaned up in this method, which will be called on destruction.

The three of these classes, when combined together, can be used to create licensable controls that stop developers using your control without first having acquired a valid license for that control. Without the presence of the license (in a format you can choose if you define your own `LicenseProvider`) then the developer cannot make use of your component in their application. Before we show you how to make use of these classes to build your own licensing framework, we will show how to use one of the most straightforward methods of licensing your component.

A derived class that inherits from the `LicenseProvider` class has been provided in the .NET Framework class library and this performs a standard way of validating your components against a specific kind of license. It isn't secure (as the license can be copied with the component) but by including the legal text of the license agreement within this file, you can perform minimal licensing requirements. This works in the same way as the licensing framework that existed for COM components.

LicFileLicenseProvider

This license provider contains the required `GetLicense()` method, and an `IsKeyValid()` method. The `GetLicense()` method checks to see if a file of the same name as the full name of the licensed class, but with a `.LIC` extension, exists in the same directory as the assembly. If it does, then it passes the first line of this file to the `IsKeyValid()` method. This method confirms that the first line has some specific text. If the class was called `WroxComponent`, then the first line of the license file must be: "`WroxComponent is a licensed component. `" Notice that there is a space after the period at the end of this sentence. If they match, then a license is generated and this first line becomes the key of the newly created license.

The best way to see how this works is to see it in use. For this chapter, assume that you have created a component called `NumericTextBox` that will only allow numeric values to be entered. Its code is shown below:

```
Imports System.Windows.Forms
Imports System.Drawing
Imports System.ComponentModel
Imports System.Globalization

Public Class NumericTextBox
  Inherits System.Windows.Forms.TextBox

  Sub New()
    MyBase.New()
    ' Additional construction to be entered here
  End Sub

  Private Sub NumericTextBox_KeyPress(ByVal sender As Object, _
                                      ByVal e As KeyPressEventArgs) _
                                      Handles MyBase.KeyPress
    If e.KeyChar = Convert.ToChar(Keys.Back) Then
      e.Handled = False
    Else
      Dim separator As String = _
        NumberFormatInfo.CurrentInfo.NumberDecimalSeparator
      e.Handled = Not ((e.KeyChar = CType(separator, Char) And _
        sender.Text.IndexOf(separator) = -1) Or _
        Char.IsNumber(e.KeyChar) Or _
        (e.KeyChar = NumberFormatInfo.CurrentInfo.NegativeSign _
        And sender.SelectionStart = 0))
    End If
  End Sub
End Class
```

This is a straightforward textbox that will only allow valid numeric values, including a negative sign at the start and zero or one decimal points. It uses the values of the current locale to allow the "," symbol, for instance, to be used as the decimal separator. This is the kind of component that you might wish to license so that each and every developer that uses it needs to pay for a license. However, once it was part of an application, you would allow the company employing the developers to license their software however they like, without the need for each user to have a license for your component too.

Here is the code you would add to this component to allow it to be licensed using the scheme implemented by the `LicFileLicenseProvider` class:

```
Imports System.Globalization

<LicenseProvider(GetType(LicFileLicenseProvider))> _
Public Class NumericTextBox
```

```
Inherits System.Windows.Forms.TextBox

Private Lic As License

Sub New()
  MyBase.New()
  Lic = LicenseManager.Validate(GetType(NumericTextBox), Me)
End Sub
...

Protected Overloads Overrides Sub Dispose(disposing As Boolean)
  If Not Lic Is Nothing
    Lic.Dispose()
    Lic = Nothing
  End If
  MyBase.Dispose(disposing)
End Sub
End Class
```

The `LicenseProvider` attribute provided on the `NumericTextBox` class is required so that the CLR can determine that this class requires a license to be instantiated, and how to acquire this license. The `LicenseProvider` attribute has one attribute, and that's the type of the license provider class. In this case, it is `System.ComponentModel.LicFileLicenseProvider`. It is always advisable to dispose of the license when you dispose of the object.

Compile this project and start a new one. The results can be unpredictable if you don't compile the assembly first and reference this, and in real life you wouldn't be providing the code anyway. This is because the directory the license file should be present in changes if the project is referenced. Reference the DLL, add the component to the Toolbox, and attempt to put it on the form. It will fail and throw an exception:

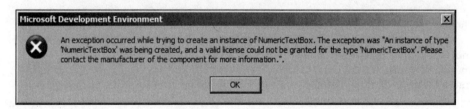

This is because a valid license file was not found and so it throws a `LicenseException`. It is quite straightforward to get this working. Just create a text file called `NumericTextBox.LIC` that contains: "`NumericTextBox is a licensed component. `" (remember the trailing space), and save it in the same location as the DLL that you have added to your toolbox; use the one saved in the `NumericTextBox\obj\Debug` or `Release` directory. The text file must be saved wherever the component file you're referencing is located.

The license file is required during development only. Once the application is compiled and linked to the component, the license is compiled and becomes embedded in the compiled assembly and the application no longer needs the presence of the .LIC file to run.

You can derive a new class from the LicFileLicenseProvider class. This system is similar to the COM licensing scheme and you may wish to employ something similar in your own application, but with a less predictable key. If the key will be stored in the first line of a text file of the same name, then you can just override the IsKeyValid() method so that it performs a different check. The IsKeyValid() method looks like the following:

```
Overridable Protected Function IsKeyValid(key As String, _
                            type As System.Type) _
                            As Boolean
```

The key to be validated is passed in the first parameter, and the type of the component requiring a license in the second; the method returns True if the key is valid. If you wanted to use a different key, you would only need to override this method in the derived type and make the relevant changes to the attribute and argument passed to the Validate() method in the NumericTextBox class. This isn't the most complicated licensing scheme, however, and you may require something more advanced.

Creating a New LicenseProvider

Adding to the code in the NumericTextBox class in a similar way to what you did above for the LicFileLicenseProvider class, you can build your own licensing scheme for design time and/or run time validation of a component that is as complex as you require. For this section we will use the same component we were using before.

The method used here is to confirm that a digital signature contained within a specific license file matches the hash code of some registration details. The signature is created and validated using a public-private key pair and so the Validate() method will know that a trusted third party who holds the private key has confirmed the values entered. This is likely to be the component maker. This license provider can test for validity at design and run time. This example only performs tests at design time, but it would be trivial to add additional code for run-time validation. We could almost achieve the same result here by deriving from the LicFileLicenseProvider class and overriding the IsKeyValid() method in the following example, but we have built it up from scratch in this case.

The License

Create a new class library project and change the contents of its class file to the following:

```vbnet
Imports System
Imports System.ComponentModel
Imports System.Security.Cryptography
Imports System.IO
Imports Microsoft.VisualBasic

Friend Class ComponentLicense
    Inherits System.ComponentModel.License

    Private key As String
    Private owner As String

    Sub New(ByVal key As String, ByVal owner As String)
        MyBase.New()
        Me.key = key
        Me.owner = owner
    End Sub

    Public Overrides ReadOnly Property LicenseKey() As String
        Get
            Return Me.key
        End Get
    End Property

    Public Overridable ReadOnly Property LicenseOwner() As String
        Get
            Return Me.owner
        End Get
    End Property

    Public Overrides Sub Dispose()
        ' No implementation necessary
    End Sub
End Class
```

This is the license that will be granted to valid calling applications so they can use this component. An additional property has been added to the licenses, LicenseOwner, which will contain the name of the person or company that owns the license.

The Dispose() method needs no real implementation, as strings are the class's only fields. However, remember that the Dispose() method of the License class must be overridden in a derived class. It has been given Friend accessibility to help keep its details to only those components in this assembly. Alternatively, it could be defined as a private nested class of the following LicenseProvider derived class.

The LicenseProvider

The `LicComponentLicense` class will be the license provider used in this project. Its definition starts as follows:

```
Public Class LicComponentLicense
    Inherits LicenseProvider

    Private Lic As License

    Public Overrides Function GetLicense( _
                        ByVal context As LicenseContext, _
                        ByVal type As System.Type, _
                        ByVal instance As System.Object, _
                        ByVal allowExceptions As Boolean)
                        As License
```

This function will be called by the `Validate()` or `IsValid()` shared methods of the `LicenseManager` class. If the `Validate()` method is called, then `allowExceptions` is set as `True`. If `IsValid()` is called, then `allowExceptions` is set as `False`.

Now we'll check that the passed in parameters are legal:

```
If context Is Nothing Then
    Return Nothing
ElseIf type Is Nothing Then
    Throw New ArgumentNullException("type")
ElseIf instance Is Nothing Then
    Throw New ArgumentNullException("instance")
End If
```

If `context` is `Nothing`, then it just returns `Nothing` as there is no execution context specified. The constructor throws an `ArgumentNullException` if the other parameters are `Nothing`. As this is called automatically, then all these parameters should be defined anyway.

```
Dim licenseFile As String
Dim fs As StreamReader
Dim ID As String
Dim Owner As String
```

`licenseFile` will contain the name of the license file, which should be present in the same location as the assembly. `ID` and `Owner` will contain the license key and license owner once the registration details have been validated using the digital signature contained in the license file. `fs` will be used to read the file.

Design Time Licensing

```
If context.UsageMode = LicenseUsageMode.Designtime Then
    Dim GUID As String = "00-A0-CC-CB-44-9F"
    licenseFile = "NumericTextBox.ctlic"
```

Remember that `context.UsageMode` contains an enumeration that indicates whether this component is being referenced before compile time or at run time. The `GUID` variable's contents would normally be retrieved from some method that in this case would inspect and retrieve the unique ID of the computer's network card. It's as good a mechanism for determining valid installation as any. For brevity, the network card's GUID has been hard coded into the variable in this case. The `licenseFile` variable contains the name of the file that contains the signature for the registration details. The `.ctlic` file extension indicates that this is a design- (or compile)-time license file.

```
Try
    fs = File.OpenText(licenseFile)
    Dim signature() As Byte = _
        Convert.FromBase64String(fs.ReadLine)
    Dim registrationDetails As String = "00-A0-CC-CB-44-9F" & _
        ControlChars.NewLine & "Wrox Press" & ControlChars.NewLine
    If DecryptLicense(signature, registrationDetails) Then
        Dim firstRecord As Integer = _
            registrationDetails.IndexOf(ControlChars.NewLine)
        ID = registrationDetails.Substring(3, firstRecord - 3)
        Owner = registrationDetails.Substring(firstRecord + _
                                                    8).Trim()

        If ID = GUID Then
            Lic = New ComponentLicense(ID, Owner)
        End If
    End If
End If
```

The license is a file containing the signature for the registration details. These would be stored in an external file, but here, for brevity, they are hard-coded in a string. The signature inside the license file is stored in a Base64-encoding format. The code first opens the file, reading it as ASCII, and then converts this Base64-encoded string into a byte array, `signature`. The `DecryptLicense()` private method returns a Boolean indicating if the hash code of the registration details matches the digital signature stored in the license file. This method will be detailed later, but it uses the methods of the `RSACryptoServiceProvider` object to verify the contents of this file. The key value pairs, concatenated together in this example, would look like the following:

```
ID:00-A0-CC-CB-44-9F
Owner:Wrox Press
```

The `firstRecord` variable contains the index of the first newline character in the string. `ID` is given a substring that will include everything following `ID:` up until the newline character. `Owner` contains everything from `Owner:` onwards, with the whitespace removed from the end.

If `DecryptLicense()` returned `False`, then we know that the registration details weren't successfully verified, so the license file has probably been tampered with. Therefore, a license isn't stored in the `Lic` variable. If the ID is the same as that stored in the `GUID` variable, then the method returns a new `ComponentLicense`. This is the end of the `Try` block, but before we go on to describing the `Catch` blocks, let's look at the contents of the `DecryptLicense()` method first.

```
Private Function DecryptLicense(ByVal signedData() As Byte, _
                      ByVal data As String) _
                As Boolean
    Const PUBLICXMLKEY As String = _
    "<RSAKeyValue><Modulus>r6oymH2xYs6T0H8QmcKXmNSmiMCC1M2ieoLxP1mQKpYQFe2
    C77JXUue1P7KwvbYRQzDG3IeuC0ItAUfXPugwWsASZr1v6+rJMN2HujjumSWXIKO1WEF6U
    FGfIWUM8kyawo49GuwF5RnHArnCx65JWEvP4ekBIRDTVQ2HHVxcEIc=</Modulus><Expo
    nent>AQAB</Exponent></RSAKeyValue>"
```

Here you can see that the public key is hard-coded into a constant. If the key were retrieved from an external file, say, then someone could just replace the contents of that file with their own public key and so create their own valid license file. Paired with strong-naming your assemblies, explained in the previous chapter, this provides you with some security that the public key used for confirming the signature is the correct one.

In the code download, two command-line applications have been provided that will return public and private keys, and generate license files using the private key. It is beyond the scope of this chapter to explain much about the generation of keys and encryption of data. The code for these programs has been included in the code download file. If you generate your own public-private key pair, you'll then have to replace the contents of this constant with the different public key.

The lines that confirm the digital signature in the license file is for the registration details given as a string in the method's parameter are shown below:

```
Dim rsad As New _
   System.Security.Cryptography.RSACryptoServiceProvider()
rsad.FromXmlString(PUBLICXMLKEY)
Dim dataToVerify() As Byte = _
   System.Text.Encoding.ASCII.GetBytes(data)

If rsad.VerifyData(dataToVerify, _
                   New SHA1CryptoServiceProvider(), _
                   signedData) Then
    Return True
Else
    Return False
End If
End Function
```

The public key is entered into the RSACryptoServiceProvider object using the FromXMLString() method. The RSACryptoServiceProvider.VerifyData() method takes the details, the signature, and a hash algorithm object as arguments. The string to be verified also has to be converted into a byte array before being used. The value returned from the VerifyData() method is returned to indicate success or failure.

Let's now return to the Catch statements of this block:

```
Catch ex As FileNotFoundException
    If allowExceptions Then
        Throw New LicenseException(type, instance, _
                                   "License Not Found", ex)
    Else
        Return Nothing
    End If
```

It is possible that the license/signature file was not found. In which case, when the StreamReader object attempts to open it, it will throw a FileNotFoundException. We catch it here and if exceptions are allowed, then we throw a new LicenseException that contains the relevant message and inner exception. If not, the method returns Nothing.

```
Catch ex As Exception
    If allowExceptions Then
        Throw New LicenseException(type, instance, ex.Message, ex)
    Else
        Return Nothing
    End If
```

The remaining Catch statement will throw a new exception if permitted, or return Nothing if not. It turns the exception into LicenseException for neatness. Regardless of the reasons for failure, the problem is still that the component cannot be licensed and the exception should indicate this.

```
Finally
    If Not fs Is Nothing Then
        fs.Close()
        fs = Nothing
    End If
End Try
```

The Finally statement ensures that the StreamReader object is closed and destroyed no matter where, and if, an exception is thrown. The next code actually returns a license if the registration details were confirmed valid.

```
If Not Lic Is Nothing Then
    Return Lic
Else
    If allowExceptions Then
        Throw New LicenseException(type, instance, _
            "GUID not authorized on this machine")
    Else
        Return Nothing
    End If
End If
```

This is all perfectly straightforward. If either the data wasn't validated, or the GUID did not match the value stored in the `ID` variable, then it throws a new `LicenseException` if `allowExceptions` is `True`. Otherwise, it returns the license that was granted earlier.

Run-Time Licensing

So far we have only talked about design time licensing. What occurs if the component is instantiated during run time?

```
    Else
        Return New ComponentLicense("Runtime", Nothing)
    End If
End Function
```

You could add any validation routines you like here, but here we're just going to test for design-time validation. Therefore, we return a new `ComponentLicense`. This is the end of the definition of the new `LicenseProvider`.

```
End Class
```

Implementing the Licensing Scheme

All that is needed now is to make use of this `LicenseProvider` for the `NumericTextBox` component. We'll implement the code to make use of the `LicenseProvider` class differently this time. In this case, we make use of compiler directives to determine whether or not the component should require a license. Add the class file that contains the `NumericTextBox` class to the project. Here is the code that replaces the start of the `NumericTextBox` class, which replaces the `Public Class NumericTextBox` line:

```
  . . .
  #Const LICENSEREQUIRED = True
  #If LICENSEREQUIRED Then
    <LicenseProvider(GetType(LicComponentLicense))> _
    Public Class NumericTextBox
  #Else
  Public Class NumericTextBox
  #End If
      Inherits System.Windows.Forms.TextBox
```

Compiler directives are not inserted into the assembly as MSIL once compiled, they are processed before compilation and they determine what will be present in the compiled code. In this case, if `LICENSEREQUIRED` is `True`, then the `LicenseProvider` attribute is added to the class definition, and it is omitted if `False`. When the component is ready for release, just change the value of the `LICENSEREQUIRED` constant.

Add the following directives around the constructor:

```
#If LICENSEREQUIRED Then
    Private Lic As License
#End If

    Sub New()
        MyBase.New()
#If LICENSEREQUIRED Then
        Lic = LicenseManager.Validate(GetType(NumericTextBox), Me)
#End If
    End Sub
```

The constructor will only attempt to retrieve a license if LICENSEREQUIRED is True. The code is identical to the code that was added to NumericTextBox when using the LicFileLicenseProvider class. The code added to the Dispose() method is also identical.

If you compile this component and try to embed it in a form, a similar exception to what you saw when the LicFileLicenseProvider class was used will be thrown – only this time it will say: "License not Found". So all that's now required is to create a valid license and try this out.

Supplied in the code download are two command-line applications, EncryptLicense, and GenerateKeys, which are used to generate the encrypted license and the public-private key pairs, respectively. The public-private key pair used in this example, which works with the public key coded in the DecryptLicense() method, looks like the following:

```
<RSAKeyValue><Modulus>r6oymH2xYs6T0H8QmcKXmNSmiMCC1M2ieoLxPlmQKpYQFe2C
77JXUue1P7KwvbYRQzDG3IeuC0ItAUfXPugwWsASZr1v6+rJMN2HujjumSWXIKO1WEF6UF
GfIWUM8kyawo49GuwF5RnHArnCx65JWEvP4ekBIRDTVQ2HHVxcEIc=</Modulus><Expon
ent>AQAB</Exponent><P>3ivYQBC75B1OisTgufXPZAMOD1EWZxc+PRpdG3cSWIhO1SiU
x4B6ZRWZADmMqGmOLu0YdLQdZ2d9q3eyDNiinw==</P><Q>ymmMjOHP56c9Gb8V5vsLv80
H8jhqUQABbMPWoN5QBcT4iNT15TfRSWC9DHpmvEyxFzLEaElDU2kJCgAX2RRxGQ==</Q><
DP>rdtXpYKy1ebq7TD1vvAJs/TkCr5krpWOwbIgzD5Yn+1gedzA2IHExdep3FAsrxmzByv
IqILOQ73rzMOlFIJudw==</DP><DQ>kOBYBIGeWztaAun1iBToRj91YXxTM9waLUMHV/6D
Hr9dw0WSIZAKzCP5RCOjq6brSiIfqnJp7TtDXSgWMVFiuQ==</DQ><InverseQ>PWtTwbM
9sZ7EpuNyNY/9c21OhsjBTDM40T1uozuzJ8wEdUV64vj4/WRozuRmmC9+YxXR1O8TikxL6
1C4GyFpWQ==</InverseQ><D>DV6q0yhd4+NNJMVHAizpVNx6gFYGmkS8ZQ6qRdCTRGp/d
uvI121/b/Pqu5piEU5WKgMAX7CD8p9qxXouS79oTp+XCBpzwGkb8oLoYm6jBV81Qw3riJA
QViguaug4cF/2ytXsQJJQ2ahtT3csdcPTykfAieHMNOtUk1focrXE5ME=</D></RSAKeyV
alue>
```

You've seen the ID and Owner pair that gets encrypted earlier, and as you have seen, this is hard-coded into the application:

```
ID:00-A0-CC-CB-44-9F
Owner:Wrox Press
```

By running the `EncryptLicense` program, a file called `EncryptedLicense.LIC` is saved that contains the digital signature of the above registration details. It looks like the following:

```
o2tgnrhIs26xsKZEBKAattHjNLExEdSmW8NXdrCnBJzQXMBfLOUMXZAIou2R5Znn/3yGRh
mx1MqE1zmMLrrSMaCRZ8zEGhLglhucfwLAVaqx+Qonnwx5ARwC8bLroeqaM/BXFUBMevkR
W3vSSEalfBeWzvOJWJ8C2N61UTsxFbY=
```

If you rename this file to `NumericTextBox.LIC` and save it in the same place the component is located in, then the component can be used fine.

Summary

In this chapter you have seen the various different kinds of license and examples of how they can be implemented. You've also seen some of the consequences of these licensing policies. The latter part of this chapter discussed developer licensing and showed how to make use of the Licensing framework provided by the .NET Framework.

Licensing is a large issue and something that can only be covered perfectly in discussion with lawyers. However, you have seen here how to implement many of the licensing models you may wish to take advantage of. Paired with strong-naming assemblies, you can provide secure methods of licensing with Visual Basic .NET.

VB.NET

Deployment

Handbook

7

7

Protecting Your Intellectual Property

When deploying an application there is typically a list of concerns and issues that comes to mind immediately. For example, there are the usual problems of physical deployment, distribution, maintenance, and installation that the book has been covering so far. How often do you think of protecting the intellectual property contained within the code when you think of deployment, however?

This can finish at the bottom of the list of concerns. Realistically, it should be given a far more prominent spot on your to-do list of preparing the application for deployment, *especially* when developing .NET applications. The reason for this is that if you don't properly deal with this problem, then the application can be broken, tampered with, reverse engineered, and you can even have proprietary information or trade secrets stolen from the *compiled* (intermediately compiled) code even though the thief does not have access to the original source code.

This chapter will take you on a tour of the various ways in which malicious individuals, organizations, thieves, and curious customers can steal or access your intellectual property, and then you'll see some of the tools and techniques you can employ to protect your intellectual property.

What Is Intellectual Property?

This chapter is about the protection of your intellectual property (**IP**). In order to protect it, you should know what it is. Intellectual property is a type of property that generally refers to things such as patents, copyrights, trademarks, and trade secrets. The patent system was designed to protect an inventor from the theft of their inventions and processes of invention. It has been extended to include any unique design or process that could result in a tangible product; this includes, controversially, the genetic blueprint of various life forms once discovered. If a unique algorithm is created, like the various encryption and compression algorithms, then this can be patented. Once patented, the full design and specification is published and copying requires permission from the inventor, which usually involves some remuneration.

Copyright is an older method of protecting intellectual property and was designed to protect writers of text from having their work stolen and printed without payment by a rival printer/publisher. Copyright can be transferred to other bodies, or shared. This is what happens in book publishing today, and has happened in the title you're reading now. Any copying and publishing of this content cannot occur without permission from Wrox Press. Copyright has been extended to include much more. Source code can be copyrighted, although this does not prevent someone from compiling it and redistributing that. Other items now have the ability to be copyrighted, such as music (and not just the sheet music on which a specific recording is based).

Trademarks are titles by which companies or products are identified. Wrox is a trademark and this prevents other publishers from sticking a Wrox label on a book and trading on our name. Product names are also trademarks and this prevents the mis-selling of a product or service. Trade secrets can be any product or process, and this includes source code, that you don't want to other party to be aware of. Contracts can be drawn up for employees and partners to protect trade secrets so that, for instance, the source code for Microsoft Office isn't distributed and any copy protection or overly distinguishing features circumvented once recompiled and distributed. This prevents those parties that translate the Office product into another language from sticking the code on some publicly accessible server.

In less technical terms, you should think of your Intellectual Property as the unique designs and creations made by you or your company. Those designs, ideas, and trade secrets are things that make your product the unique product it is and comprise information that you do *not* want anyone outside your company to have or use. A major concern with Intellectual Property is that different countries might have different definitions, rules, and procedures regarding the protection of IP, if they have any policy concerning it at all. The TRIPs (Trade Related Intellectual Property rights) agreement set up during World Trade Organization round table discussions set certain minimum standards for implementation of IP legislation that have to be implemented by all countries and governments that wish to take part in global trade. This has helped this issue, but the TRIPS agreement has come under much criticism due to the inclusion of genetic material and pre-existing indigenous methods that haven't yet been patented. However, any subsequent agreements are likely to include legitimate innovative concepts in software design.

Some other examples of intellectual property in software include private encryption keys, proprietary algorithms for performing certain tasks (such as high performance image compression, streaming media, etc.) or even things as simple as literals and constants contained within your code that you don't want the user to know about.

Property Theft

There are a variety of ways that your property can be stolen. When we think about the ways that secret or proprietary information has traditionally been stolen in the past, not much has changed. One of the most common ways of stealing intellectual property is through a process called Reverse Engineering, which will be discussed shortly. In addition to this, people can steal other intangible things such as the application's look and feel, which is just as much a unique part of your application as your algorithms.

> **It's not for this book to tell you exactly what can and what cannot be legally protected, for that you will have to take legal advice, as the law can vary depending on country and time.**

Reverse Engineering

Reverse Engineering is the process by which your compiled code is examined, analyzed, and turned back into source code. In the past, this was accomplished by turning an x86 executable binary file into machine or assembly code. This was usually accomplished with a piece of software called a **decompiler**. Programmers and hackers alike would then spend countless hours poring over the results of the decompilation to figure out the original flow, logic, and purpose of the compiled code. Such reverse engineering produces cheats for games and malicious programs such as software that can generate valid serial numbers for piracy-protected software, allowing unlimited reproduction and pirated distribution. In the past, your compiled code was raw binary, or, in the case of Java, compiled bytecode. The result of a .NET compilation, however, is an easy-to-read Intermediate Language.

There is one simple fact to keep in mind when thinking about your own application and your own intellectual property:

> **Someone who reverse-engineers your code *will always* find a use for the information that you did not expect.**

There are a couple of different reasons why people might be disassembling your code. The first and most obvious is to avoid paying for it. If someone decompiles your code and can determine from the decompiled code how you validate your serial numbers, they can avoid paying for your product. This is definitely a malicious intent.

Other decompilation might fall into the realm of curiosity. For example, a curious game player decompiles an Assembly and finds out a way to give his character in the game infinite health. They still paid for your game, and are still playing it; most manufacturers consider this type of "tampering" fairly harmless.

Another more insidious use for decompilation is to find a way to use your application to produce a virus. Everyone knows how many different viruses have been spread through the various loopholes discovered in Microsoft Outlook. If someone can disassemble your code and examine it, they might be able to figure out how to use your application as a weapon.

For example, a game manufacturer releases a video game that has piracy protection enabled in the form of serial number validation. It is a common scenario (albeit oversimplified): each game produced includes a single valid code that authorizes the customer to use that game. If someone manages to reverse engineer the compiled form of that game, they can decipher the algorithm used to validate the codes, which then allows that programmer to write software that does nothing but produce valid codes. Many times people think that just because they invented a particular algorithm, other people will be unable to figure it out. Another fact of life is that no matter how good your algorithm is someone else will have enough spare time and resources with which to decipher it.

A subtler example might be in some online commerce transaction software. Assume that a company has produced a graphical client that communicates over the Internet with the central bank to perform transactions. Can you imagine the amount of damage, fraud, and money that would be lost if people were able to reverse engineer the communications protocol used to send these transactions? That kind of intellectual property must be protected at all costs. In a well-designed application, such transactions would be performed on the server and the client would have no control over how these processes are performed. However, some network communication is likely to occur even at the server end, and so these communication transactions must be protected from reverse engineering.

Before you see how you can protect yourself, let's look at some of the tools that hackers and customers have at their disposal.

MSIL Disassembler

The Microsoft Intermediate Language (MSIL) Disassembler Tool, `ildasm.exe`, is both the programmer's best friend and worst nightmare. It is a tool that allows a programmer to inspect the internals of any .NET Framework Assembly. This means that, using this tool, you can examine every class, enumeration, structure, method, member, and namespace contained within an Assembly. What's worse is that you can examine the IL (Intermediate Language) for any given method.

Let's examine the `ildasm.exe` tool by taking a look at a method of a standard console application. It simply calculates the square of a number and prints out its value to the console:

```
Imports System

Module Square
    Sub Main(args() As String)
        Dim number As Single = CType(args.GetValue(0), Single)
        Console.Write(number*number)
    End Sub
End Module
```

We can examine the contents of `Main()` method with the `ildasm.exe` tool using the following command-line statement:

> **`ildasm.exe Square.exe`**

When the tool opens, expand the Square node and then double-click on the Main : void(string[]) node to see the following window.

```
Square::Main : void(string[])                                              _□×
.method public static void  Main(string[] args) cil managed
{
    .entrypoint
    .custom instance void [mscorlib]System.STAThreadAttribute::.ctor() = ( 01 00 00 00 )
    // Code size       22 (0x16)
    .maxstack  2
    .locals init (float32 V_0)
    IL_0000:  ldarg.0
    IL_0001:  ldc.i4.0
    IL_0002:  callvirt    instance object [mscorlib]System.Array::GetValue(int32)
    IL_0007:  call        float32 [Microsoft.VisualBasic]Microsoft.VisualBasic.CompilerServices.SingleType::FromObject(object)
    IL_000c:  stloc.0
    IL_000d:  ldloc.0
    IL_000e:  ldloc.0
    IL_000f:  mul
    IL_0010:  call        void [mscorlib]System.Console::Write(float32)
    IL_0015:  ret
} // end of method Square::Main
```

Even if you have never seen the Intermediate Language before, it isn't all that difficult, even for the average programmer, to interpret what's going on in the above listing. We know that method calls are stack-based, so we see that the first command-line argument is loaded on the stack. Then the value 0 is added (which represents the memory allocation for the number variable). Then we can see the values multiplied using the two `ldloc.0` lines, followed by the `mul` instruction, before being passed to the `Console.WriteLine()` method.

So, if the above code listing is pretty easy for even the IL-neophyte to interpret, think about how even the most complex code can be read like an open book in the hands of someone familiar with IL. Since the IL is actually an industry standard (Microsoft has submitted its IL to the ECMA standardization body), it takes only a few minutes to download the IL Language Reference from the Internet.

Being good programmers, we always use meaningful names for our variables, for class members, for classes, and for namespaces. If code was written by a good programmer, a method that validates a serial number is likely to be named `ValidateSerialNumber()`, or similar. Without protecting our code from intrusion, that method will stick out like a blinking neon sign to anyone who knows how to use `ildasm.exe`.

Reflection and API Consumption

I've always been surprised by how infrequently we take into account that our customers might be programmers, or they might employ programmers. This (mis)assumption is quite dangerous, *especially* when the platform is the .NET Framework. The reason for this is that all CLR-compliant code performs the same way, and .NET provides us with something called Reflection.

Reflection allows us to examine, in detail, every single member, method, namespace, and more within any Assembly we want, regardless of who wrote the Assembly. This means that, yet again, good programming habits might turn out to hurt us in the end. If, as good programmers, we have produced libraries of common or related functionality to work as an API of sorts for our application, then anyone can use it.

If, for example, you'd produced a library for your own development team that was placed in the Assembly `MyCompany.BankCommunication`, then if you lacked enough foresight to protect your code, then it is possible for other programmers or even your own customers to simply examine all of the classes and methods available in the `BankCommunication` Assembly and use it themselves. Not only does this potentially allow them to abuse the system, but if they've managed to steal the use of the `BankCommunication` Assembly, then they might decide that they just don't need to pay you for our application any longer, and simply maintain their own wrapper for your wonderful set of tools.

So, not only can your code be looked at and examined in the form of Intermediate Language, but it can also be browsed in any Object Browser, including the one that ships with Visual Studio .NET, and any API you produced for your own application can easily be used for someone else's. When customers usurp your own libraries, they will generally decide that they don't need to pay you for services, since you no longer hold any power over the library of useful functions.

Mistaken Identity

Identity is a vulnerability that exists more with .NET programming than it does with other, more traditional methods, like COM programming. This actually involves a few aspects of the .NET Framework. We'll briefly cover them here, but you should be familiar with the concepts of Code Access Security (CAS) and Strong Naming in order to be fully aware of this vulnerability. For more information on these concepts, you can consult the Wrox book *Visual Basic .NET Code Security Handbook* (ISBN: 1-86100-747-7) or you can look them up in the MSDN reference that installs with the Framework SDK.

Let's remind you of the concept of Strong Naming. When you strong-name an Assembly, you provide the following four pieces of information about that Assembly:

❑ File name

❑ Version

❑ Culture

❑ Public Key

These four pieces of information indicate how the .NET Runtime determines the uniqueness of any given Assembly. The problem arises when developers don't supply all of this information. An Assembly that has not been strong-named is *extremely* vulnerable to identity theft.

An assembly that does not have a strong name cannot have a *strong reference*. This means that without a strong name, any other assembly that references the weak-named assembly can only have a weak reference. This weak reference only includes partial evidence such as a file name, version, and culture. On the surface there doesn't seem to be all that much wrong with this situation. The problem is in the weak reference. A weak reference allows hackers or malicious customers to *replace* portions of your application easily. Let's say we had (regrettably) decided to place our serial number validation code in a single method in a single assembly. An adventurous programmer could easily write their own Assembly that provides a method simply returning true regardless of the serial number. Without the public key information, an assembly can be produced that the executable thinks is a legitimate part of the application.

While the serial number example has been used far too often, let's look at something more deliberate and more destructive. Let's say you had neglected to strong-name your assemblies, and so all of the building blocks of the application are linked through weak references. If the application is a web site, and a hacker found a vulnerability to gain access to the site's /bin directory, they could very easily start dropping in assemblies that cause destructive behavior, because our application has no idea that the assemblies came from a malicious source.

Protecting your Code

So far we've taken a look at some of the most common ways in which people can steal valuable intellectual property from your application and your code. This next section of the chapter will cover some of the steps that you can take as a developer to ensure that your Intellectual Property is as protected as it can be.

Legal Protection

Whenever you talk about protecting Intellectual Property, you can't avoid a discussion about legal terminology and protection. There are fleets of lawyers who practice patent law and software-related cases that know far more about it than this author. However, there are a couple of things that you can do that will give you an added measure of legal protection.

Most authors of Shareware know that it doesn't take anything more than a simple Copyright notice embedded in the source code of their application to legally grant that author the copyright of the code. Code is probably one of the easiest things to legally copyright.

There is a simple issue that you might want to keep in mind when building your application, however. It is possible for people to contest the validity of a copyright for a particular piece of software. These contests are usually settled easily, so long as the right evidence is there. For example, if you place copyright notices in the comments of an application's source code, then that information vaporizes as soon as the application is compiled, as comments don't end up in the compiled Assembly.

However, there are two attributes that you can place on an Assembly that will give you legally binding evidence that both the compiled Assembly and the source code belong to you (or your organization). Those attributes, usually found in the `AssemblyInfo.vb` file, look like this:

```
<Assembly: AssemblyCopyright("")>
<Assembly: AssemblyTrademark("")>
```

You use these attributes to fill in legal ownership information. The copyright information is the standard copyright information that you can assign to the Assembly. In order to fill in the trademark information, a lawyer will actually have to be involved.

Here's an example of a properly documented and copyrighted Assembly that uses these attributes. The following is a screenshot taken of an Assembly that Wrox produced for a recent book that contained a large sample web application:

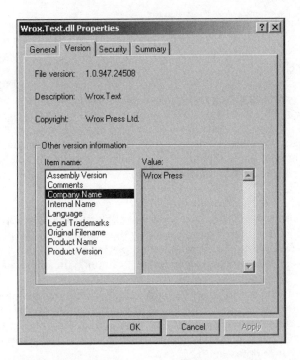

As you can see, the Copyright information is clearly visible. Also, contained in the dialog box you can see a navigation interface for browsing the other versioning information that belongs to the assembly.

Obfuscation

Obfuscation is the act of disguising code to make Reverse Engineering difficult. Obfuscate is a verb that means *to make obscure* or *darken* or *confuse*. Essentially this process changes symbol names, class names, method names, variable names, member names, and essentially any other metadata in your code to confusing, preferably randomly-generated names of some length. This produces Intermediate Language that is positively painful to read as a human and generally useless to a program that attempts to reverse engineer IL into C# or VB.NET.

Before you see *how* to obfuscate your code, there are a couple of things that should be mentioned first. The following point is something that you should make sure you keep in mind when thinking about obfuscation:

No obfuscation of your code is 100% perfect. There will always be *someone* who can reverse-engineer your code.

With that simple fact in mind, the key thing to remember is that your goal is to make your code complex enough to reverse engineer that it is not worth the time and money involved. In other words, the costs of reverse engineering your application should far outweigh any benefits involved.

Obfuscation tools work by taking namespaces, classes, method names, arguments, and public and private members and renaming them to something that is meaningless. Some obfuscators actually use some form of mathematical algorithm that generates the names. The problem with this is that algorithm itself can be reverse engineered, so it is possible for people with enough patience and ability to restore the original names and find that method entitled `DoSecretMathFormula()`, etc.

You can find countless obfuscation tools that are designed to obfuscate the IL stored in your assembly or application. The better tools will obfuscate an entire application (preventing you from having to worry about what the obfuscated name of a particular method might be) and will use an algorithm for replacing metadata that is one-way. That means that there is no mathematical algorithm that can undo the obfuscation changes.

Unfortunately, obfuscation only makes it hard to find something being looked for. The truly determined reverse engineer will find what they're looking for by reading every single line of IL code in your application until they find the information they need. The reason for this is that string constants and numeric literals are still completely visible in your IL code, even after obfuscation.

The following little snippet of code validates a serial number:

```vb
Sub Main()
    Dim licenseCode As String
    Dim codeValid As Boolean

    Console.WriteLine("Enter the license code:")
    licenseCode = Console.ReadLine()

    codeValid = False
    If licenseCode.Length = 14 Then
        If licenseCode.Chars(0) = "7" Then
            If licenseCode.Chars(13) = "7" Then
                codeValid = True
            End If
        End If
    End If

    If codeValid Then
        Console.WriteLine("Your code is valid")
    Else
        Console.WriteLine("Your code is invalid")
    End If
End Sub
```

The code validation rules require that the number start with 7, end with 7, and contains exactly 14 characters. This is a fairly simple algorithm but let's take a look at what our IL looks like for this before obfuscation. Use `ildasm.exe` to examine this:

```
ValidateNumber::Main : void()                                    _ □ ×
.method public static void  Main() cil managed
{
    .entrypoint
    .custom instance void [mscorlib]System.STAThreadAttribute::.ctor() = ( 01 00 00
    // Code size       109 (0x6d)
    .maxstack  3
    .locals init (bool V_0,
             string V_1)
    IL_0000:  ldstr       "Enter the license code:"
    IL_0005:  call        void [mscorlib]System.Console::WriteLine(string)
    IL_000a:  call        string [mscorlib]System.Console::ReadLine()
    IL_000f:  stloc.1
    IL_0010:  ldc.i4.0
    IL_0011:  stloc.0
    IL_0012:  ldloc.1
    IL_0013:  callvirt    instance int32 [mscorlib]System.String::get_Length()
    IL_0018:  ldc.i4.s    14
    IL_001a:  bne.un.s    IL_0053
    IL_001c:  ldloc.1
    IL_001d:  ldc.i4.0
    IL_001e:  callvirt    instance char [mscorlib]System.String::get_Chars(int32)
    IL_0023:  call        string [Microsoft.VisualBasic]Microsoft.VisualBasic.Compil
    IL_0028:  ldstr       "7"
    IL_002d:  ldc.i4.0
    IL_002e:  call        int32 [Microsoft.VisualBasic]Microsoft.VisualBasic.Compile

    IL_0033:  ldc.i4.0
    IL_0034:  bne.un.s    IL_0053
    IL_0036:  ldloc.1
    IL_0037:  ldc.i4.s    13
    IL_0039:  callvirt    instance char [mscorlib]System.String::get_Chars(int32)
    IL_003e:  call        string [Microsoft.VisualBasic]Microsoft.VisualBasic.Compil
    IL_0043:  ldstr       "7"
    IL_0048:  ldc.i4.0
    IL_0049:  call        int32 [Microsoft.VisualBasic]Microsoft.VisualBasic.Compile

    IL_004e:  ldc.i4.0
    IL_004f:  bne.un.s    IL_0053
    IL_0051:  ldc.i4.1
    IL_0052:  stloc.0
    IL_0053:  ldloc.0
    IL_0054:  brfalse.s   IL_0062
    IL_0056:  ldstr       "Your code is valid"
    IL_005b:  call        void [mscorlib]System.Console::WriteLine(string)
    IL_0060:  br.s        IL_006c
    IL_0062:  ldstr       "Your code is invalid"
    IL_0067:  call        void [mscorlib]System.Console::WriteLine(string)
    IL_006c:  ret
} // end of method ValidateNumber::Main
```

You can see everything in here from the 14-character length test, to the test of index 0 (`ldc.i4.0`) on the character string array, to the test of the ending character against the final index (13). After we run this code through an obfuscator, the main method will be renamed, the variables will all be renamed, and even the class and namespace could be renamed. The problem is that all of the method calls to all of the standard services (such as `StringType::StrCmp`) will all be completely visible, as will the numbers 14, 7, 13, and 0. Every numeric and string constant used in the code will be untouched by obfuscation.

As said, obfuscating your code makes it *difficult* to reverse-engineer but does not make it anywhere near *impossible* to reverse engineer. Always keep in mind that anything stored in literal form as a constant, a variable, an argument to a method, or even in a resource file, will be visible in your assembly somewhere. Your goal is either to make it so that the information that those literals convey is harmless, or that you do something within your code itself to further obscure the information, such as build various numbers or strings at run time to gain more benefits from obfuscation.

Let's take a look at an example of what obfuscation can do for us (and what it can't). We'll use an obfuscator from a company called 9rays.NET. This obfuscator uses a sequential algorithm to produce obfuscated member names. First, you need to load the assembly into `ildasm.exe`, and dump the contents into an `.IL` file, via File | Dump. The first screenshot shows what the obfuscator (and anyone with a decompiler) can see inside the IL code:

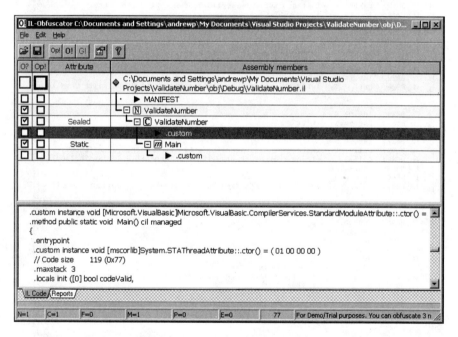

As you can see, there's a namespace called `ValidateNumber` (inserted by default with Visual Studio – Note that currently a namespace has to be present in the assembly), a class by the same name, and the `Main()` method. The main method is the first place people look for essential code logic. In a real-world example, there would be several classes with varying purposes and more complex IL code. Now let's at what the obfuscator does for this IL:

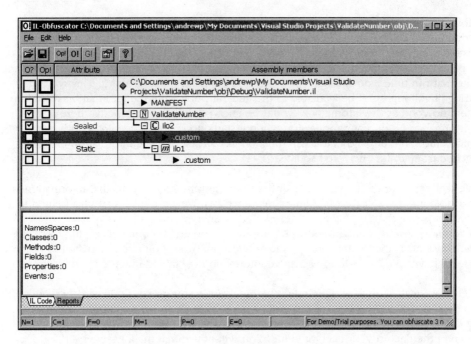

As you can see, many of the human-readable symbol names in the IL have been modified to something less than useful. However, you can see that there is a pattern and that there is a sequential order involved in the method renaming. It may be possible for someone with enough patience to figure out where the important code is, even with obfuscation.

The key here isn't to think that obfuscators will save your code from intrusion. The point is that obfuscating your code is something that is quick, painless, and easy to do before deploying your code, and it adds another measure of complexity to the task of decompiling.

Encryption

As early as the peak of the Egyptian empire and even earlier than that, encryption has been used to hide important information from the wrong eyes. Encryption will always be a reliable way of protecting your sensitive information (assuming the encryption algorithm itself is reliable). If your application needs to store information on disk that it needs to keep private, it can encrypt that data.

However, what about information that is *part* of your application? For example, the string literals that we talked about in the previous section on obfuscation are still visible to anyone with access to `ildasm.exe` or any other disassembler. One way to protect that information is to store the information at compile time in encrypted form. Then, at run time, you can decrypt the information and make use of it. This way, the string literal might still be available to the general public, but the information would do them no good as the information would be encrypted. If done properly, there is a performance hit on your application when it starts up so it can decrypt its private information, but beyond that it will function just as fast as if the information had been cached from an un-encrypted source.

We won't go into the in-depth use of the Cryptography API here, as that information is available in other .NET programming references. However, the general idea behind this concept is that the Cryptography API is used to encrypt the constants (probably through the use of some in-house development tool) and then the encrypted form of the constants is then compiled into the application. At no point does a customer or a hacker have any access to the sensitive information contained in the encrypted string

Here is a small sample of what might be involved in storing your private data in an encrypted format. This type of example is good because it makes no difference whether your assembly can be decompiled, anyone who does so won't be able to decrypt the data in your encrypted file. You will notice that the keys we used for encrypting and decrypting are stored as literal constants. Note that these constants will be visible to a decompiler, so for a production-quality application you might want to implement some misdirection to hide where the symbols are.

Below is some code that writes a string to a data file in encrypted form and then reads it (and decrypts it) and displays it to the user, showing how easy it is to protect your vital data from prying eyes.

```
Imports System
Imports System.IO
Imports System.Security.Cryptography
Imports System.Collections
Imports System.Resources

Module EncryptData
   Sub Main()
      Dim fs As FileStream
      Dim RMCrypto As RijndaelManaged
      Dim CryptStream As CryptoStream

      Dim Key As Byte() = {1, 2, 3, 4, 5, 6, 7, 8, 9, 10, 11, _
                           12, 13, 14, 15, 16}
      Dim IV As Byte() = {1, 2, 3, 4, 5, 6, 7, 8, 9, 10, 11, _
                          12, 13, 14, 15, 16}

      RMCrypto = New RijndaelManaged()
```

```
      If (Not (File.Exists("privatestuff.supersecretfile"))) Then
          fs = New FileStream("privatestuff.supersecretfile", _
                         FileMode.CreateNew)
        CryptStream = New CryptoStream(fs, _
                     RMCrypto.CreateEncryptor(Key, IV), _
                     CryptoStreamMode.Write)
        Dim SWriter As New StreamWriter(CryptStream)

        SWriter.WriteLine("Top Secret Value: 42")
        Console.WriteLine("Top Secret Information Written to the File")

        SWriter.Close()
        CryptStream.Close()

        fs.Close()
      End If

      fs = New FileStream("privatestuff.supersecretfile", FileMode.Open)

      CryptStream = New CryptoStream(fs, _
                   RMCrypto.CreateDecryptor(Key, IV), _
                   CryptoStreamMode.Read)
      Dim SReader As New StreamReader(CryptStream)

      Console.WriteLine("Line Read from File: " & SReader.ReadLine())
      SReader.Close()
      CryptStream.Close()
      fs.Close()
    End Sub
End Module
```

Here's what the encrypted file looks like in notepad:

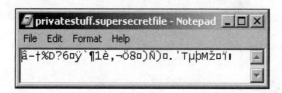

You can combine this technique with using Isolated Storage in your application to allow your application to still write secure, private information even if it was downloaded from the Internet (which, by default, does not have permission to write to the user's hard drive). Here's what the console output looks like, illustrating that the original line we wrote to the file is able to be read intact, even though it was encrypted:

Misdirection

Misdirection is yet another technique to avoid exposing the sensitive innards of your code to unwanted, prying eyes. If someone is determined enough to attempt to reverse-engineer a complex application, they have some experience. That experience has taught them where to look for sensitive information, and taught them how to recognize various patterns when looking at assembly code, and more recently, when looking at IL code. The problem with IL code is that it is so high level. It supports such notions as arrays, classes, instances, constructors, etc. This makes it easier to understand, interpret, and reverse-engineer than lower-level languages such as machine code and assembly language.

The concept behind misdirection is that the information you consider sensitive and private isn't located in the typical places to store private and hidden information. For example, when people store hidden information, a cursory attempt at hiding it from reverse engineering is to concatenate it from several string constants. This sort of thing is easy to detect and really doesn't fool anyone.

.NET assemblies can maintain internal resources that have string-type indexing. Often times these resources are used to store error messages, informational messages, warnings, or even globalization information such as various prompts stored in multiple languages. One caveat here is that error messages that provide a lot of useful information to the user can provide contextual clues about the operation of your application to a hacker. To avoid this people often include simple numbers and terse messages that only make sense to the application's developers when a customer calls the Tech Support line. These places are very common places to store non-sensitive, publicly visible information and most people looking to reverse-engineer an application spend little time glancing at public resources (unless they're searching for the clues mentioned above). This is what makes this location all the more appealing for storing your sensitive information. If you're worried about the occasional intruder that might actually find your information cleverly hidden out in the open, just encrypt the data in the resource and they can't immediately do anything with the information they find anyway.

> **The easiest way to make your code easy to reverse-engineer is to make private information *look like* private information. Consider various ways of misdirecting a potential intruder.**

Let's look at an example of how to use misdirection and why. In the previous example, you saw how to encrypt your private data to make it unreadable to people who have access to your application and its IL. To see where the problem is, let's look at this IL produced by the previous example:

```
EncryptData::Main : void()                                                _ □ ×
.method public static void  Main() cil managed
{
  .entrypoint
  .custom instance void [mscorlib]System.STAThreadAttribute::.ctor() = ( 01 00 00 00
  // Code size       402 (0x192)
  .maxstack  4
  .locals init (class [mscorlib]System.Security.Cryptography.CryptoStream V_0,
           class [mscorlib]System.IO.FileStream V_1,
           unsigned int8[] V_2,
           unsigned int8[] V_3,
           class [mscorlib]System.Security.Cryptography.RijndaelManaged V_4,
           class [mscorlib]System.IO.StreamReader V_5,
           class [mscorlib]System.IO.StreamWriter V_6,
           unsigned int8[] V_7)
  IL_0000:  nop
  IL_0001:  ldc.i4.s   16
  IL_0003:  newarr     [mscorlib]System.Byte
  IL_0008:  stloc.s    V_7
  IL_000a:  ldloc.s    V_7
  IL_000c:  ldc.i4.0
  IL_000d:  ldc.i4.1
  IL_000e:  stelem.i1
  IL_000f:  ldloc.s    V_7
```

The problem is that anyone with an IL reference manual can find out *exactly* what bytes are being used as our encryption keys. If a hacker gets hold of that data, they can just write their own application just as we did that will decrypt your file and get at the sensitive data contained within.

You have a couple of options, including using more encryption to actually encrypt your encryption key (we won't go into that here). Another option is to use misdirection to hide the various pieces of your encryption key in subtle places. If your code is suitably obfuscated and the bytes of your key are in separate places, the chances of someone deciphering the byte array are fairly small.

Copy the previous example to a new directory, EncryptData_Misdirection. Change the declaration of the byte array so that instead of referencing literals, it references members of other classes in other assemblies. This produces the following IL:

```
Module1::Main : void()                                              _ □ x
.method public static void  Main() cil managed
{
  .entrypoint
  .custom instance void [mscorlib]System.STAThreadAttribute::.ctor() = ( 01
  // Code size        458 (0x1ca)
  .maxstack  4
  .locals init (class [mscorlib]System.Security.Cryptography.CryptoStream V_
          class [mscorlib]System.IO.FileStream V_1,
          unsigned int8[] V_2,
          unsigned int8[] V_3,
          class [mscorlib]System.Security.Cryptography.RijndaelManaged V_4,
          class [mscorlib]System.IO.StreamReader V_5,
          class [mscorlib]System.IO.StreamWriter V_6,
          unsigned int8[] V_7)
  IL_0000:  nop
  IL_0001:  ldc.i4.s   16
  IL_0003:  newarr     [mscorlib]System.Byte
  IL_0008:  stloc.s    V_7
  IL_000a:  ldloc.s    V_7
  IL_000c:  ldc.i4.0
  IL_000d:  ldsfld     unsigned int8 [MiscAssembly1]MiscAssembly1.MiscClass1
  IL_0012:  stelem.i1
  IL_0013:  ldloc.s    V_7
```

As you can see, the references in this section of code are for other class members, and not for actual literals. If you examined the other classes, you might find those literals. However, if you obfuscate your code, and occasionally use a simple set of math to set up one or two of the bytes in your key, it should be *extremely* difficult for probing hackers to figure out your encryption key to load your data file and examine its contents.

There is a definite drawback to this approach: Misdirection generally creates somewhat sloppy looking code. The casual observer might think that the code was cluttered and unorganized because bits and pieces of values were strewn across the solution. You'll have to weigh the cost of misdirection against the benefit of making it even harder for someone to obtain access to your Intellectual Property.

Strong Naming

Identity theft is a big problem these days with credit cards, online commerce, check forgery, and many other crimes that are very damaging, annoying, and are often hard to prosecute. Unfortunately, Identity theft has worked its way into the programming world. This involves the way in which .NET assemblies reference other .NET assemblies, and the way in which Code Access Security (CAS) is enforced. We'll discuss each issue separately.

Weak References

As said before, a weak reference is a reference from one assembly to the other that does not involve the use of a complete strong name. This reference only uses an assembly filename, and possibly a version number or culture. There is no public key information to guarantee the authenticity of the Assembly being referenced.

This allows someone to replace your Assembly with their own, either circumventing logic in a desktop-deployed application, or to damage or shut down a public web site through other vulnerabilities that might exist in the web server application. Take, for example, a virus that came out a while ago that would send itself into a destination machine's IIS system and display some "You have been hacked" message to users. If a hacker had the ability to replace entire Assemblies of useful functions in your application, they could at best cripple your application, and at worst, completely hijack the functionality of it, stealing private information from your database and your customers.

The bottom line here is that the only way to combat the vulnerabilities made available by building applications with weak references is to build applications with strong references by strong-naming all of your assemblies.

To strong-name an assembly, as you learned in Chapter 5, you need to create a file that contains a public-private key pair that represents a digital signature. This digital signature is then used to sign each of your assemblies. No one else can create an assembly with the same digital signature as yours, so long as you are the only one with a copy of your signature file.

Every Assembly signed with the same .snk *file will have the same Public Key.*

The fact that every assembly signed with the same file has the same public key is a *very* important aspect of this procedure to remember. It has two important impacts: Strong references and Code Access Security. The importance of this is that the assemblies must all have the same public key to prove that they all came from the same source.

After you have created the central signature file that you will be using to sign all of the assemblies in your application, you can then create strong references, preventing anyone from producing an assembly that has the same strong name as yours. This means that it is impossible for someone to produce an assembly that will be called instead of your own authentic assemblies. It ensures that your application will always be using 100% authentic and verified legitimate assemblies at all times, regardless of how many copies of assemblies with the same file name reside on the customer's hard drive.

Code Access Security

Code Access Security is something that arrived with the .NET Framework and the Common Language Runtime. This facility allows administrators to define policies to dictate which permissions your various applications will have at the enterprise, network, machine, or even user level. For example, an administrator can indicate that by default, the entire enterprise gives full trust to all Microsoft code, but that specific machines run Microsoft code with less permissions enabled, such as local hard-drive file I/O. Microsoft code is either specified by a digital publisher certificate (such as those provided by Verisign) or by specifying the public key of assemblies produced by Microsoft. In fact, if you look at your security policy (In Administrative Tools under .NET Configuration) you'll see that there is already a code group set up for Microsoft code, giving it Full Trust.

The same thing can apply to your application. An administrator can grant to or take away from your application any privilege they like. Your application will not be able to do anything that the administrator doesn't want you to (assuming you don't exploit security holes such as COM Interop or Platform Invoke, if Platform Invoke has been permitted).

This should immediately raise a concern: if someone calls your code to accomplish a task that they themselves don't have permission to accomplish, they might be able to get around the security limitations. By default, security permissions are additive. In other words, you start with nothing and are granted permissions. If your code attempts to perform a task for which it has not been granted permission, the Common Language Runtime will throw an exception and your code will be prevented from performing that task. Also, it is very easy for an administrator to get the policy configured wrong and not explicitly deny permissions to a set of suspect code (there is an extra step involved in denying code permission rather than granting it).

So, how do you defend yourself? How do you prevent your application from being abused if it has been given a high security level? How do you prevent your application from being used by the wrong people?

Tighten Security

There is no way that you can anticipate all of the ways in which your application might be abused if someone manages to get into the system. They might use your application to discover private information that you thought was well concealed (for example, you provide a method called DecodeHiddenPassword() and don't obfuscate the method name) or they might use your application's trusted security status to destroy files on a customer's machine.

The best way to prevent this type of hijacking is to tighten your own security. Do not allow your code to do anything that could harm anything that your code uses. For example, if your code will never delete a file in normal operation, then *explicitly* define in the security policy that your code cannot delete files. If your application is being deployed to desktops, then ship a file containing the security policy that users can install. If your application is a web site, then make sure that you lock down the security settings on all of your web servers before you start up the web server. Your code should *only* be allowed to do those things that it must do to function properly. Any attempt to do anything beyond that should be considered an abuse of your code and you should have the Code Access Security feature block such attempts.

Prevent Code Abuse

Intellectual property isn't just static information sitting in your application. It is the control of your application itself. Intellectual property also concerns the way in which your application behaves. The fact that your application's business objects are used by your application's presentation tier should be considered a rule that deserves to be enforced.

The good news is that, assuming you followed the previous advice and strong-named every single assembly in your application, you can actually enforce this rule. By using the Code Access Security system within your code, you can write methods that simply will not execute unless the assembly calling the method was strong-named with a particular public key. This means that you can essentially create an attribute that indicates that only assemblies compiled by your company can call the method. Once this is done, any attempt by a third-party application that your company did not compile against your central SNK file to invoke methods on your assembly will fail. An exception will be thrown by the Runtime itself and the method will never be called.

Relocation

The last solution we'll discuss to prevent theft of Intellectual Property is hard to accomplish: simply don't give users any access to your intellectual property. What this means is that any code you consider sensitive that you want to be 100% tamper-proof will actually reside on *your* machine (or your company's). If you are deploying a Windows Forms application, the backend for that application might be exposed through a web service rather than deployed directly to the desktop. This prevents prying eyes from being able to disassemble your code, because the code simply won't be on the desktop. The same thing can be accomplished via Remoting. For example, you might deploy an intranet application to thousands of employees in a giant network of companies, but make sure the business layer for that application stays in a safe, protected location that is only accessible via Remoting. There are ways around this approach too, but if you've been following all of the advice gone through so far, the loopholes in this approach won't get the hacker or curious customer any more information than you want them to have anyway.

Theft

So far we've talked about the various ways that customers, hackers, and people outside your organization can gain access to intellectual property. One thing we haven't covered yet is how people *within* your organization can do damage with that same property. As much as we would like to deny it, the danger of a disgruntled employee simply walking out the door on their last day with vital trade secrets is a very real danger.

Some employees will actually accumulate trade secrets such as this throughout the term of their employment, to prepare for the day they leave the company. The more our applications rely on proprietary designs, trade secrets, and other vital, private information, the more vulnerable we are to attacks from within.

Some companies have policies that deny employees access to the vital information as soon as the employee gives notice to leave or is fired. The problem with that solution is that it assumes that the employee doesn't have a cache of the company's intellectual property sitting on their hard drive at home.

There are no really good solutions to this problem. Monitoring employees like a "Big Brother" typically results in low morale and resentment. Not monitoring employees at all can sometimes result in productivity loss and more property theft than would otherwise occur. The only solution is to reach a compromise of security that allows the programmers to feel respected and allows the company to feel as though its property is safe from theft.

Summary

This chapter has been about intellectual property, how people will try to take it from you, and how you can try and keep them from achieving their goals. We talked about the ways in which people can try to reverse-engineer your application, and what you can do to make the information obtained from reverse engineering as close to useless as possible. There is nothing you can do that will prevent people from stealing your intellectual property 100% of the time, but you can certainly prepare your organization and your application to make it so that if that theft occurs, minimal damage and loss will occur.

The key to securing your Intellectual Property *and* still being able to make a profit on your applications lies in the juggling act you must perform when balancing security versus resources. Each of the above solution ideas presented has a tradeoff: each takes a certain amount of development effort to produce. It is up to you to determine how much development effort and resource cost should be spent in preventing the potential loss of intellectual property. Unfortunately, the accuracy of your decision is only measurable if someone tries to take your Intellectual Property. At that point, your decisions were either accurate and you prevented the loss, or you made the wrong decision and hadn't tried hard enough to prevent it.

VB.NET

Deployment

Handbook

Appendix A

Using Active Directory to Deploy the .NET Framework

For a .NET application to be installed and run on any computer, that computer must have the .NET Framework installed. The .NET Framework Redistributable package is available as a standalone executable called Dotnetfx.exe. The redistributable package may be installed on a computer in various ways, such as through the Windows 2000 Active Directory, as we shall see in this appendix.

> **The redistributable package available from the Microsoft web site for download is called Dotnetredist.exe. This file contains the Dotnetfx.exe file that must be used for deployment. Double-click on Dotnetredist.exe to extract its contents.**

Client Computer Requirements

Before the .NET Framework can be installed on a client computer using Active Directory, that client computer must meet two criteria:

- ❑ It must meet the minimum configuration requirements in order to install the .NET Framework (see Chapter 2 for details).

- ❑ It must have Windows Installer Version 2.0 installed. Note that Windows Installer Version 2.0 itself is not designed for deployment through Active Directory.

Once these criteria have been met, the first task is to extract the Dotnetfx.exe file that will be used to deploy the .NET Framework.

Extracting Dotnetfx.exe

To extract the files from Dotnetfx.exe, use the following procedure: Firstly, open the command prompt and create a folder called C:\dotnetfx. Then use the following command to extract the files:

```
> dotnetfx.exe /T:C:\dotnetfx /C
```

Next, check that the contents of the folder have been correctly extracted.

Once the contents have been verified, move the dotnetfx folder and its contents to the network location that you wish to use for deployment.

Creating an Active Directory Software Installation Package

The next step in creating an Active Directory software installation package is to open the Active Directory Users and Computers MMC snap-in located under Administrative Tools.

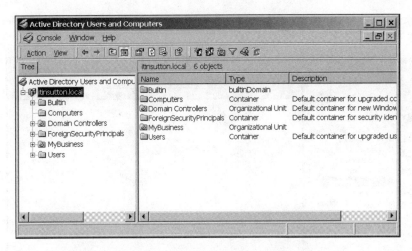

Right-click on the domain name and select Properties. Select the Group Policy tab from the Properties dialog box.

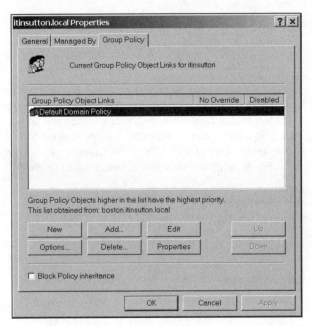

Now click the Edit button to display the Group Policy window. There are two alternatives to choose from when deciding how your software will be installed:

❑ Computer Configuration – This option is used to set policies that are applied to computers no matter who logs on to them.

❑ User Configuration – This option is used to set policies that are applied to users no matter which computer they log on to.

247

For the purposes of this demonstration, expand the User Configuration node and select Software Settings.

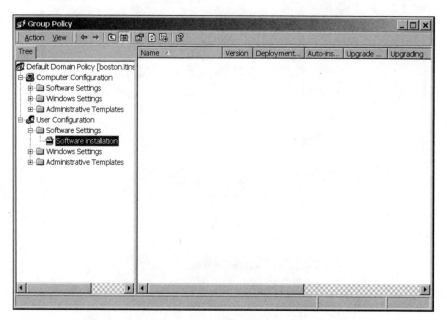

To create a new package, right-click on Software installation and select New | Package... to open a dialog box from which you can navigate to the network share (navigate to the share name not the folder) that contains our dotnetfx folder and select the netfx.msi file. Once you have pressed OK you will be presented with the Deploy Software dialog box that allows you to select the deployment method. For the purposes of this demonstration, choose Advanced published or assigned and press OK.

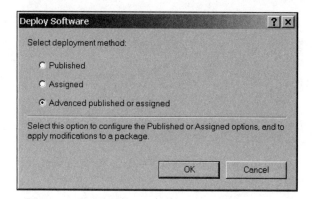

You will now be presented with a Properties dialog box. On the Deployment tab you can choose Assigned to install the package on all computers in the domain the next time they boot up, or Published to allow users to install the package if they wish to. For the purposes of this demonstration, choose Published.

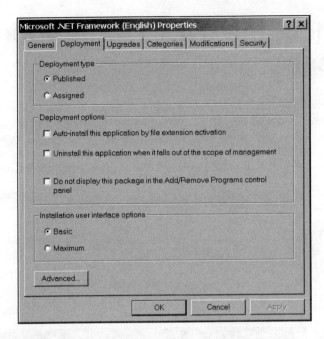

The package will be added to the **Group Policy** window and be available for users to install from their machines.

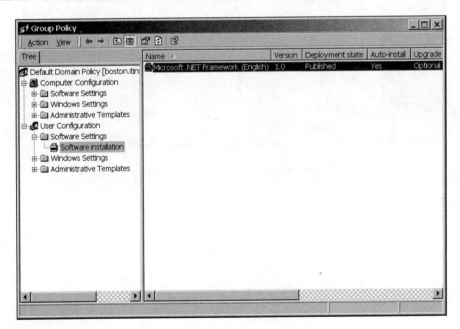

Installing the .NET Framework Package

In this demonstration we published the package so that it does not install itself automatically the next time the user starts their computer, as would have been the case if we had assigned the package. To see how a user can install our package, log on to a client computer that is part of the domain. From the Control Panel select Add or Remove Programs. Click the Add New Programs button and the .NET Framework package should appear in the list of available packages in the Add programs from your network: section.

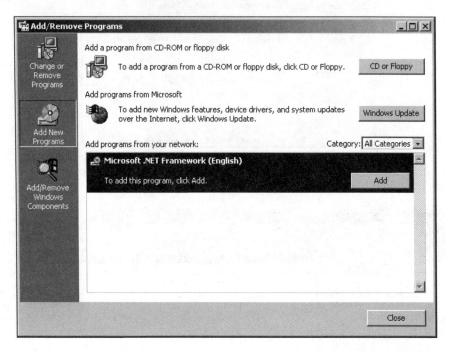

We can click the Add button to install the package (providing the computer meets the minimum requirements stated earlier).

VB.NET

Deployment

Handbook

Appendix B

B

Deploying the .NET Framework with an Application

In this appendix we will demonstrate how to create a single setup program that will first install the .NET Framework, if necessary, and then your .NET application. We will use Microsoft's `setup.exe` bootstrapper example that can be downloaded from http://msdn.microsoft.com/downloads/default.asp?URL=/code/sample.asp?url=/msdn-files/027/001/830/msdncompositedoc.xml.

The `setup.exe` bootstrapper example consists of two files:

❑ `setup.exe` – This file launches both the `Dotnetfx.exe` file used to install the .NET Framework and your .NET application's `.msi` file. It is written using unmanaged code because it must be able to run on a computer that does not yet have the .NET Framework installed.

❑ `settings.ini` – This file is used by `setup.exe` to determine the locations of `Dotnetfx.exe` and your .NET application's `.msi` file, the language version of the .NET Framework that is required, and any custom strings used in dialog boxes by `setup.exe`.

The `setup.exe` bootstrapper performs the following three actions:

1. It checks the registry of the target computer to see if the specified version of the .NET Framework is installed.

2. If the specified version is not installed, it launches a silent installation of `Dotnetfx.exe` (a reboot may be required).

3. It installs your .NET application. If a reboot is required in the previous stage, it is suppressed until the .NET application has finished installing.

Detecting if the .NET Framework is Installed

The `setup.exe` bootstrapper checks the version number obtained from the `Dotnetfx.exe` file against the following registry key:

```
HKLM\SOFTWARE\Microsoft\.NETFramework\policy\v1.0
```

If there is not a match, the .NET Framework will be installed. If you want to check for the language version you must specify the culture name in the `settings.ini` file (more on this later), otherwise the English language version is installed by default. The following screenshot shows the relevant registry key.

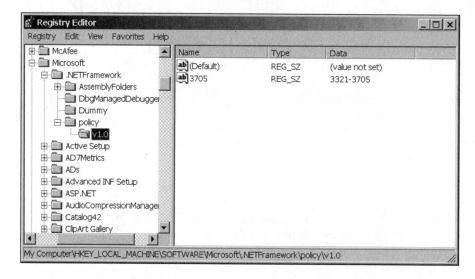

Detecting if MDAC is Installed

For any .NET applications that include data access, MDAC 2.6 or later must be installed. The `setup.exe` bootstrapper can be extended to include a silent installation of `MDAC_typ.exe`, which is a standalone executable used to install MDAC.

The `setup.exe` bootstrapper will check the following registry key to see if the value of `FullInstallVer` is 2.6 or greater:

```
HKLM\SOFTWARE\Microsoft\DataAccess
```

The following screenshot shows the relevant registry key.

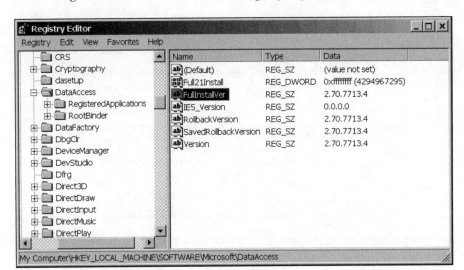

For more details, see http://support.microsoft.com/default.aspx?scid=kb;EN-US;q257604.

Customizing the Installation

The `setup.exe` bootstrapper uses an external file called `settings.ini` to determine the following:

❑ The locations of `Dotnetfx.exe` and your .NET application's `.msi` file

❑ The language version of the .NET Framework you wish to install

❑ Any custom strings for `setup.exe` to use in dialog boxes during the installation

You can create a `settings.ini` file manually or customize the one provided by Microsoft in the download. The file must contain the path to both the `Dotnetfx.exe` and your .NET applications `.msi` file, which can be specified as absolute or relative paths. All other settings are optional.

The following example gives absolute paths to `DemoAppSetup.msi` and `Dotnetfx.exe` (note that the name of the `.msi` file must be specified, but only the path to `Dotnetfx.exe` should be specified), and supplies a value of `DemoApp` for the `ProductName` key:

```
[Bootstrap]
Msi=C:\Deployment\DemoAppSetup\Debug\DemoAppSetup.msi
'LanguageDirectory=
ProductName=DemoApp
```

```
'DialogText=
'CaptionText=
'ErrorCaptionText=
FxInstallerPath=C:\Deployment\dotnetfx
```

If you specify the `ProductName` key without the `DialogText` or `CaptionText` keys, the user will be presented with a dialog box like the following when they run `setup.exe`.

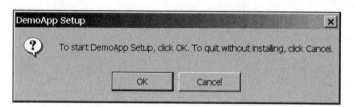

If the `ProductName` key is not specified, **Application Setup** will be displayed to the user. If you wish to customize the message to your users, you can specify the `DialogText` and `CaptionText` keys, as the following example demonstrates:

```
[Bootstrap]
Msi=C:\Deployment\DemoAppSetup\Debug\DemoAppSetup.msi
'LanguageDirectory=
ProductName=DemoApp
DialogText=Welcome - Click OK to install DemoApp or Cancel to quit.
CaptionText=This is the DemoApp setup program
'ErrorCaptionText=
FxInstallerPath=C:\Deployment\dotnetfx
```

This version of `settings.ini` will produce the following dialog box.

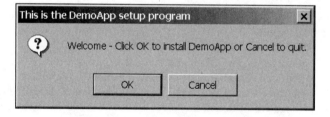

You can also customize the `ErrorCaptionText` that will be displayed to the user upon a setup error. For instance, you could specify the following:

```
ErrorCaptionText=My DemoApp Error Text
```

If an error occurs, the user will see the following dialog box.

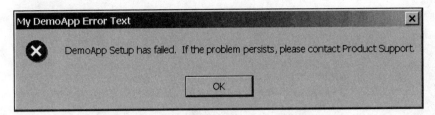

If you need to install a language version of the .NET Framework other than the default English version, you can do that by specifying the LanguageDirectory key. For example, the following will specify the German language version of Dotnetfx.exe:

```
LanguageDirectory=de
```

Supplying a Readme File

It is good practice to supply a readme file along with your setup package. At a minimum this should include setup instructions and the minimum requirements to run your .NET application. For example, the .NET Framework requires Windows 98 or later and .NET applications that use data access require MDAC 2.6 or later. If there are any extra requirements for you application, you should specify these as well.

VB.NET

Deployment

Handbook

Appendix C

An AutoDeploy Component

Throughout this book you have seen examples of different kinds of deployments. The example developed here was written by Rockford Lhotka and is Chapter 4 of *Visual Basic .NET Solutions Toolkit* (ISBN: 1-86100-739-6). It loads and executes code from both DLLs and EXEs on a client machine *without* having to manually copy files.

Note that this only works with .NET DLLs and EXEs. If the application also includes COM components, they will need to be deployed and registered using traditional deployment methods.

Scenario

When deploying a networked Windows Forms application the biggest challenge is getting the application out to the client workstations. In VB6/COM DLL versioning issues, the Windows Registry, and so forth, complicated this. The .NET platform solves these issues, allowing us to deploy applications by simply copying files to the client machine.

However, copying files to hundreds or thousands of client machines is still a big issue. It would be great to have true *zero touch* installation of applications, so they auto-deploy to the client workstations as needed. With minimal code, .NET provides this functionality virtually out of the box. All that's required is that the client machines have the .NET Runtime installed.

Technology

The technology required to auto-deploy assemblies to a client is built into the .NET Framework via reflection. Reflection allows us to write code that examines and interacts with .NET assemblies, types, and objects. We can use reflection to dynamically load an assembly into memory from a URL (or the hard drive). Once the assembly is in memory, reflection allows us to interact with it.

We can place .NET assemblies in a virtual directory on a web server, and .NET can download the files to each client machine automatically. On the server this requires nothing special, just a virtual directory or other directory that can be accessed via URL from the client. Into that directory we can place all the EXE and DLL files required by our application. The web directory does not need to be browsable, nor does it need any aspx, asmx, or other web-related files.

Once the files are accessible via a URL, the client workstation can use them. In fact, it is possible to simply create a web page with a link to the remote executable. When the user clicks on that link, .NET will automatically download the EXE and run it on the client. If the EXE depends on any DLLs, they will also be automatically downloaded as needed.

These automatically downloaded files are placed into a user-specific client-side cache. On subsequent attempts to run the application, the cached version is checked against the server version and any updates are downloaded automatically. If updates are not required, the cached version is run.

There are three problems with the standard implementation:

1. If you create a desktop shortcut or attempt to use Start|Run to launch an application via URL, the browser will appear, then disappear and the program will launch. This is because any use of a URL invokes the browser, which then detects that it isn't needed and so it goes away.

2. There is a bug in .NET that prevents auto-downloaded code from using the SoapFormatter or BinaryFormatter to deserialize objects. This can be a serious limitation in application design since it precludes the use of distributed objects.

3. If the web server has .NET installed, the application will be unable to read its configuration file. All files with a .config extension are unavailable for download after ASP.NET is installed on a server. This precludes the use of normal application configuration files for auto-downloaded code, and that is a serious problem in many cases.

Fortunately, with a small amount of code wrapped into a reusable library, we can overcome all three limitations. We will be able to auto-download applications from a URL using a desktop shortcut or from Start|Run without the annoying browser flicker. The auto-downloaded application will be able to deserialize objects and can employ distributed object technology, and we'll have a partial, but good, solution to the configuration file issue.

If the assembly is an EXE available via a URL, we'll be able to launch the program from the client, causing .NET to auto-deploy a .NET program from a URL to our client workstation and then run it. This allows us to run virtually any .NET program on our client workstation, with the only deployment effort being to put the program's files into a virtual root on the web server.

If the assembly is a DLL available via a URL, we'll be able to create objects by using the classes defined in the DLL. The DLL will be automatically downloaded to the client and loaded into the client process. Once that's done we can create instances of objects from the DLL and use them within our application. This allows client-side applications to dynamically access DLLs from a web server as needed.

In either case, any other DLLs that our auto-deployed EXE or DLL require will be auto-deployed to the client on demand, with no extra work on our part at all. .NET automatically detects when an EXE or DLL requires another DLL, and it automatically goes back to the directory or URL where the original file came from to look for any of these required files. If the file is not available, then the application will fail. This can happen because the file doesn't exist at the URL, or because the network has become unavailable.

For instance, say you run an EXE from a URL. If that EXE requires a DLL, .NET will automatically detect this and will automatically look at that same URL to find the DLL. If the DLL is there, it will be automatically downloaded to the client. If it is not there, the application will fail because the DLL is unavailable. This is no different from putting a program into a local directory on the client hard drive. You are effectively using a remote URL as if it were a local directory.

Design

Though not a lot of code is required to implement the auto-deployment functionality, it is very powerful code.

Remember that this code will all be running on the client machine. On the server the only requirement is that we set up a virtual directory or other web directory accessible via URL into which our application files (EXEs and DLLs) will be placed.

You need to understand how this works at a high level. On the client, you need to manually deploy both the .NET Runtime (if it isn't already installed) and a bit of custom code to each client to start from. Typically this custom code will be in the form of a program that the user launches, and then this program will use auto-deploy to invoke any other assemblies that are required. You can think of this program as a client-side launcher or shell application.

Preventing Browser-flicker

By having a client-side launcher, we are able to prevent the **browser flicker** effect that occurs when an application is run from a URL via a desktop shortcut, or the Start|Run command. The client-side launcher causes .NET to download and run the application, bypassing the need to invoke the browser at all.

Of course this client-side launcher or shell application must be deployed to the client first. This is typically done by creating a standard setup program to install the launcher, or by using XCopy to get it to the client workstation. As you'll see, the launcher can be totally generic and so this is typically a one-time effort, after which we can auto-download all of our applications as needed.

The class we'll create here can be used to create a variety of launcher applications ranging from a generic launcher that can run any .NET program from an URL to a cohesive MDI menuing application that dynamically creates its menus, and loads its components, using auto-deployment.

As stated earlier, there are two caveats we need to address in this launcher class. First, auto-deployed code is treated a bit differently from code from a local source and so we need to catch an event from the `AppDomain` to ensure that deep serialization (deserialization using the `SoapFormatter` or `BinaryFormatter`) works properly for auto-downloaded code. Second, an auto-deployed EXE can't read its own configuration file. Instead, it will use the one from the EXE we originally ran on the client.

Solving the Deserialization Issue

In the auto-deployment class itself, we'll include code that catches the event that occurs when deserialization fails and we'll fix the issue. This will allow our auto-deployed code to use all the features of .NET.

The problem with deserialization is this. Auto-downloaded assemblies are loaded into our client `AppDomain` just fine, but within the `AppDomain` there are two separate lists of assemblies. One list contains assemblies loaded locally; the other list contains auto-downloaded assemblies. Almost all code in .NET treats these two lists the same, but the `SoapFormatter` and `BinaryFormatter` only look at the local list when deserializing objects, and so they fail to find the assembly containing the appropriate code. When this happens, the `AppDomain` raises an event indicating that there was a failure to locate the assembly. We can handle this event, providing a reference to the 'missing' assembly by merely scanning the complete list of assemblies loaded in the `AppDomain` to find the one it needs.

Supporting Application Configuration Files

As noted earlier, files ending in a `.config` extension are not available for download from a web server when ASP.NET has been installed. Therefore, our application configuration files will become unavailable when provided through IIS. The ability to have a configuration file with an `<appSettings>` block is very powerful and is a feature you wouldn't want to lose just because your clients are auto-downloading the code.

Before we get too far into this, remember that an auto-downloaded program is not written in any special way. A .NET EXE run from a local installation can be auto-deployed simply by placing it into a virtual directory and then launching it from the client. The caveat is that it then loses access to its configuration file.

What we really want is a way for a program to automatically detect whether it is auto-downloaded so it can read the local configuration file if running directly from the hard drive, or a remote configuration file if it was auto-deployed.

To solve this issue, we'll create a class that is a drop-in replacement for `System.Configuration.ConfigurationSettings`, providing transparent access to either the local application configuration file or a remote configuration file, depending on whether the EXE was launched via auto-deployment or directly.

Any application using our new `ConfigurationSettings` class will run as normal when run locally from a hard drive, and will also run just fine when run via auto-deployment.

The final issue is one of security. All auto-deployed code runs in a sandbox and thus will have restricted security. In fact, .NET SP1 precludes running remote code entirely by default. When the .NET Runtime is installed on a client workstation, the installation includes the tools necessary to change security for a specific URL, so that we can grant the appropriate level of trust to our remote code and so run it safely on the client workstations. Alternatively, we could strongly name your executables and assemblies so that the local client code will specifically allow signed assemblies to execute with enough permissions from that location, This means we don't need to alter the security settings on every client machine. However, strong-naming assemblies is out of scope for this book.

Implementation

The following is the complete code with an explanation for each important section.

Create a new file called `AutoDeploy.vb`, and create two classes in this project: one to launch or load EXE and DLL files via URL, and one to take care of remote application configuration files. Ensure the root namespace has been removed in Visual Studio .NET by inspecting the property pages.

Launcher Class

The `Launcher` class will dynamically create an object from a DLL that is accessible via a URL. It will also include functionality to run an EXE that is accessible via a URL, and will contain the code to work around the bug with deserialization, as mentioned earlier.

As you'll see later, this class can be used to create a generic launcher application, or a shell program, to dynamically run code on the client. The `Launcher` class itself will run on the client and it auto-downloads any required DLL or EXE files as required. The `System.Xml` and `System.Collections.Specialized` namespaces have been imported for use in the next class, but they are shown here:

```
Imports System.Reflection
Imports System.Xml
Imports System.Collections.Specialized

Namespace Wrox.Toolkit.Util
  Public Class Launcher
    Private Sub New()
      ' Prevent instantiation of the class
    End Sub

    Private Shared Sub New()
      Dim CurrentDomain As AppDomain = AppDomain.CurrentDomain

      AddHandler CurrentDomain.AssemblyResolve, _
        AddressOf MyResolveEventHandler
    End Sub
```

This defines a class that cannot be instantiated; we want this behavior because the methods we'll be adding are shared and so there is no need to create an instance of the `Launcher` class.

We've also defined a shared constructor. The shared constructor method will be automatically called before any other method on the class is invoked, so we can use it to initialize any members of this class. We'll be defining a handler method later and this attaches the method to the `AssemblyResolve` event.

Now let's add a shared method to create an object from an auto-deployed DLL. Add this method to the class:

```
Public Shared Function GetObject(ByVal AssemblyURL As String, _
                                 ByVal TypeName As String) _
                                 As Object

    Dim RemoteAssembly As [Assembly]

    RemoteAssembly = [Assembly].LoadFrom(AssemblyURL)
    Return RemoteAssembly.CreateInstance(TypeName)
End Function
```

This method uses the LoadFrom() method of the Assembly class to load an assembly from a URL. The result of this method call is that the client-side cached assembly version is compared to the version on the URL, and the assembly is automatically downloaded from the server to the client if it isn't present locally, or if the client version is out of date. It is placed in a local cache for the current user. To see what is in the current user's cache we can use the gacutil command-line utility:

> **gacutil -ldl**

This will list all the assemblies in the current user's download cache.

Once the assembly has been downloaded, it is also loaded into memory in the current process. This makes all its types available for our use. The final line of code in the method creates an instance of the requested type and returns it as a result.

A similar thing happens when downloading an EXE from a URL. Add the following method to the class:

```
Public Shared Sub RunApplication(ByVal AssemblyURL As String)
    Dim RemoteAssembly As [Assembly]

    RemoteAssembly = [Assembly].LoadFrom(AssemblyURL)
    AppDomain.CurrentDomain.SetData("RemoteEXE", AssemblyURL)
    RemoteAssembly.EntryPoint.Invoke(RemoteAssembly.EntryPoint, _
                                     Nothing)
End Sub
```

Again, we are using the LoadFrom() method on the Assembly class to download the assembly to the client's cache and to load the assembly into memory.

However instead of creating an instance of a specific class, in this case we are launching an application. All .NET applications have a specific method called an **entry point**. The entry point is the method that the .NET runtime calls to launch the application, and the compiler creates it automatically when we build any application. The assembly object dynamically loaded has an `EntryPoint()` method, which returns a reference to this special method. In addition, we have set some data in the current domain to indicate that a remote assembly has been called. This will add further functionality to the application, as we shall see later.

Any DLLs required by this EXE will be automatically downloaded from the same URL by .NET. No extra work or special coding is required for this to happen – it's automatic. Using the `EntryPoint` property, we can call its `Invoke()` method to run that method – effectively launching the application just as if we were the CLR itself. The result is that the application begins running as it would normally.

As we mentioned earlier, auto-deployed code is loaded differently from locally loaded code, and because of a bug in the Soap and Binary formatter objects we are unable to deserialize objects in auto-deployed code without raising an error. Fortunately we can avoid this error by trapping an event on the `AppDomain` object.

Let's add the event handler to the class:

```
Private Shared Function MyResolveEventHandler( _
                ByVal sender As Object, _
                ByVal args As ResolveEventArgs) _
                As [Assembly]
  ' Get a list of all the assemblies loaded in our appdomain
  Dim Assemblies() As [Assembly] = _
    AppDomain.CurrentDomain.GetAssemblies()

  ' Search the list to find the assembly that was not found
  ' and return the assembly from the list
  Dim asm As [Assembly]
  For Each asm In Assemblies
    If asm.FullName = args.Name Then
      Return asm
    End If
  Next
End Function
End Class
```

The problem is that, even though the auto-deployed assembly is loaded into memory, the deserialization code only scans through the list of *locally* loaded assemblies. Thus it is unable to find our dynamically loaded assembly when it tries to do the deserialization.

To overcome this, all we need to do is loop through the list of assemblies loaded in our `AppDomain` (which *does* include the dynamically loaded ones) and return a reference to the assembly.

When .NET fails to find an assembly, the `AppDomain` object raises an `AssemblyResolve` event, allowing us to dynamically resolve the assembly on its behalf. All we have to do is handle this event with the code we just wrote, and that happens in the shared constructor, as shown earlier.

Since the shared constructor is always called before the `GetObject()` and `RunApplication()` methods, we can be certain that the class is initialized and the event handler registered before any assemblies are dynamically loaded.

That's the end of this class, but we now need to add another class, `ConfigurationSettings`, to this namespace.

ConfigurationSettings Class

At this point, we have everything we need to create objects from dynamically loaded and auto-deployed DLLs. We also have everything we need to launch any .NET executable from a URL as long as that program doesn't use an application configuration file.

The thing to consider with configuration files is that they are loaded automatically, and the runtime always loads the configuration file for the currently running program. This will always be our shell or launcher program, rather than the dynamically loaded EXE.

As mentioned earlier, we're typically auto-deploying our EXE from a web server, and if that web server has ASP.NET installed, then you cannot access any files ending in a `.config` extension. This file extension is protected so that no one can read a `web.config` file, for instance. While this is a very good security feature in most cases, it does get in the way when you want to use the configuration file in auto-downloaded code.

What we'll do to overcome these issues is to create a clone of the `ConfigurationSettings` class from the .NET Framework, which understands auto-deployment. If the program has been auto-deployed, this new `ConfigurationSettings` class will read a `.remoteconfig` file from the URL, instead of trying to read the `.config` file.

The `.remoteconfig` file might be created by simply copying an existing `.config` file. As implemented here, the code will read the `<appSettings>` element from the `.remoteconfig` file assuming the same syntax as if it were in a regular `.config` file.

This is the one change that needs to be made to the dynamically launched EXE for it to work correctly with the launcher code: it will need to use `Wrox.Toolkit.Util.ConfigurationSettings` instead of `System.Configuration.ConfigurationSettings`. Other than this one small compromise, we'll have created an infrastructure where any .NET EXE can be launched via a URL.

Create a new class in this namespace:

```
Imports System.Xml
Imports System.Collections.Specialized
...
   Public Class ConfigurationSettings

      Private Shared LocalCache As NameValueCollection

      Private Sub New()
        ' Prevent instantiation of the class
      End Sub
```

Since the only method on this class will be shared, we're preventing an object from being created from external code by implementing a private `New()` method.

We're declaring a shared variable named _Cache as well. The configuration file should only be read once, since it requires us to go back to the server to get the file. After we've loaded it the first time, we'll cache the results in this variable.

The only part of the configuration file that we'll support in this case is the `<appSettings>` element. Since this is simple XML, we'll just load the remote configuration file into an `XmlDocument` and read through it.

Of course we only want to use the remote configuration file in the case that we're being launched via auto-deployment. Remember that there is no reason the application can't be run from a local hard drive instead of from a URL, except because of this `.config` file issue. To make sure it works as expected when run directly from a hard drive, it should read from a regular `.config` file. However, when run via auto-download from a URL, it should read from a `.remoteconfig` file. This way we not only support both scenarios, but we have an easy way to have some different application configuration settings for auto-downloaded code from locally deployed code.

All you need to do now is check to see if the application is being run locally or remotely. Remember that there was a line in the `RunApplication()` method as follows:

```
AppDomain.CurrentDomain.SetData("RemoteEXE", AssemblyURL)
```

This line of code puts the URL of the remote EXE into the application domain's shared memory space as a name-value pair. The value is now available to any code running in the AppDomain; including the ConfigurationSettings class.

It's time to add some more code to the ConfigurationSettings class. Since we're only dealing with the <appSettings> element, a typical .remoteconfig file might look like this:

```xml
<?xml version="1.0" encoding="utf-8" ?>
<configuration>
  <appSettings>
    <add key="MyValue" value="Remote" />
  </appSettings>
</configuration>
```

This is no different from what would be put in a standard .config file, which is good news, since we're trying to keep as much parity as possible between code run locally and code run via a URL.

First, we'll write a method that reads a configuration file's <appSettings> element into a NameValueCollection. The NameValueCollection is the type returned by the usual AppSettings property:

```vbnet
Private Shared Function LoadSettings(ByVal config As String) _
                        As NameValueCollection
    Dim col As New NameValueCollection()

    Dim xml As New XmlDocument()
    xml.Load(config)
    Dim root As XmlElement = _
       xml.GetElementsByTagName("configuration").Item(0)
    Dim settings As XmlElement = _
       root.GetElementsByTagName("appSettings").Item(0)

    Dim cmd As XmlElement
    For Each cmd In settings.ChildNodes
      Select Case cmd.Name
        Case "add"
          col.Add(cmd.GetAttribute("key"), _
                  cmd.GetAttribute("value"))
        Case "clear"
          col.Clear()
      End Select
    Next

    Return col
End Function
```

Given the name of a configuration file, this function simply finds the `<appSettings>` element and uses its instructions to populate a `NameValueCollection`. This collection is then returned as the result of the function.

Notice that this method is `Private`. Before it is called, we need to determine if we are running directly from the hard drive or via auto-deployment, so we know which `appSettings` to return. If we're running from the hard drive, then we should just use the normal `.config` file, while if we're running from a URL then we should return the `.remoteconfig` file.

Add this property (which is the same as the method signature as that on the `System.Configuration.ConfigurationSettings` class):

```
Public Shared ReadOnly Property AppSettings As NameValueCollection
  Get
    Dim URL As String = _
      AppDomain.CurrentDomain.GetData("RemoteEXE")

    If Not (URL Is Nothing Or String.Empty) Then
      ' We are running remote exe and need to load config manually
      If LocalCache Is Nothing Then
        Try
          LocalCache = LoadSettings(URL & ".remoteconfig")
        Catch
          LocalCache = New NameValueCollection()
        End Try
      End If

      Return LocalCache
    Else
      ' We are running normally and can just use regular config
      Return _
        System.Configuration.ConfigurationSettings.AppSettings
    End If
  End Get
End Property
End Class
End Namespace
```

This property retrieves the URL of the application (if any) and uses this value to determine if we're running locally or remotely. Remember that this value won't exist unless the program was run via `Launcher` so it can be used to detect if we are local or remote.

If we are remote, the URL is used to derive the name of the `.remoteconfig` file, which is then loaded and the resulting `NameValueCollection` is returned. If we are local, then `AppSettings` from `System.Configuration` is returned.

This can now be compiled as `AutoDeploy.dll`.

Demonstration

To demonstrate how `AutoDeploy` is used, we need to create two projects – a shell launcher application that we'll call `Launcher`, and a test program (`TestApp`) that is launched remotely.

Any shell program can be as simple as a program to launch a remote EXE or a complete client-side application that dynamically loads DLLs via a URL. This shell program must be installed on the client either via a standard setup program, or via XCopy, and the client machine must already have the .NET Runtime installed as well.

The test program is a simple Windows Forms application; the only difference is that it needs to use `Wrox.Toolbox.Util.ConfigurationSettings`, instead of `System.Configuration.ConfigurationSettings`, to retrieve its `.config` file. For this example, we'll also create a simple class that uses serialization to establish that deserialization works in the code.

This application should be placed in a virtual directory or web directory that is accessible from the client via a URL. From there, it will be auto-downloaded to the client by the CLR.

Create a new Windows Application and name it `TestApp`, renaming `Form1.vb` to `TestApp.vb`, and the `Form1` form to `TestApp`. Add a reference to the `AutoDeploy` assembly through the **Add References** dialog. Remove the default namespace in the Property pages.

Add a class to the project that contains the following:

```
<Serializable()> _
Public Class SampleObject
   Implements ICloneable
   Private SomeData As Integer

   Public Function Clone() As Object Implements ICloneable.Clone
     Dim Buffer As New IO.MemoryStream()
     Dim MyFormatter As _
       New Runtime.Serialization.Formatters.Binary.BinaryFormatter()

     MyFormatter.Serialize(Buffer, Me)
     Buffer.Position = 0
     Return MyFormatter.Deserialize(Buffer)
   End Function
End Class
```

This is a simple, but serializable class that contains a `Clone()` method that uses deep serialization to make an exact duplicate of the original object.

Now add two buttons to `TestApp` named `btnClone` and `btnConfig`. At the top of `TestApp`, place an `Imports` statement:

```
Imports Wrox.Toolkit.Util
```

Then put the following code behind the two buttons:

```
    Private Sub btnClone_Click(ByVal sender As System.Object, _
                               ByVal e As System.EventArgs) _
                               Handles btnClone.Click
      Dim obj As New SampleObject()
      obj = CType(obj.Clone(), SampleObject)
      MsgBox("Clone worked OK")
    End Sub

    Private Sub btnConfig_Click(ByVal sender As System.Object, _
                                ByVal e As System.EventArgs) _
                                Handles btnConfig.Click

      MsgBox("Config setting: " & _
        ConfigurationSettings.AppSettings ("MyValue"))
    End Sub
```

The first button simply creates an instance of `Class1` and clones it – establishing that deserialization works in the auto-deployed code.

The second button retrieves a value from the application configuration file. When auto-downloaded from a URL, it should retrieve the value from the `.remoteconfig` file, and when run directly from a hard drive, it should retrieve the value from the `.config` file.

Add an application configuration file to the project in Visual Studio by using Project | Add New Item. Name it `TestApp.exe.config` and create the following entries:

```
    <?xml version="1.0" encoding="utf-8" ?>
    <configuration>
      <appSettings>
        <add key="MyValue" value="Run from hard drive" />
      </appSettings>
    </configuration>
```

In the Solution Explorer click the Show All Files button so the `bin` directory is visible, and then move this `.config` file into this directory. Now hide those files again. Notice that the `bin` directory remains visible since it now contains a non-hidden file.

Do the same thing to create a `TestApp.exe.remoteconfig` file in the bin directory
with the following:

```xml
<?xml version="1.0" encoding="utf-8" ?>
<configuration>
  <appSettings>
    <add key="MyValue" value="Auto-deployed from URL" />
  </appSettings>
</configuration>
```

Note the different value in each file.

Now build the solution. Using the Internet Services Manager found under
Administrative Tools, create a virtual root or web directory and copy the `TestApp\bin`
directory's contents into that web directory.

> *Technically the PDB (debug) files are not required, only the DLLs,*
> `.config` *and* `.remoteconfig` *files are needed.*

Use the .NET Framework Configuration tool found under Administrative Tools to add a
security entry for this web directory (URL) and give it a setting of `FullTrust`. To do
this, right-click on the LocalIntranet_Zone entry and choose New to launch a wizard that
walks through the process of defining the URL and the trust level desired. The result is
a new node in the security configuration:

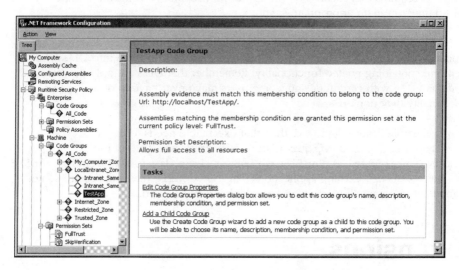

Now you can create a launcher application. Create a new Windows Application project
and name it `Launcher`. Add a reference to the `AutoDeploy` assembly, and remove the
root namespace using the Property pages.

Add a button to `Form1` named `btnObject` and put the following code behind it:

```
Private Sub btnObject_Click(ByVal sender As System.Object, _
                            ByVal e As System.EventArgs) _
                            Handles btnObject.Click

   Wrox.Toolkit.Util.Launcher.RunAppliation( _
     "http://localhost/TestApp/TestApp.exe")

End Sub
```

Change the URL as appropriate to point to the location where your test application resides on the server. Now build and run the program and it will auto-deploy and launch `TestApp.exe`. Click the buttons on the form to see that serialization and the `.remoteconfig` file both work as desired.

We can also go to the `TestApp\bin` directory on the hard drive and run the application by double-clicking on `TestApp.exe`. In this case, we'll see that the `.config` file is loaded rather than `.remoteconfig`.

Limitations

This code requires that security be set up for the URL that contains the remote DLLs or EXE so they run in an appropriate sandbox.

There are obviously some bandwidth considerations here too. When designing an application for auto-deployment, the application should be broken into DLLs, with each one containing related functionality. Remember that DLLs are only downloaded on demand, so with careful design, some users may never have to download DLLs for functionality they don't use.

If an executable is auto-deployed, then that executable needs to use the `Wrox.Toolkit.Util.ConfigurationSettings` class instead of the `System.Configuration.ConfigurationSettings` class to read from its `.config` file. This means that existing applications that use `.config` files will require some change before they will work in an auto-deployment scenario.

Extensions

A major benefit of .NET is that we avoid DLL hell and it solves numerous deployment issues. However, with just a bit of extra code we can create applications that provide truly zero-touch deployment.

You can use the GetObject() method shown here to create a shell application that creates an entirely dynamic menu structure in an MDI window or other UI style. All the code to actually implement the application's functionality can be auto-deployed by calling GetObject() to download and create Windows Forms, controls, or business objects as needed.

The RunApplication() method shown here can be used to create a simple and generic launcher application that can be used to run any .NET program from a URL. This is a powerful solution, as it allows us to create regular .NET Windows Forms applications and deploy them to clients at essentially no cost.

This chapter has been taken from Visual Basic .NET Solutions Toolkit, a co-branded book between Wrox Press and Magenic Technologies Incorporated. This book incorporates 30 different Visual Basic .NET components to do a vast array of different useful tasks, and is divided up into five distinct sections, each covering a different area. It was written by various consultants from Magenic and edited by the same team of editors who work on the different books in the Handbook series. Its ISBN is 1-86100-739-6.

VB.NET

Deployment

Handbook

Appendix D

Support, Errata, and Code Download

We always value hearing from our readers, and we want to know what you think about this book: what you liked, what you didn't like, and what you think we can do better next time. You can send us your comments, either by returning the reply card in the back of the book, or by e-mailing us at feedback@wrox.com. Please be sure to mention the book title in your message.

How to Download the Sample Code for the Book

When you log on to the Wrox site, http://www.wrox.com/, simply locate the title through our Search facility or by using one of the title lists. Click on Download Code on the book's detail page.

The files that are available for download from our site have been archived using WinZip. When you have saved the attachments to a folder on your hard-drive, you will need to extract the files using WinZip, or a compatible tool. Inside the Zip file will be a folder structure and an HTML file that explains the structure and gives you further information, including links to e-mail support, and suggested further reading.

Errata

We've made every effort to ensure that there are no errors in the text or in the code. However, no one is perfect and mistakes can occur. If you find an error in this book, like a spelling mistake or a faulty piece of code, we would be very grateful for feedback. By sending in errata, you may save another reader hours of frustration, and of course, you will be helping us to provide even higher quality information. Simply e-mail the information to support@wrox.com, your information will be checked and if correct, posted to the errata page for that title.

To find errata, locate this book on the Wrox web site (http://www.wrox.com/ACON11.asp?ISBN=186100771X), and click on the Book Errata link on the book's detail page:

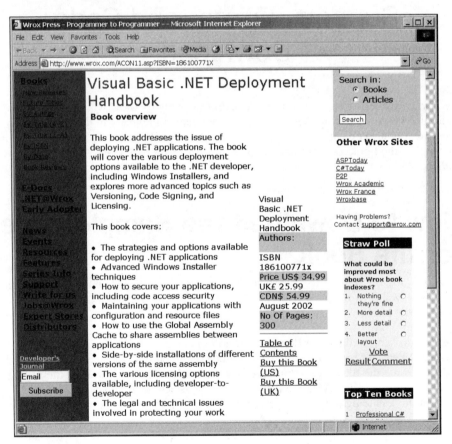

E-mail Support

If you wish to query a problem in the book with an expert who knows the book in detail then e-mail support@wrox.com, with the title of the book, and the last four numbers of the ISBN in the subject field of the e-mail. A typical e-mail should include the following:

❑ The name, last four digits of the ISBN (in this case 771X), and page number of the problem, in the Subject field

❑ Your name, contact information, and the problem, in the body of the message

We won't send you junk mail. We need the details to save your time and ours. When you send an e-mail message, it will go through the following chain of support:

❑ **Customer Support**

Your message is delivered to our customer support staff. They have files on most frequently asked questions and will answer anything general about the book or the web site immediately.

❑ **Editorial**

More in-depth queries are forwarded to the technical editor responsible for that book. They have experience with the programming language or particular product, and are able to answer detailed technical questions on the subject. Once an issue has been resolved, the editor can post the errata to the web site.

❑ **The Authors**

Finally, in the unlikely event that the editor cannot answer your problem, they will forward the request to the author. We do try to protect the author from any distractions to their writing (or programming); but we are quite happy to forward specific requests to them. All Wrox authors help with the support on their books. They will e-mail the customer and the editor with their response, and again all readers should benefit

The Wrox support process can only offer support for issues that are directly pertinent to the content of our published title. Support for questions that fall outside the scope of normal book support is provided via our P2P community lists – http://p2p.wrox.com/forum.

p2p.wrox.com

For author and peer discussion, join the P2P mailing lists. Our unique system provides Programmer to Programmer™ contact on mailing lists, forums, and newsgroups, all in addition to our one-to-one e-mail support system. Be confident that the many Wrox authors and other industry experts who are present on our mailing lists are examining any queries posted. At http://p2p.wrox.com/, you will find a number of different lists that will help you, not only while you read this book, but also as you develop your own applications.

To subscribe to a mailing list follow this these steps:

- ❑ Go to http://p2p.wrox.com/
- ❑ Choose the appropriate category from the left menu bar
- ❑ Click on the mailing list you wish to join
- ❑ Follow the instructions to subscribe and fill in your e-mail address and password
- ❑ Reply to the confirmation e-mail you receive
- ❑ Use the subscription manager to join more lists and set your mail preferences

VB.NET

Deployment

Handbook

Index

Index

A Guide to the Index

The index is arranged hierarchically, in alphabetical order, with symbols preceding the letter A. Most second-level entries and many third-level entries also occur as first-level entries. This is to ensure that users will find the information they require however they choose to search for it.

A

X

Z

Visual Basic .NET Threading Handbook:

Author(s): K. Ardestani, F. C. Ferracchiati, S. Gopikrishna, T. Redkar, S. Sivakumar, T. Titus
ISBN: 1-861007-13-2
US$ 29.99
Can$ 46.99

All .NET languages now have access to the Free Threading Model that many Visual Basic Developers have been waiting for. Compared to the earlier apartment threading model, this gives you much finer control over where to implement threading and what you are given access to. It does also provide several new ways for your application to spin out of control.

This handbook explains how to avoid some common pitfalls when designing multi-threaded applications by presenting some guidelines for good design practice. By investigating .NET's threading model's architecture, you will be able to make sure that your applications take full advantage of it.

What you will learn from this book
- Thread creation
- Using timers to schedule threads to execute at specified intervals
- Synchronizing thread execution - avoiding deadlocks and race conditions
- Spinning threads from within threads, and synchronizing them
- Modelling your applications to a specific thread design model
- Scaling threaded applications by using the ThreadPool class
- Tracing your threaded application's execution in order to debug it

Visual Basic .NET Text Manipulation Handbook:
String Handling and Regular Expressions

Author(s): François Liger, Craig McQueen, Paul Wilton
ISBN: 1-861007-30-2
US$ 29.99
Can$ 46.99

Text forms an integral part of many applications. Earlier version's of Visual Basic would hide from you the intricacies of how text was being handled, limiting your ability to control your program's execution or performance. The .NET Framework gives you much finer control.

This handbook takes an in depth look at the text manipulation classes that are included within the .NET Framework, in all cases providing you with invaluable information as to their relative performance merits. The String and Stringbuilder classes are investigated and the newly acquired support for regular expressions is illustrated in detail.

What you will learn from this book
- String representation and management within the .NET Framework
- Using the StringBuilder object to improve application performance
- Choosing between the different object's methods when manipulating text
- How to safely convert between String and other data types
- How to take advantage of .NET's Unicode representation of text for Internationalization
- The use of regular expressions including syntax and pattern matching to optimize your text manipulation operations

Visual Basic .NET Class Design Handbook:
Coding Effective Classes

Visual Basic .NET Class Design Handbook: Coding Effective Classes

Author(s): Andy Olsen, Damon Allison, James Speer
ISBN: 1-861007-08-6
US$ 29.99
Can$ 46.99

Designing effective classes that you do not need to revisit and revise over and over again is an art. Within the .NET Framework, whatever code you write in Visual Basic .NET is encapsulated within the class hierarchy of the .NET Framework.

By investigating in depth the various members a class can contain, this handbook aims to give you a deep understanding of the implications of all the decisions you can make at design time. This book will equip you with the necessary knowledge to build classes that are robust, flexible, and reusable.

- **What you will learn from this book**
- The role of types in .NET
- The different kinds of type we can create in VB.NET
- How VB.NET defines type members
- The fundamental role of methods as containers of program logic
- The role of constructors and their effective use
- Object cleanup and disposal
- When and how to use properties and indexers to encapsulate data
- How .NET's event system works
- How to control and exploit inheritance in our types
- The logical and physical code organisation through namespaces and assemblies

wrox
Programmer to Programmer™

p2p.wrox.com
The programmer's resource centre

A unique free service from Wrox Press
With the aim of helping programmers to help each other

Wrox Press aims to provide timely and practical information to today's programmer. P2P is a list server offering a host of targeted mailing lists where you can share knowledge with four fellow programmers and find solutions to your problems. Whatever the level of your programming knowledge, and whatever technology you use P2P can provide you with the information you need.

ASP Support for beginners and professionals, including a resource page with hundreds of links, and a popular ASP.NET mailing list.

DATABASES For database programmers, offering support on SQL Server, mySQL, and Oracle.

MOBILE Software development for the mobile market is growing rapidly. We provide lists for the several current standards, including WAP, Windows CE, and Symbian.

JAVA A complete set of Java lists, covering beginners, professionals, and server-side programmers (including JSP, servlets and EJBs)

.NET Microsoft's new OS platform, covering topics such as ASP.NET, C#, and general .NET discussion.

VISUAL BASIC Covers all aspects of VB programming, from programming Office macros to creating components for the .NET platform.

WEB DESIGN As web page requirements become more complex, programmer's are taking a more important role in creating web sites. For these programmers, we offer lists covering technologies such as Flash, Coldfusion, and JavaScript.

XML Covering all aspects of XML, including XSLT and schemas.

OPEN SOURCE Many Open Source topics covered including PHP, Apache, Perl, Linux, Python and more.

FOREIGN LANGUAGE Several lists dedicated to Spanish and German speaking programmers, categories include. NET, Java, XML, PHP and XML

How to subscribe
Simply visit the P2P site, at http://p2p.wrox.com/

WROX PRESS INC.

Wrox writes books for you. Any suggestions, or ideas
about how you want information given in your
ideal book will be studied by our team.
Your comments are always valued at Wrox.

Free phone in USA 800-USE-WROX
Fax (312) 893 8001

UK Tel. (0121) 687 4100 Fax (0121) 687 4101

NB. If you post the bounce back card below in the UK, please send it to:
Wrox Press Ltd., Arden House, 1102 Warwick Road, Acocks Green, Birmingham. B27 9BH. UK.

Registration Code :   771X7X4M6K5Y7FQ01

Visual Basic .NET Deployment Handbook - Registration Card

771X

Name
Address

City
Country   State/Region
E-mail   Postcode/Zip
Occupation
How did you hear about this book?
☐ Book review (name)
☐ Advertisement (name)
☐ Recommendation
☐ Catalog
☐ Other
Where did you buy this book?
☐ Bookstore (name)   City
☐ Computer Store (name)
☐ Mail Order
☐ Other

What influenced you in the
purchase of this book?
☐ Cover Design
☐ Contents
☐ Other (please specify)

How did you rate the overall
contents of this book?
☐ Excellent   ☐ Good
☐ Average   ☐ Poor

What did you find most useful about this book?

What did you find least useful about this book?

Please add any additional comments.

What other subjects will you buy a computer
book on soon?

What is the best computer book you have used this year?

Note: This information will only be used to keep you updated
about new Wrox Press titles and will not be used for any other
purpose or passed to any other third party.

Check here if you DO NOT want to receive further support for this book. ■

771X

wrox

PROGRAMMER TO PROGRAMMER™

BUSINESS REPLY MAIL

FIRST CLASS MAIL   PERMIT#64   CHICAGO, IL

POSTAGE WILL BE PAID BY ADDRESSEE

WROX PRESS INC.
29 S. LA SALLE ST.,
SUITE 520
CHICAGO IL 60603-USA